GRANT NOTLEY

GRANT NOTLEY

The Social Conscience
of Alberta

Howard Leeson

THE UNIVERSITY OF ALBERTA PRESS

First published by
The University of Alberta Press
Athabasca Hall
Edmonton, Alberta
Canada   T6G 2E8

Copyright © The University of Alberta Press 1992

ISBN 0-88864-244-X cloth

Canadian Cataloguing in Publication Data

Leeson, Howard A., 1942–
  Grant Notley, the social conscience of Alberta

  Includes bibliographical references and index.
  ISBN 0-88864-244-X

  1. Notley, Grant, 1939-1984.   2. Politicians—Alberta—Biography.
3. Alberta New Democratic Party—History.   4. Alberta—Politics and government — 1935-1971.   5. Alberta—Politics and government—1971–   I. Title.
FC3675.1.N67L43 1992   971.23'03'092   C92-091247-8
F1078.25.N67L43 1992

Frontispiece of Grant Notley courtesy of Alberta NDP.

Printed on acid-free paper. ∞

Typesetting by Pièce de Résistance, Ltée., Edmonton, Alberta, Canada

Printed and bound in Canada by
John Deyell Company Limited.

Ede and I would like to dedicate this book to Nancy Eng.
Like Grant Notley, Nancy was taken from us too early in life.

CONTENTS

PREFACE

WHEN THE EUROPEAN SETTLERS streamed into this land a hundred years ago, the prairies seemed a vast almost unending region, a *tabula rasa* awaiting only the imprint of their collective hands. It was virtually unspoiled and unresisting. Over the years the settlers changed the prairies dramatically, building farms, homes, towns, and eventually cities. Just as importantly, they also built new social structures. The experiences of isolation, oppression, and alienation plowed new social furrows beside those in the land. These cultural roots remain with us today. They nourish us, providing us with a sense of heritage, a stability, a sense of place in a world which constantly seeks to change our values and norms.

As you might expect, we look to our community leaders for verification of these values, for personification of what we hold closest. Some leaders stand out in this respect. They are almost archetypal, so vividly familiar that we immediately identify with them. Somehow they reflect a truth about ourselves which demands our attention.

Such a man was Grant Notley. In the society and politics of Alberta he stood out. Albertans felt intuitively that he represented a part of their collective being, and his untimely death touched them deeply. When he died, a bit of Alberta died. He was us, and we miss him.

ACKNOWLEDGEMENTS

I WOULD LIKE TO acknowledge the help of many people in the preparation of this manuscript. In particular I wish to thank Sandy Notley Kreutzer for taking the time to talk to me about Grant, and to thank all of those people who permitted me to record their observations and recollections. As well, I am grateful to Mark Zwelling who sent me his tapes of conversations with Grant, to Linda Sarafinchan who provided many useful documents and to Bill Dryden and Anne Hopp for their help in interviewing and consultation. Finally, I would like to acknowledge Leanne Overend for enduring the many extra typings of the manuscript caused by my constant need to keep changing everything.

The photographs of Grant Notley were provided by the Alberta New Democrats. A special thanks to Tom Sigurdson, MLA, for allowing us the use of photographs from his personal photo albums.

I wish to acknowledge the University of Regina President's Fund and the University of Alberta for financial help in the preparation of this work. The Alberta Foundation for the Arts also provided funds towards publication.

INTRODUCTION

In this House, where 74 of the members represent one philosophical view, and I represent another, I am here to challenge some of the basic assumptions . . . . It is the difference between a passive philosophy of government and an activist view of government that distinguishes today's conservative from today's socialist . . . . Whether government should plan ahead or anticipate problems, or simply react when disaster strikes: whether one backs public ownership with pride or backs into public ownership only when unavoidable. In my view, passive government is bound to fail despite the sincerity of its advocates.[1]

"Today's socialist" strange words to be heard in the Alberta legislature. When Grant Notley spoke about today's socialist in his maiden speech he was well aware of the momentous change that had taken place in Alberta during the election of 1971. After 35 years the mighty Social Credit party was out of office, beaten by Peter Lougheed and the Progressive Conservatives, and Grant Notley had been elected in Spirit River-Fairview, the first full-term New Democrat in the Alberta Legislature. There was proof at last that Alberta was not impervious to social and political change. Along with the rest of North America it had finally succumbed to urbanization and liberal capitalism. For the first time "today's socialist" faced "today's conservative" across the floor of the Alberta House. The old order of politics had been put aside, soon to be relegated to the political attic of past curiosities.

xiii

Grant obviously understood these changes. He was well aware of his role as a bridge between the politics of today and yesterday. Together with Peter Lougheed he personified the metamorphosis of the province's twin political streams. What had begun as contradictory elements of prairie populism had finally matured into the more modern class basis of an urbanizing society. The province of "major experiments," as C.B. MacPherson put it, would soon settle into the more comfortable modes of contemporary Canada. The challenge for Grant Notley was to mobilize the remnants of a truncated and defeated Cooperative Commonweath Federation (CCF), the urban poor, and the working classes, into a single political force at a time when the entrepreneurial right in the province had ascended to power and covered Alberta politics like a blanket. Despite his own enthusiasm he understood well how tenuous the position of his political movement was. Properly nurtured it might grow. Improperly led, it would surely die.

Two pictures always hung in Grant Notley's office, usually over a fireplace, or behind his desk. One was of J.S. Woodsworth, the first leader of the CCF, the other of Bill Irvine, a former Alberta leader of the CCF. These pictures symbolized his strong sense of history, his connection with the principles of the prairie reform movement. They graphically illustrated that he was not an isolated man, adrift in a sea of personal ambition. He was not, as are so many, involved in politics by accident or personal whim. He had chosen to be a democratic socialist, and in so doing inherited a dogged and steadfast determination to continue the social change begun by his predecessors.

And yet, he was not simply the last extension of an already established social movement. He was one of the bridges between a CCF which had exhausted itself against the prosperity of post World War II Canada, and the New Democratic Party (NDP), which was attempting to forge a new alliance with Albertans and Canadians. He understood and appreciated the vision of the CCF, its evangelical desire to change the social, economic, and political life of our country. And yet, like Neil Reimer, his predecessor, he understood the need to capture office, to win the electoral struggle, to use the state to wrest power from the privileged classes in Alberta. It produced in him a curious mixture of electoral zeal and social gospel, of modern politician and prairie social reformer.

Contradictory impulses are typical of Albertans. Indeed, they seem mandatory. Grant Notley often exhibited these schizophrenic tendencies.

Although a committed Canadian, he was also a proud Albertan. Economically radical by comparison with his fellow citizens, he was often socially conservative. Optimistic in his belief that social change could and should be undertaken, there was nevertheless a dark streak of prairie pessimism in his nature. One of his favorite phrases was "all things considered equal, they'd rather not."

From the time of early settlement in Alberta this pessimism has been a part of the culture. The promise of the prairies has been tempered and often broken by the "stingy reality"[2] of life in the region. Promises of abundance have proven false for each succeeding generation of prairie settlers as their subordinate position in the Canadian economy betrayed them. Boom cycled with bust. There were far too many busts, and far too few booms. How could such cycles be explained? Obviously they were not a failure of the land itself. It was often tough and sometimes unyielding, but it was incredibly fertile, growing unbelievable crops in good years. Neither could failure be explained by a lack of effort on the part of the settlers. They worked hard, often under unendurable circumstances. If the crop failed, it was because of drought, frost, hail, or grasshoppers. These were beyond the control of men or the land. They must be stoically endured. However, once the crop was harvested the settlers faced yet another obstacle. How to sell their grain, and what the price would be. When it was not successfully marketed it was usually the fault of other men, not the farmers. These "other men" ran the railways, banks, and grain companies and could readily be identified. Failures of this type had to be dealt with through action by the settlers.

Thus, a mixture of stoicism and activism settled into the political culture of Alberta. It taught patience, endurance and longevity of purpose, but it also encouraged collective organization, radical behavior, and a certain insularity. Liberal capitalism fed the belief that everyone could succeed according to his own effort. But the all too apparent manipulation of the settlers in the interest of eastern Canadian capital also generated the view that failure could be explained by a rigged economic system, one designed to ensure a subordinate position for the settlers and their region. Economic emancipation therefore, lay not in individual effort but in collective effort. Two views. One counselled acceptance, the other rejection. One taught prayer, the other political action. Both were accepted, and both were embedded in the political psyche of Alberta.

The practical result of this was two brands of prairie activist. The first tended to refrain from collective action, seeking temporary changes during very tough economic times. In part this reaction was rooted in his view of himself as the independent yeoman farmer; impervious to the urban vices of despair, and hasty action. His position as a small landholder reinforced his general support for the system since it gave him a stake in preserving property relationships. His psychological and economic needs could be reconciled in programmes that challenged the dominance of those oppressing him, but not the dominance of the system itself. He sought, therefore to repair the system, to find moral fault in particular individuals outside of the region.

The second prairie activist sought to change the system, accepting an analysis which criticized capitalism both inside and outside the region, rooting political action in the belief that, as Bill Irvine said, " . . . . In a mixed economy the bank accounts of the wealthy will not be mixed with the bank accounts of the wage earners. The incomes of the monopolist protectors will not be mixed with that of the semi-bankrupt farmers . . . ."[3] Social action was not only permissible for a Christian yeoman farmer, but mandatory if one was to combat evil on earth.

These groups were united on some matters. They both supported the family farm. They both opposed large outside private interests, especially the banks, and believed the region to be unfairly treated by private interests which were in league with the federal government. Regional alienation was common to both groups. They supported collective or cooperative enterprise as an eventual method of gaining control of their own economic destiny. They rejected the party system and parliamentary structures as unsuitable to the needs of their society. Finally, they accepted the necessity of collective, regional political action, directed toward the federal government, although they often differed on what should be done. Naturally, unity was strongest during political or economic crises, but once the immediate crisis had passed, disagreement emerged, leading to the eventual split of the farmer's movement into several factions.

In Alberta the result was the United Farmers of Alberta (UFA), first a farmer's movement, and then a political party, which captured power in 1921. Between 1921 and 1935 the UFA governed Alberta. It represented and articulated the interests of a radicalized farm community. By 1935, however, under the weight of 14 years in office, personal scandal, and the Great Depression, the UFA failed. Its social base was appropriated by a newer, more socially conservative movement, a movement which promised immediate cash relief, The Social Credit Party.

Between 1935 and 1971, prairie radicalism in Alberta was thus split into two streams. The first, Social Credit, developed along a predictable path. After an initial burst of radical activity, it settled into the more comfortable tasks of provincial management. Aided by the return of prosperity after WWII, and the increasingly buoyant revenues guaranteed from oil, Social Credit remained in power for 36 years. During that time it exorcised itself of any "radical" elements, providing sound, scandal free, conservative government. It became increasingly the handmaiden of foreign capital, blessing the economic development and urbanization which would eventually prove to be its own undoing. When Peter Lougheed and the Conservatives won the election in 1971, it was because the Social Credit administration had prepared the way for them. One branch of prairie radicalism had swallowed itself.

The other stream ventured further into socialism, with some success in Saskatchewan. In Alberta, however, the CCF was too intimately associated with its UFA predecessor to escape the election of 1935. In rejecting the UFA, the people of Alberta also rejected the CCF. The question of whether or not this meant a rejection of socialism is not of great importance. Albertans were comfortable with Social Credit and increasingly comfortable with their "stake" in the system. The CCF simply withered after World War II.

As with all dying social movements, pockets of activity remained. Thus, when the disaster of 1958 hit the national CCF, and the leadership determined to forge a new alliance with organized labour, there were still those in Alberta who were willing to undertake the arduous task of "building the left anew." But it would not be the left of 1933, nor the left of 1921. It would be a new left, reaching out in a new approach to organized workers and all working people. There would be an attempt to wed prairie populism and urban socialism.

In Saskatchewan this marriage succeeded. In Alberta it was only partially effected. Significant elements of the old CCF could not reconcile themselves to the new party, to its "electoral orientation," and to its less traditional approaches to matters of foreign and domestic policy. In Grant's own words:

Embittered, the whole CCF movement in Alberta was scarred by years and years of defeats. They had been part of the UFA, in government, then swept away.[4]

The movement split in 1961, with some going to the New Party, and others going to a group called the Woodsworth-Irvine Fellowship. The second stream of prairie populism had also transformed itself.

Educated in the CCF, but dedicated to the creation of the NDP, Grant Notley was one of the living links between the prairie populism of the CCF and the social democracy of the NDP; between the new urban base, and the remaining rural support; between the now old leadership of the UFA, and the as yet untested leaders to come. He could speak with passion about both movements; he could articulate the premises and interests of each group. In a socially eloquent way, he was the perfect ideological hybrid. But, as with most hybrids, he was never fully accepted by either side. Too "rural" for some New Democrats, he was branded as "an upstart" by CCFers.

And yet, he commanded a tremendous personal loyalty from those who came in contact with him. Most of his closest associates agreed that once you were one of "Notley's people," you never were free of him. He not only kept track of his former friends and associates, but could draw them back to Alberta, and to his cause, when really needed. Election campaigns in Alberta became reunions, as various generations of "Notley's Crew," came in contact with each other.

What prompted such loyalty? How could a shy, solitary, and socially retiring person take such a grip on people? The answer lies somewhere in his hard work, his own devotion to social change, and in the ideals of those that he sought to enlist. He never abused their trust, or proved unfaithful to their general goals. He was prodigious in his work, and personally incorruptible. Never did his people feel that he had used them for his own personal gain; and thus, they could always be exhorted to further work for the good of the party. Simply put, his goals, his willingness to work, his "practical idealism" always found resonance in some, and thus they gave unstintingly.

Those goals, his personal integrity, his obvious dedication to social change, his "practical idealism," made him the social conscience of Alberta. He bridged the old and the new, he provided the necessary hard work to forge a link that ensured the continuation of a progressive social party in Alberta. Practical party worker, social conscience, pragmatic idealist, Grant squared the circle of contradictions that one finds in the social and political history of Alberta. He embodied a phase of social change. That change is now almost complete. It remains to be seen if Grant Notley's "bridge" has led to a new phase of progressivism, or if the external forces of North American capitalism were simply delayed a little by the efforts of a single man whose dedication could not revive that which rightly ought to have passed into history.

1 A PRAIRIE CHILD

AS YOU COME into Olds, Alberta, it could be any town on the prairies. It is neat, clean and unlike smaller towns, it does not yet betray a sense of imminent demise. There is a mixture of the old and the new. A Dairy Queen restaurant in one part, the normal small business of main street Alberta in the other.

The region around Olds is a prosperous farming area. It was originally known as the "Lone Pine" district, a stop-over place somewhat to the northeast of the present site. Several names were considered for the town, including Lone Pine, Sixth Siding, and Shannon, the latter after the local farmer who gave up his land to the CPR for the present townsite. In the end, as with so many prairie towns, the name Olds was chosen for George Olds, a CPR traffic manager.

As you go west from Olds the beauty and variety of the Alberta landscape unfolds. There is little to equal the rolling prairie fields with the mountains in the background. The Innis Lake district affords a kind of magical view where the loneliness of the flat prairie meets the excitement of the jagged cliffs of the Rockies. A short walk down the road west of the Notley farm, with that collision of view before you, suggests much about Grant Notley's love for his province.

Walter Grant Notley was born in this area on January 19, 1939. His parents farmed there for most of their life. On the paternal side Grant traced his lineage to Suffolk, England. His great-grandfather was in charge of an estate there. Grant often joked that his great grandfather came over to Canada because of a drinking problem, something that

1

might have been partially true. His grandfather and grandmother came to Alberta from Ontario in 1892. They eventually moved to Olds, where Grant's father, Walter Notley, was born.

On the maternal side his grandparents were a mixture of United Empire Loyalist, Scottish and Danish. His maternal grandfather came to Alberta from Ontario. He arrived in the town of Frank in 1905, just two weeks before the famous Frank slide, an enormous mountain slide which buried the town. Eventually he taught school, first near Calgary, and then at Olds. Later he became the Town Clerk in Olds for many years.

Grant recalled little about the politics of his grandparents, except for his paternal grandfather, whom he described as a "rock ribbed conservative, small c, who never supported the UFA." He remembered his grandfather's politics because of his grandfather's opposition to public ownership. In 1948 there was a provincial referendum along with the election. The referendum was on public power. Grant's grandfather "gave his grandmother holy hell, because she had voted in favour of socialized, or public power." She had voted for it because she wanted her children to have electric power. His grandfather chastised her for this view, replying that this would mean higher rates, and was dead set against it. The referendum failed by only a few hundred votes, province-wide. That failure obviously made an impression on Grant, who was at the time, only nine years old.

Francis Notley, Grant's mother, was born Francis Grant in Olds, in 1910. She had four sisters. After finishing school in Olds, she continued her education at Normal School, eventually teaching in the area for a number of years. Grant's father Walter was born on a farm near Olds. He finished school in Olds as well, going on to the agricultural college nearby. He was part of the first graduating class. Both of Grant's parents were well educated for their time, something that had a profound influence on his life. They were married in Calgary in 1938.

The Notleys were not a political family, except for being anti-Aberhart. Francis Notley admits to voting Social Credit in 1935, but became convinced against the party after that time. She remembers several "lively" discussions with her sisters, one of whom was a strong CCFer. Eventually she settled on support for the CCF. Walter Notley's family was strong Conservative, but he too became a supporter of the CCF, after discussion with a local Scandinavian friend. Eventually Grant's father attended CCF conventions in the late 1940s. There was no local organization for them to attend, and Francis recalls they were supporters, but not card carrying members. It is clear that they were politically different from most of their neighbours, who were Social Credit. Indeed, some of those neighbours described the Notleys as "odd" for supporting the CCF, but this did not detract from their respect for the family.

Grant was born in Didsbury, at the hospital. The choice of Dibsury was made on the basis that the road there was better than the road to Olds, something that one considered carefully in January of 1939. By then the Notleys had taken up farming on a quarter section in the Innis Hill District, west of Olds. When Grant was two years of age they moved to the Eagle Hill area. When he was four they moved again, this time to the Westerdale District, about 13 miles west of Olds.

Grant's description of the family farm betrayed his great love for Westerdale:

> The area west of Olds is a very beautiful area, you see the foothills, and walking to school when the sun would come up in the east, it would shine against the mountains, making a beautiful sight. The seasons were so clear, the trees green in the spring, the colours in the fall. It was a very beautiful area of the province. Still is.

His recollections of the farm were very precise partly because of the state of the home quarter.

> When my parents got the farm though, that was the one quarter section that was barren. It was parkland in the area, but their farm was just absolutely barren. So they . . . had 3000 trees planted, got a garden tractor . . . and cultivated these trees and now, its a beautiful place.

It is clear that the Notley farm was both a home and a refuge for Grant, something not replaced until he acquired his own "home quarter" near Fairview.

Francis Notley remembers Grant as an active baby. When he learned to walk, he also learned to run. She also recalls that he had a "darned blanket" that went all over the farm with him. He would not part with it, forcing his mother to gradually reduce the size of the blanket by cutting off pieces, until it was only a little over a foot square. When he was two and a half he finally abandoned the now diminished blanket, albeit reluctantly.

Grant was an active and imaginative child. When he was four, living at Eagle Hill, he decided to have his own play. He was the director and his young playmate was one of his actors. Grant, naturally, took the lead in this play, ensuring that his friend did everything according to the way that he thought that it should be. From the recollections of others it is obvious that he was given to a bit of "longwindedness" even as a child.

His mother recalls that he used to write everything into "books," so much so that she was convinced that he would be a writer. (Later in life he confided to his mother that after his life in politics he wanted to retire on his Peace River farm and write.) He also listened avidly to the radio, with an ear to every programme that he could. The family had a wind electric radio, so that saving on batteries was not a problem. It is not difficult to come to the conclusion that Grant was a gifted child, soaking up every experience possible in a limited rural setting.

Family life for Grant during his childhood was quite normal for the time. The farm demanded hard work from everyone, children included. Grant had his chores to do, including tractor work on what he described as "that damn tractor." His chores consisted of the usual things, cleaning the barn, fetching the cows, and feeding the dogs and cats. At school he recalled that he was responsible for splitting the kindling, among other things.

There is little that was unusual about Grant's relationship with his family and friends during those early years. He made light of his ancestral connections, seeming to be unimpressed with his grandparents. They appear to have had little influence on him. His relationship with his parents seems to have been more important.

His mother was most decisive in his life. While this is not unexpected, it went beyond the usual mother-son relationship, since she had also been the school teacher at the one room Westerdale school. Francis Notley is a reserved person, intelligent, personable, and guarded. She has been described by some as both unemotional and distant. Her relationship with Grant seems to have been consistent with her personality. They were obviously close, according to Grant and others, but not in a public way.

Throughout her life Francis Notley has been hard-working, responsible, and dutiful, traits which Grant possessed. It is difficult not to conclude that Grant derived much of his drive and view of life from his mother. Indeed, one person commented that much of Grant's life was spent trying to measure up to his mother's expectations, a reasonable conclusion if one considers the dual role of mother and teacher which Francis Notley played.

The role of Grant's father, Walter Notley, is less clear. Grant was named after his father but always used his second name, his mother's maiden name. His recollections of his father during his childhood are kindly. He remembered him as an active community man, with an obvious sense of pride, and was quick to enumerate his father's public activities.

> There was a commitment to community service, particularly on my father's part, that was very, very strong. He was a cooperator, President of the Innis Lake Local of the FUA, he was one of the first people to bring in hail suppression, . . . my father would go out night after night and have meetings all over the damn place. Gradually it was picked up by the government so that the whole business of weather modification as we know it in the province stems from the work of himself.

Sandy Notley recalls her father-in-law Walter Notley as a kindly man whom she was quite fond of. He was not particularly talkative, and would spend long hours in the barn by himself. The contrast between his public and private activities is apparent, just as it was later with Grant. There is little to indicate, however, that Walter Notley was a role model for his eldest son. While he was an active CCFer later in life, and appreciated his son's position and accomplishments, he was not the driving force in Grant's life. Indeed, Sandy Notley remembers clearly that Francis and Walter were not "stage parents," pushing their son to a career that he was unprepared for.

Grant had one brother, Bruce, who was two years younger. Grant and Bruce spent a good deal of time together, but Bruce seems not to have played much of a role in Grant's life. Bruce is described by those who knew him as bright, creative, and well behaved. His mother recalls that Grant used to be "bossy" with Bruce, while teachers and other students recalled that Grant always "pushed" Bruce.

Their relationship was clearly that of the dominant and dominated, of the older brother pushing a younger sibling to live up to elder's expectations. It is a picture of an ambivalent relationship in which an older brother feels responsible for a younger brother, and worries about that responsibility. And yet, his constant willingness to respond to the problems of his younger brother also leads one to conclude that there was a genuine affection between them. Grant's attitude toward Bruce tells us a great deal about his own sense of duty and responsibility, about his dedication and willingness to work hard to achieve a goal. Although his political commitment was to fairness, equality and compassion, he was uncompromising with those who did not measure up, or would not work.

Grant started school in 1945, the year the war ended, at Westerdale School. It was to the west of his farm, about a mile and a half. He walked everyday. There is some disagreement as to what his first day at school was like. His mother recalled that he walked down the lane by himself. "I watched him all of the way," she said. But his teacher, Lois Buckley recalls that he was very shy and terrified at school. "His first day his mother came with him," she said, "and he hid in her skirts." It is likely that the two days involved are different, but the persistence of his shyness is a theme. For example, when Halloween came, the children all dressed up in costumes, but the costumes scared Grant, and the teacher made the children take them off. All of this is in contrast to another trait mentioned by school friends, the fact that he "talked all the time," and much of it about politics. This inconsistency remains unexplained, but his interest in politics, and the ability to overcome his personal reluctance when speaking about politics, are significant deviations for a shy, and sometimes solitary young man.

Grant's years at school were busy, productive and seemingly happy. It was the post-war period in Alberta. Social Credit had been in power for ten years, and the discovery of oil at Leduc would soon propel the economy of Alberta into prosperity. But it would be another decade before this prosperity would mature and reach rural Alberta. For the children of the time things were changing, but if opportunities were more numerous, they were still few in number and had to be won with hard work.

Grant's teachers remember him as a boy who read and talked a lot, was thoughtful and well spoken, but also a bit of a "wimp." He was often teased, and sometimes bullied. But his mother recalls that he "never showed hurt," as a child or later. But he did respond to outside opinions of himself. For example, he thought that his ears were too prominent, and even tried to tape them down to keep them from sticking out so much. He was gangly, with no chin, his mother recalls, but it grew. He took his shirt off in Spring, and put it on again in Fall. He always participated in the events of the school, especially the Christmas concerts, which were quite important in rural areas.

Francis Notley remembers that teachers were "made or broken" on their Christmas play, unlike today:

. . . in the rural [areas] they made a big thing of the Christmas concerts. Every kid took part in 101 different things on the programme. They were used to being in public and people from miles around would come to the Christmas concert. And so the matter of stage fright was just something that from grade 1 on they [the kids] just got over.

Grant got some early training in being "on stage," something which his mother thinks helped him with public speaking.

It would be easy to conclude that the children of Grant's era were deprived of social stimulation because of their relative isolation. Such was not the case. As with the concerts, every activity was utilized to the full, every opportunity for participation seized. Thus, when there was a graduation, as an example, every child gave a speech, not just the valedictorian. In this area Grant seemed to show early promise. Not only did he like to talk, but was able to think on his feet. Francis Notley recalled being at a 4H meeting during which the young boy who was to give the speech "ducked out." The director asked Grant to give a speech without any preparation. He did so, and did a good job. At his graduation, he gave such a good speech that the school principal, Mr. Wiggins, came down and remarked to his parents that he was sure that "Grant was going to be a preacher."

Grant recalled later that he had "good teachers" at Westerdale, Norma Buckley being the one who stood out in his mind. His mother supplemented what he learned at school with some home education. He moved ahead very fast, his teachers describing him as "meticulous about himself and his work." Other students had kindly memories of him. "My bike kept breaking down," one student recalled, "and Grant would push his bike and walk beside me so I would not be left behind. When I had no bike he would wait and double me so that I would not have to walk the mile or so more from school." Another remembered him as "neighbourly" with a "concern for others." "He always seemed to be able to put himself in the other person's situation." Some of his activities were what we would consider now to be quite normal.

Grant would spend his noon hours (when we couldn't go outside) drawing modernistic cars on the blackboard. Now we would probably consider them 1986 cars.

Other activities were a little more unusual, but showed an early penchant for politics. Apparently he and some friends decided to turn the outhouse into "parliament" where they initiated the "political process."

When he left Westerdale he was the first boy in two decades to go to high school. Up until then everyone else had stopped at grade nine. The school prophecy was that he would become prime minister.

No one remembers Grant as overly competitive in his school years. He did not participate in athletics to any great extent. Work on the farm, and the need to take the bus home limited his ability to do so. He had to bike two miles after he left the bus, making it even more difficult in high school. He finished his grade 10 at Olds, but the bus route changed, and he completed his high school at Didsbury.

He did not have a wide variety of friends, in part because of his farm origin, and in greater measure because of his own personality. He was shy with girls, partly because he was usually younger than his female classmates. He was active in the 4H, keeping his own Holstein cows and showing them. During this period he competed with another young man named Bob Clark, who was later elected as the Social Credit member from Olds, served as a cabinet minister, and eventually became Leader of the Social Credit Party. The two were active contemporaries in the early 1950s. Local opinion is that Grant used to win the "confrontation of the cows."

The origin of Grant's interest in CCF politics is obscure. Olds was the bedrock of Social Credit. It was an area where the party could run anyone, and elect him, especially in the 1950s. By contrast the CCF had never been a factor in local politics, did not have an organization in the area, and could not always field a candidate.

Grant had very little early recollection of politics, or of why he was CCF. He remembered a good deal about early American politics, and how he and his family were impressed with Adlai Stevenson, especially with Stevenson's humanity. It is clear however that his parents' political values were passed on to Grant, most particularly his distaste for Social Credit.

By the time that Grant became interested in politics Social Credit had settled into a safe, comfortable, conservative style. Gone were the radical trappings of the 1930s. In the 1944 election Social Credit directed all of its energies against the CCF in an anti-socialist campaign. The results were productive, with the CCF gaining only two seats, and Social Credit winning by a landslide. It was a lesson not lost on the Social Credit leadership, who continued to champion free enterprise in every subsequent election. For the CCF, which had hoped to recover the position of the UFA, it was a bitter defeat. Although the CCF was in power in Saskatchewan, its prospects seemed dim in Alberta. Nevertheless a solid base of party members existed, and continued the party's activity throughout the 1940s and 1950s. In the Olds area this was particularly difficult however, since Social Credit dominated the constituency completely.

In trying to recall his first political activities Grant thought that he remembered the 1952 election. He certainly remembered the public power debate in 1947; but nothing of the CCF. His father did not take him to any party meetings. He remembered the words "CCF" being used often, because his parents had great respect for M.J. Coldwell, then national leader of the party. Television was not factor in those days, although radio was. His parents listened faithfully to CBC, especially the news at 6:00 p.m. Of course, E.C. Manning, then Premier, also used the radio very effectively with his Sunday *Back to the Bible Hour.*

Grant did not come in contact with any "live" CCF politicians in Olds. As he said later, the party had ceased to exist there by the mid-1950s. The first CCF candidate that he listened to was in the 1957 federal election, a man by the name of Sandy Mansen. Grant remembered later that Mansen seemed very nervous and awkward at the meeting in Sundry.

Early on Grant determined that he wanted to go to university. This was unusual for his generation and area, but not surprising given his family background. His decision was undoubtedly made easier by the fact that he was very allergic to grain dust, probably part of a larger allergy to grass pollens. He loved the farm. He never rebelled against his chores or duties, but he was not "farm minded" as Francis Notley put it, in large part because he could not be around grain dust. He was so intent on going to university that he came home one day and announced to his parents that they would have to buy his cows, or else, because he would need the money to go to Edmonton. In the spring of 1957 he graduated from high school. In the fall he started at the University of Alberta.

Several things stand out when one looks at Grant's childhood. Early on he developed a passion for education, for learning. He read a lot, was bright, and could assimilate and use facts, something which later served him quite well. He was fortunate to have a family committed to encouraging him. It is difficult to know which is most important in this process, his natural ability, or the family stimulation.

Grant was also a hard worker, a goal oriented, meticulous person, destined to become an achiever. His mother's influence was dominant in this respect. Although he had all of the tools for accomplishment, they needed to be encouraged, which she did. His distaste for "laziness," as he put it, would stay with him all of his life.

Grant was always an articulate child, willing to express himself and able to do so. Indeed, many concluded that as a child he was overly endowed in this respect. Yet, despite this ability, he was never dominant in school life. He was not a leader at this point. No one remembers him as such, including himself. Despite being articulate he was also solitary, dispasionate and a bit of a "loner." The combination of public ability and a solitary disposition led to a dual personality, one of which was at ease in public, and another which was secluded and unknown to his public colleagues.

Finally, it is clear that Grant's interest in the CCF, his inclination to public affairs, and his passion for politics, came from his family. These attitudes were not deliberately taught to Grant by his parents. Rather he "soaked them up" in the socialization process. As with so many, however, these family values were open to change by outside influences, especially when removed from the family setting. For Grant, his university days would become decisive, molding and extending his early value systems. Although he acquired a tentative bias toward the CCF at home, it required the strengthening that would occur at the University of Alberta in order for it to develop into a life-long commitment to progressive politics.

2 UNIVERSITY YEARS

BY THE TIME GRANT started university in 1957, the old order of politics in the prairies had begun to crumble. For twenty-five years the political culture of the region had been dominated by memories of the Depression. A generation of people and opportunities had been "lost" to an economic catastrophe. It was difficult for voters to forget the lessons of that time. This change was very disruptive for the Alberta CCF.

The failure of the CCF to succeed the UFA in Alberta has prompted much debate. Most explanations settle into two groups. The first, socio-economic in character, stresses the conjunction of economic, social, and religious variables which provided fertile ground for Social Credit.[1] The second group of explanations centre on the historical circumstances, in effect arguing that the CCF was doomed by the failure of its UFA predecessor and the consequent rise of Social Credit in 1935. Both arguments are important, and perhaps not entirely mutually exclusive. Common to both, for example, is the notion that Social Credit initially occupied the political "space" of the CCF in Alberta, preventing it from amalgamating both the alienated prairie populist, and the genuine prairie socialist, as happened in Saskatchewan. The result was a situation in which two parties competed for much of the same vote until 1944-1948. After that time, as the Cold War progressed, the electorate grew increasingly conservative and Social Credit metamorphised into a business party, able to keep much of its prairie roots intact by portraying its prairie rival as a godless, socialist, communist menace. In the competition for

11

the populist prairie vote in Alberta the CCF had been defeated by its appearance in the wrong place, at the wrong time.

Coupled with these general explanations are arguments that the leadership of the Alberta CCF also blundered in its approach to politics: that it emphasized the wrong issues, and failed to deal adequately with matters of organization and practical leadership. As Bill Glass, later a member of "Notley's Motley Crew" at the University of Alberta, remarked, there was a contest between the "Ivory tower types" and those who wanted to organize and capture power. This characterization surfaces often throughout the 25 year history of the CCF from 1935 to 1960. The "Ivory tower types" insisted that the CCF remain true to its socialist purposes. They characterized the other group as reactionaries who wanted to wean the CCF away from socialism, to remake the party into another Liberal Party, and were interested in power for power's sake.

They were generally successful in keeping control of the Alberta CCF. Some argue that this led to an emphasis on issues which were of marginal interest to the voting public. Speaking about the 1944 election, a watershed in Alberta politics, author Myron Johnson said:

> One might ask here why the CCF did not do even better indeed, why it did not defeat the Social Credit. [In the 1944 election] . . . . To some extent, . . . the problem was the nature of the CCF campaign, which "lacked the practical appeal of Tommy Douglas" approach in Saskatchewan. There was "too much abstract theory and not enough live ammunition."[2]

Johnson goes on to say that the Alberta CCF did not emphasize matters, like markets, prices, farm crops, and health. Indeed, especially after 1948, the party concerned itself increasingly with international affairs, something which frustrated people like Elmer Roper, former CCF leader and later Mayor of Edmonton.

This split persisted, and grew worse in the 1950s. It was blamed by some for the catastrophic decline of the party in Alberta from 24.9% of the popular vote in 1944, to 4.3% fifteen years later. Indeed, Ivor Dent, later Mayor of Edmonton, interviewed in 1976, specifically drew attention to the fact that the provincial party had concentrated far too much on international politics and points about socialism, and too little on organization. By contrast, Betty Mardiros, a supporter of the position of Irvine and Johnson, argued that the rest of the CCF had abandoned its socialist principles. She and others believed that in far too many cases electoral expediency had overridden principled stands on issues.

The internal split was at its worst between 1952 and 1960. For example, in his biography of Bill Irvine Tony Mardiros noted the uproar caused by Bill Irvine's trip to the Soviet Union in 1956, and the fact that remarks attributed to him that the Soviet Union was "more democratic than Canada" drew intense internal criticism in Alberta. He quotes Irvine from a letter:

> As you truly say, there does not appear to be any valid reason why any-one should have taken objection to our visiting Russia . . . . You may be interested to know that we are all on trial before the Provincial Board which meets on November 10. This was inspired by Mr. Roper, who I have reason to believe is acting under the urging of Coldwell and Lorn Ingle. So we are prepared for western-style liquidation.[3]

Irvine also said that the CCF leaders had "soaked up American propaganda," and "oozed poison like a Dulles." An attempt was made by the CCF board members to censor Irvine. Elmer Roper called for his removal from the post of President on the grounds that he had damaged the CCF. These actions were rejected by the CCF Executive Board.

To understate the case, there was "some disharmony" in the CCF during this period. It was exacerbated by the fact that the party fell to fourth place, behind the Liberals and Conservatives in the provincial election of 1955, and appeared to be a spent force in Alberta in the mid-1950s, badly divided internally, with little hope of reconciliation.

However, new political winds were spreading across the prairies at this time. The Conservative Party, which had been politically dead on the prairies since the depression, was about to experience a dramatic revival. Memories of "Bennett Buggies," and the role of the Tories in the Depression had dimmed. Prairie radicalism seemed to have ebbed. More importantly, a new Conservative leader, John George Diefenbaker, a Saskatchewan MP, was set to change the political map of Canada. In the election of 1957, the Liberals were defeated, ending a 22-year reign in office. More importantly, however, the PCs revived in the west, capturing three seats in Alberta. Social Credit still retained 13 seats. By contrast, a year later the Conservatives elected all 17 members in Alberta, a complete sweep. At the same time the CCF was reduced to just eight members in the House of Commons. A new political dynamic was being forged in Alberta, unfortunately, at the time of a new low for the CCF.

This then was the state of the CCF in the province when Grant Notley entered the University of Alberta in the fall of 1957. He started out in the Faculty of Arts, not knowing what his major would be. He was torn between English and History. He had done well in Social Studies in school, particularly in the history part. But he also loved to read English literature. The lure to politics came naturally from his Social Studies and History background, while his background in English added a broader dimension to his character. He was gangly, raw boned, and unkempt when he entered the university. His clothes always had a "well washed" look to them. Later, Sandy Notley recalled that Grant got married in the only white shirt that he owned that had no holes in the elbows. He was there on his own resources and had nothing to spare for an extensive wardrobe.

He stayed at a rooming house in the old Garneau district. His landlady, Mrs. Keen, lived close to the university. Because of this, meetings were never held at Grant's place; they were always somewhere else. His parents gave him what money they could, but he had to work in the summers, on road construction, in a cheese factory, and even selling encyclopedias. Often he would hitch-hike home for visits since he had no money for bus fare. He had good memories of his first years at the University of Alberta, however, enjoying his studies. He was not active in any campus clubs during his first year. There had been a CCF club started in 1955 by two senior students, Bill Glass and Keith Wright, but it had not been reactivated in the Fall of 1957.

Grant's first political activity, according to his own recollection, came in the federal election of 1958. He says he was "conned" into driving an old Austin up and down Whyte Avenue by Ivor Dent, then a member of the CCF provincial executive. The car had a big "Vote CCF" sign on it. Later he also put up posters for the candidate in his area, a man called Arnie Holmes. The 1958 campaign was not the best one for a bright, young, new activist to become involved in. The CCF was almost eliminated by the Diefenbaker onslaught with the leader M.J. Coldwell and even Manitoba MP Stanley Knowles losing their seats. Needless to say, Arnie Holmes did not win. As Grant later said, "That was a miserable night, I'll tell you."

This involvement however, was significant for Grant. He had not been active with the CCF in Olds, primarily because of a lack of opportunity.

In Edmonton, although the party was still small, there was a chance to work with candidates in campaigns. Grant was vague on the reason for his initial involvement. From the vantage point of thirty years later it is still not clear. However, two or three factors provide clues. First, he was interested in politics at home. It was natural that he should seek this activity out when given the opportunity to do so. Second, he liked to "perform" at home, to give speeches, to talk to groups, and to participate in them. He already knew how to become involved in a group, making it easier to do so in Edmonton. Third, the CCF was desperate for people. Anyone who wanted to help was welcomed with open arms; there was no long waiting line.

Although Grant spoke disparagingly of being "conned" by Ivor Dent, he had nothing but admiration and respect for the then city alderman. He established a continuing friendship with Ivor that lasted long after both men were no longer involved together in daily provincial politics. Grant especially liked Ivor's sense of getting on with the job.

> When I think of campaigns and people busy doing things, I always think of Ivor Dent.

Ivor's appreciation of hard work appealed to Grant, who had little patience with those whom he perceived to be wasting time. His friendship with Ivor set him in conflict with the establishment of the CCF, which did not favour Dent or his approach to politics. As the former Mayor recalled later, one of the common impressions of the CCF leadership in Alberta was that they would rather play bridge than campaign.

Such a statement was not entirely fair. People like Nellie Peterson, Floyd Johnson, Betty and Tony Mardiros and others had worked hard for the party over the years. Indeed, the conflict really had little to do with campaign styles, and much more to do with the goals of the CCF in Alberta, its orientation on issues, and control of the party. The election defeat of 1958 set in motion far reaching changes which culminated in the creation of the New Democratic Party in 1961.

If the defeat of 1958 was dismaying to young people like Grant, the prospect of being involved at the start in the creation of a brand new party was quite exciting. It is not surprising then, that Grant remained active following his initial contact in the federal campaign.

After the federal campaign Grant decided to attend other activities in the CCF. He recalls his first meeting of the party with bittersweet fondness.

The first CCF meeting I went to was at a place called the Odd Fellows Hall. There were about sixty or seventy people there. Most of them were older people. I went in and the fellow who was chairing the meeting, a fellow by the name of Bob Atkins came up to me, and of course it had been so long since they had seen a young person at a CCF meeting that he said, "you must be from the Edmonton Journal." He thought I was a cub reporter sent out to cover the story.

He also remembered attending his first CCF Convention in 1958:

I remember the first CCF convention I went to. The average age was well into its sixties. I was the only person my age. I was nineteen at the time. And I thought, what am I getting into?

Despite the lack of young people there was still some resistance to the involvement of young members.

Some of the people thought that we were opportunists. My God, to be an opportunist in the Alberta CCF, that was hilarious. That was the claim. Better watch these obstreporous young upstarts, they may take us away from the tried and true.

Even years later, when he was speaking of this "welcome" into the CCF, there was still an edge of bitterness in Grant's voice. It is clear that he resented the implication of opportunism, and even more, he resented the implication that young people his age could not be involved for genuine reasons of principle.

Despite these early problems, and his own apprehensions, Grant decided to remain active in the CCF. When he returned to university in the fall of 1958 he became involved with a number of other students in reactivating a CCF campus group. The people he met then were to have a substantial impact on his career, and the friendships that he formed would stay with him throughout his life.

The initial meeting of what was later to become "Notley's Motley Crew," was held on campus in September of 1958. Only a few people attended. Keith Wright, who had been at university in 1955 and started a campus club in 1956, had returned, and was eager to take up the challenge again. Keith was from Lacombe, Alberta. His mother was Social Credit, and his father was CCF. In high school he remembers being a bit of a Liberal. At the University of Alberta he was active in the Student Christian Movement, which led him to the left of the political spectrum, and the campus CCF.

At the beginning of the Fall 1958 semester, after a year out of school, he was put in contact with Grant by Betty Mardiros, a long time CCF activist in Edmonton,[4] who was then working in the CCF office. Keith and Grant had lunch in the cafeteria, and decided that they should organize a campus CCF club. "All two of us," as Keith put it later. They also decided, even at that point, that Keith would be leader of the club during the coming year, and that Grant would be leader the following year, taking good advantage of the fact that there were only two of them.

They called a public meeting, attended by seven individuals. Later others would join, including Kathy Wright, Keith's wife. She had grown up in a staunch Social Credit home, but a very political family. Then, as she later recalls, "she had an instant conversion called love," and became very active in the Youth Club of the CCF.

Others at the initial meeting were Dan de Vlieger, a young man who had been born in Holland in 1935, but emigrated with his mother and brother to Lacombe in 1951. Dan had worked in various jobs, ending up at the Red Deer training school between 1953-1958. He decided that he wanted to attend university and upgraded his initial education by correspondence. He had been interested in politics prior to 1958, and by virtue of his European experiences tended toward the CCF. He was attracted to the organizing meeting by a notice circulated by Keith Wright and Grant Notley.

Bob Gordon and Janice Omners rounded out those attending the first meeting. A first-year student in Arts, Bob lived in Edmonton with his parents. His fellow students remembered him best for being a bit "uncoordinated," and for always being "dressed up." He could be counted on to come to campus with a shirt, jacket and tie, and even a vest. Janice was an education student in the same year as Dan and Bob Gordon. She was to be the mainstay of the club amongst future teachers at the University.

The meeting was held in a classroom in the old Arts building. Given the less than massive turnout, there was little question about who would be elected to the Executive. Everyone was awarded a position. As previously arranged, Keith Wright became leader, and Grant was Chairman. Bob Gordon was selected Vice-Chairman, and Janice Omners Secretary-Treasurer. (As Keith Wright said years later, "In those days women were always selected Secretary.'') Rounding out the Executive, Dan de Vlieger became Publicity Convenor.

Right from the beginning the club was energetic and busy. They put out a campus newsletter entitled *The Progressive Student*. The first issue came out October 24, 1958. It was typed and run off on a Gestetner duplicator.[5] In it they announced the formation of the campus club, its goals, officers, and the role of the newsletter. As well, they included a column called, "CCF Forum." It began with an explanation:

> This is to be a regular-feature of *The Progressive Student*. It will consist of a series of questions and answers pertaining to the CCF, its organization, policies, and platform. It is hoped by means of these the student will acquire a knowledge that will enable him to make a wise choice at election time.

The "wise choice" involved was, of course, to be the CCF candidate. The issues stressed in the first forum give us an insight into what the students thought was important in the fall of 1958.

Q. What is the CCF?
A. The CCF is a political party dedicated to the principle of "humanity first." The CCF believes in economic planning based on political and social freedom.
Q. Is it true that public ownership has been a failure in Saskatchewan?
A. On the contrary, looking at public ownership from the dollars and cents point of view, it has been extremely successful. Total investment in the enterprises by the Saskatchewan government has been 9m and the *net* profits have been 13m.

Other questions were:

Q. Should Canada get back to a two party system?
Q. Will it ever be possible for the CCF to replace one of the established parties? (answer—"very definitely")
Q. How do you account for the effectiveness of the CCF in parliament?

These themes are still familiar within the NDP, stressing the democratic goals of the CCF, debunking propaganda about public ownership, dealing with the "third party" arguments.

Also in the first issue was an announcement that a city-wide CCF youth club would be formed. Dan de Vlieger was put in charge of this exercise. Finally, the club proudly announced in its lead story that the "brilliant young CCF House leader," Hazen Argue would speak to a meeting on Campus on October 27, 1958.

In conclusion, we in the campus CCF are proud to announce that the man many call the unofficial leader of the opposition, will be on campus next week. Come out and hear him, won't you.

The price of the newsletter was set at "your interest."

A second edition of *The Progressive Student* was published on November 10, 1958. It announced that Ivor Dent, a "prominent city High School teacher," would speak on campus on November 14. His topic, aptly, was, "Let's Get to Work." A "Flash" noted that Harold Winch, "Canada's most controversial MP," would speak on campus on November 24. A founding meeting of the CCF Youth in Edmonton on November 13 was also announced. The *CCF Forum* in the newsletter answered questions like, "Would the CCF nationalize everything if it was elected?" "Will labour dominate the new political party proposed by the CCF and CLC?" "Will support from labour drive the farmer supporters away from the CCF?" The latter question, of great importance in Western Canada, was answered:

No it won't. Today farmers realize that their prosperity depends on the prosperity of the working man and vice versa. As the interests of these two groups are similar they will tend to work together even more in the future.

While not very original, it continued the ever hopeful answer of the CCF in Western Canada.

The campus club remained active, and was successful in attracting more people. It soon became apparent to everyone that this was in large part due to the "tenacious" hard work of Grant Notley. Grant early exhibited the dual qualities of idealism and zeal, of dedication and hard work. As the Wrights would put it later, he could make his contemporaries feel "guilty" about not working hard enough for the cause. Grant, therefore, became the doer, the person who would always ensure that things were organized, active, and productive. He would nag people about commitments that they had agreed to, until they would be compelled to complete them. It was an important lesson for the young Grant Notley. He was excited about politics, interested in the CCF, yet clearly lacking in some of the natural attributes of leadership at this point. He was shy with women, had a rather high pitched voice, spoke like a preacher, was gangly, a bit unkempt, somewhat less than a bon vivant, had little money and even less in material goods than most people nor was he interested in the mainstream international ideas of the CCF at the time. He came from a limited rural social background and, generally looked younger than his age. To counter these drawbacks, he was bright, single minded, and a hard worker. Slowly, over the months, Grant became the real leader of the group. Even the older students, Keith Wright, Dan de Vlieger, and Bill Glass acknowledged that fact. He simply overwhelmed everyone else with his hard work.

At an early stage the club took on a contrary orientation to the senior party. Early in the fall semester Floyd Johnson was invited to speak to the club. His speech dealt with planned obsolescence and the work of an American author prominent in the field of the time. Dan de Vlieger recalled that he thought the speech was very impressive. However, after Floyd Johnson had left, both Keith Wright and Grant, "threw cold water" on the speech. They criticized it for its lack of practical content. They both believed it to be too esoteric and lacking in practical import. Dan remembers being disturbed by this, but also recalls that this attitude became the norm in the club. Although Keith and most others were largely interested in national and international politics, this interest took a practical bent, directed toward getting elected, putting in place a CCF government which could effect real change. Grant agreed with this attitude, but in addition he was much more interested in Alberta politics. In this he was set apart from the other club members, most of whom cared little about the Alberta scene.

A city wide Youth Club was formed in November of 1958. It involved a number of people who were not on campus. Judith Gorman (nee Levine) became active in this club. She was a recent high school graduate, who worked at a Royal Bank branch in Jasper Place, a small town adjacent to Edmonton at that time. She was shy, and not too self-confident. She became involved when Grant called her and asked if she would be interested in attending the organizational meeting of the CCF youth on November 13. She decided to go and remained active in the youth group thereafter.

In all, the city youth group never exceeded twenty people, the largest number of whom were in university at the time. Quite often the youth members outside of the university would help in the student elections on campus. Judith Gorman recalls that she took an instant liking to Grant. "He was a kind person, he had gentle ways. He wasn't self-important. Even when he had to correct someone he did it in a very nice way." She thought that Grant was extremely self-possessed.

> . . . Grant never seemed shy. He seemed to have all the confidence in the world. I don't know what he really felt inside, I guess I have never really thought about it until now, but he never seemed to have any doubts.

When the student elections came in January of 1959, the CCF fielded a full slate for the first time in years. A special issue of *The Progressive Student* was published on January 14, 1959. It was heavily oriented to national affairs, with some space for campus matters. In his open letter to students on the front page, Keith Wright stressed a national view:

> Once again Model Parliament has arrived. Model Parliament was returned to the campus three years ago . . . . Unfortunately the other parties have continually treated Model Parliament as a farce . . . only the CCF has continually made an effort to bring its unique ideas to the fore in campus elections . . . . Thus, elsewhere in this paper you will find in detail the CCF platform for this years campaign . . . . Remember that the CCF is the only political party in Canada that offers economic, social, and political freedom for all citizens.

By now other young people who would remain friends with Grant for life had agreed to join. They included Lawrence Radcliff, Robin Hunter, Floyd Johnson, Jr. and others. A front page article outlined a "tremendous" surge in support for the CCF. Grant said, "I expect a sweeping victory in the Arts division and tremendous gains in the Science section at the Faculty of Arts and Science." The official slogan was:

VOTE for **C**ourageous **C**ampus **F**ighters

But the unofficial slogan was:

Vote Left, Vote Wright

When the dust of the election settled, despite its enthusiasm and optimism, the CCF had not won. Seats were awarded by proportional representation. There were as many seats in the Model Parliament as in the Alberta legislature. The CCF got only 6% of the vote, and four seats. As Grant recalls:

The winners were always the Liberals. The Tories were usually second, the Socreds third and the CCF fourth. It was always pretty clear, we were last.

This loss did not dim the enthusiasm of the group, however. They had elected more members than in any year previous, and believed that they were "on the way up."

It is clear from conversations that by this time most people recognized Grant as the *de facto* leader of the group. He continued his own hard work, and attempted to build his own leadership abilities. A key part of this involved public speaking. With some exceptions, most of his friends thought that he was not a good public speaker at first. Dan de Vlieger remembers that he was "not a good speaker, not naturally gifted. He prepared meticulously, and practised his speeches." The Wrights recalled that his speeches were always serious, with no humour. They seemed almost like homilies, although not religious. Bill and Myrna Glass did not remember him as naturally gregarious, having to "force himself" to be so in public. They thought of his speeches as forced and strident. For them he was not a natural or spontaneous speaker. Judith Gorman has the most vivid memories of Grant's early speaking ability.

I wouldn't call Grant charismatic, he was a dreadful speaker at first. I used to wince when he got up in public to speak. He was coherent but boring, monotone. He sounded very artificial. The first few times he was on television I used to kind of slip down in my couch and hope it would be over quickly, but I really felt that I should watch. I must say that he did improve very rapidly.

Indeed, Grant did improve rapidly. In fact, by the time that he entered the legislature he was universally acclaimed by political friends and foes as a first rate speaker and debater. But as with so many other things, it came only with hard work and patience.

In Alberta an election was held on June 18, 1959. Grant and his "motley crew" were active participants. In Edmonton Northwest the CCF was seeking a candidate. Myrna Glass's father was campaign manager and in January a meeting was held in his basement. Three young men came to the meeting. They came to tell people about the campus club and what it was doing. Grant so impressed everyone at the meeting that they thought maybe he should be their candidate. As Myrna Glass recalls:

> They tried to get Grant. Second time they ever saw him in their lives. They'd never met him before, and they were so impressed with him, he made so much sense to them, they thought, if we can get this kid for a candidate, he'd be very good. Except, that he wasn't old enough. At that time you had to be 21 and Grant was only 20. So he couldn't be a candidate.

Eventually another candidate was chosen for Edmonton Northwest.

The election of 1959 was a disaster for the CCF. The party lost the only two ridings it held, and its share of the popular vote dropped to 4.3%. The party had now suffered through two bad elections, the federal in 1958, and the provincial of 1959. It was clear to the leadership of the CCF that something had to be done if a left wing alternative was to remain electorally viable.

When classes resumed at the University of Alberta campus in September of 1959, a renewal of the CCF campus organization took place. A meeting was held on October 7, 1959 to fill the various executive positions. Bill Glass attended that meeting. He had been active two years earlier at the urging of Keith Wright when both were in residence. This time he was attracted by a poster advertising the meeting. More people attended at this meeting than the year before. As they had agreed, Keith Wright did not run for leadership a second time. Grant put his name forward. However, his first position as leader was not to be won uncontested. Bill Glass recalled:

> At that meeting they were just getting themselves organized, which involved the election of officers. So Grant was running for the leader-

ship of the campus club at that time. And as I was sitting there some-body gave me a nudge in the ribs after Grant was nominated, and said, "How about for the sake of democracy you nominate me. So I said okay, for the sake of democracy." I used to kid Grant that the first time I saw him I had the good sense to nominate someone against him.

The "someone" was a young student named Archie Stone. Grant won the election handily, and Archie was later elected study group convenor. As usual, everyone at the meeting was elected to a post, including Bill Glass who was made Treasurer. As Keith and others noted later, the elec-tion only formalized what had become the real situation.

It was to prove to be an interesting year on campus. The club con-tinued to put out *The Progressive Student*, emphasizing issues like peace, the programme of the CCF, and the role of organized labour in society. The latter issue was highlighted when Claude Jodoin, then President of the CLC, came to the campus on October 22 to address an open meet-ing. As well, the club continued to stress the democratic nature of the CCF, contrasting themselves with the Communist Party in Alberta. In 1959 the linkage of the CCF to communism was still a major issue, one which required tough measures, at least in the minds of the young CCFers. A sample of the tenor of that approach is found in *The Progres-sive Student* of October 20 of 1959.

We were heartened by the latest issue of the rag published by the campus LPP [Labour Progressive Party] Club (or is it now the Com-munist Party of Canada) which stated that the local Communists are now going all out to capture the National Federal fascist vote on campus.

We are now convinced (until now we only suspected) that there is no fundamental difference between the communist and fascist.

In the past few weeks, the communists have been calling on every-one to follow them in the "swing to the left." Perhaps they should be a bit truthful for a change and admit that they are fully as reactionary as the fascists.

Such an unlikely analysis seems to have been borne of the need to clearly differentiate the CCF from its competitor on the left. The Cold War men-tality was still strong, and it caused the CCF to attack the Communists with vigour.

In addition to Mr. Jodoin, Floyd Johnson, leader of the Alberta CCF, Fred Newling of the Packinghouse Workers Union, and Carl Hamilton National Secretary of the CCF spoke to the Campus Club. Grant also gave a speech about the oil and gas policies of the Saskatchewan CCF government. In addition, the Club held study meetings in the Rutherford Library every Tuesday, and sent ten delegates to the provincial CCF convention that year. Given the place of the CCF in politics at the time, it was a remarkably active group, and all agreed that it was largely due to the perseverance of Grant.

When the student election of January 8, 1960 was fought it was not surprising that the CCF club was the most vigorous. This was a time when there were other aspiring politicians at the university. Joe Clark, who would briefly become Prime Minister, Jim Coutts, for years a senior advisor to Pierre Trudeau, and Ray Speaker, later leader of the Social Credit Party, were all involved in the Model Parliament and the student elections. Grant recalled later that it was an exciting time, and an exciting election.

Once again, the CCF club put out a special edition of *The Progressive Student*. It featured a large picture of Grant on the front page, complete with graduation gown, as well as an open letter to all students. In his letter he dealt mainly with the international situation ending with a plea, paraphrasing Woodrow Wilson, equating a vote for the CCF with "making the world safe for democracy." The platform of the club stressed pay for practice teaching, improved teachers' salaries, disallowance of Newfoundland's labour legislation, equality in immigration quotas, disarmament through the creation of a permanent United Nations Police Force, and expulsion of South Africa from the Commonwealth. Although Grant may have had his eye on provincial politics, the club continued to emphasize national and international matters.

The election turned out to be a relative success for the CCF. It doubled its members from four to eight. They were still in fourth place, but the swing was definitely up. The Liberals got 25 seats, the PCs 14, Social Credit 11, National Federalists 7, and the Communists 2. It was a minority parliament. The leader of the Liberals, Jim Coutts, formed a government. The Liberal platform in the House was designed to attract the parties opposing the Conservatives, but the Grits only narrowly survived a non-confidence motion. It was during this session that we find the first public press report of Grant Notley. As leader of the CCF group he was quoted in the Edmonton *Journal*.

CCF leader Grant Notley supported the arms and capital punishment policies [of the Liberals] and in addition asked for a study of what he called the violation of the labour act in Newfoundland.[6]

For a rural Albertan, described as primarily interested in provincial politics, a comment on the labour act in Newfoundland was a curious way to begin a public career.

The next year would see the CCF get 13 members, and the following year, after Grant had left the campus, it elected 24, to become the Official Opposition. The five people who had revived the club in the fall of 1958 could rightly feel proud of their accomplishment, and all agreed that much of the credit went to Grant Notley. He had turned hard work and tenacity into solid leadership skills during his three-year university programme, using those skills to ensure that the CCF would become a credible campus force.

While Grant was sharpening political skills, he was also forging lasting memories and relationships. Not all was politics and business, even for Grant. Although it was during this period that he established his reputation for being somewhat "parsimonious," as Keith Wright put it, he was always involved in social occasions. Often there would be weekend parties, and Grant would be at them. He could also be spontaneous, as Keith Wright remembers:

He often organized parties for us. He would call up people on Friday, and say, "What are you doing tomorrow night? Let's have a party, we'll have it at Wrights." He enjoyed the company, the political discussion and the singing. I'd get out the guitar and we'd start singing the songs, "Solidarity Forever" and "Joe Hill."

Kathy Wright also noted some "spontaneity" in Grant's behaviour.

He actually, during that period of time, was a creature of impulse. One night about two o'clock in the morning, someone came knocking at the window, Knock, knock, knock, and its Grant. "It's us, from the CCF," he said. "We've come to talk," and came barging in (we were living on a second floor apartment) through an apartment of a poor young girl who was scared out of her mind, because it was the only way into our apartment. He came barging right into her bedroom. Dan de Vlieger was with him and Floyd Johnson as well, I think. All three of them ended up in our bedroom at 3:00 a.m. talking. In later years you couldn't imagine Grant being a second storey man.

His appreciation of things nonpolitical was actually quite limited, however. For example, he accompanied the Wrights to the film *Psycho*, and thought it was the "dumbest thing he had ever seen." It did not seem real to him, not to mention being a waste of time. For Grant, even social situations had to have a political point. Songs like "Solidarity," or "Joe Hill," were favourites with him precisely for that reason.

Such was the case also with the Youth Camp at Pigeon Lake. Shortly after World War II a farmer with land adjacent to the lake had made available an area to the CCF youth. The Youth Group of the day had built a small cabin there in the late 1940s. According to some accounts (although this could be considered unjustifiable criticism from a later, less hardy group), the construction had been "mixed up," with two layers of internal shiplap on both the outside and the inside. In reality it was little more than a ten foot by fourteen foot granery, but as Bill Glass recalled later "it did the job." It was rediscovered by Grant and his youth group, and on most summer weekends after 1958 a contingent of CCF youth would spend the weekend there.

It was dubbed, "Camp Irvine," in reference to Bill Irvine. Activities consisted of singing, boating, swimming, and of course, talking politics. No "adults" attended the weekends, but the Wrights remembered that no chaperone was needed. Grant was the chaperone. He was terribly afraid that the camp would acquire the wrong reputation amongst members of the senior party. He insisted that boys sleep in a tent, while girls used the cabin. This included even the Wrights, who by this time were married. There were two outdoor toilets, one was designated "girls," and the other "boys." Since the group was a bit "irreverent," they named these outhouses "Mardiros Lounge and Trace Lounge," after two senior CCF members whom they perceived to be in the "establishment."

The memories of the group about times at the camp are uniformly positive, despite the fact that there were few amenities, many rules, and little to do other than talk politics. The tremendous camaraderie that develops in a group settled on its purpose and eager to work on a programme was evident in the CCF youth. Throughout Grant was always its leader. His sense of rural social conservatism imposed itself on their activities, but no one rebelled. His single minded devotion to politics communicated itself to all members of the group, and they responded in kind. They were idealistic, positive, and active, and found in Grant a leader who seemed to reinforce their own attitudes. They grumbled at his nagging, but he always got them to respond. It was an obvious trait of leadership, one which Grant displayed early, even in social situations.

Given his campus position after 1959, it was inevitable that Grant would be drawn into the politics of the provincial and national parties. Energy, enthusiasm, and commitment were too rare not to be seized upon by the CCF at this time. After the defeat of 1958 there was much soul searching in the party. It looked as if the movement had run out of steam only 25 years after its foundation. Even worse, it suffered not only from electoral defeat, but from what Walter Young called "the schizophrenia of socialism in Canada." How could the party remain true to the goals of the movement, if the goals of the movement meant that the party would never be electorally successful?

This tension was at the root of changes which took place in the CCF between 1956 and 1961. In effect the leadership transformed the CCF into a "new party," complete with a formal and more durable link with organized labour. This was accomplished by first passing the Winnipeg Declaration in 1956, which made the CCF more palatable to mainstream labour, and subsequently by responding in 1958 to the call of the newly created Canadian Labour Congress to "establish a consultative committee with the CCF for the purpose of developing an effective political instrument patterned along the lines of the British Labour Party." This was accomplished largely through the efforts of David Lewis, M.J. Coldwell, and others.

The creation of the NDP opened the final chapter in a continuing struggle within the CCF. Was the CCF a socialist movement, or an electoral party? Was it a vehicle for education and eventual social change, which would result in larger and larger electoral victories, or was it a political party, which ought to emphasize the most attractive parts of its programme in order to gain power and effect the remainder of its goals? As Walter Young put it:

> The development of the CCF program and ideology demonstrates the struggle within the movement to establish the party and the belief of the party leaders that the CCF's failure was somehow due to a failure to make the socialist message register. To overcome this deficiency they tried to accentuate those aspects of CCF policy that promised

more prosperity for more people. They reshaped and changed their policy to make it more consistent with contemporary socialist thought and with the middle class attitudes and values that predominated in the Canadian electorate. It was an attempt to make the message more meaningful while avoiding any dilution of the ultimate ends of socialism. They found they could dispense with social ownership and at the same time retain their moral convictions about the inherently evil nature of capitalism. Their liberalism kept them from being communists while their socialism prevented them from becoming liberals.[7]

In Alberta, the battle was quite bitter. In part because of its small size, the leadership of the Alberta CCF was able to keep the party well to left of the national party. The attempted removal of Bill Irvine in 1958 was typical of the bitterness which permeated this internal fight. From the beginning the youth had allied itself with the "organizational side," of the debate, opposing the CCF leadership. As Judith Gorman recalled:

We were having constant rows with Nellie Peterson and Bill Irvine. We didn't think. We were a self-confident, arrogant bunch, we really were. We decided that Nellie Peterson and Bill Irvine, and Floyd Johnson didn't know what they were doing . . . and we could do a much better job than they could in running the CCF.

This attitude manifested itself in party meetings, especially at conventions. Ralph Eng, husband of Nancy Eng who would later be President of the Alberta NDP, was active in the CCF in the late 1950s. When asked about the CCF youth he remembered them as, "a pain in the ass."

They were always bringing up points of order. That was one of the big things. The chairman wasn't doing things the way he should be doing them.

I could see their point in some respects. But there weren't a thousand people at them [conventions], and they [the CCF youth] were a little sticky on sticking so absolutely to the rules of order and the rest of parliamentary procedure. They were right, they were always right. But, I thought, what difference does it make at this point.

Obviously the youth group brought their experience in the model parliament to convention, with the same zeal that the "newly learned" bring their new knowledge to all tasks. In the final analysis, however, Ralph Eng estimated that the youth were a welcome addition.

> I was glad to have them around. There were some people who were not so kind. I was concerned that the more young people we got into the party the better, because at that time most of the party members were older than I was.

In all then, the youth group was somewhat of a force to be reckoned with in the salad days of the Alberta CCF.

What stands out about Grant's early involvement is that he was always careful about his reputation. Just as he was conservative in his behaviour at Pigeon Lake, so too was he conservative at party meetings. He is not recalled as one of those obstreperous types. Grant remembers some of CCF people as influential in his youth. In particular he singled out Nellie Peterson:

> Someone who I have great respect for was Nellie Peterson. She was Secretary of the CCF at the time. Nellie was very powerful, one of the most able people I've ever met in politics. Even though I was often on the opposite side of issues from Nellie, I certainly had a great respect for her.

He remembers that at his first convention Nellie changed the meeting around completely on the issue of salaries for women, just through her own eloquence. Grant was quite passionate in his recollection. Even 25 years later he was impressed with Nellie's ability, her charisma.

> She was opinionated, often wrong, but always a force, always a force.

Although he was part of the youth group, he was determined to play a role in the party as a whole. Thus, although he led the youth at this time, he also attended conventions, and other party functions in 1958 and 1959. His reputation for hard work, and his conservative demeanor made him more acceptable to the adult party. He became the link between the youth and the larger party in 1959 and 1960. As such, however, he was vulnerable to the problems of being in such a position. He often had to compromise on issues while trying to be elected to a position on the Provincial Executive. In so doing he ran the risk of alienating his youth group associates and jeopardized his position as their leader.

Grant seems to have managed this transition without great problem. The Wrights recall that at the 1959 provincial convention Grant nominated Floyd Johnson for the position of Leader, the man most of them thought ought to step aside. Kathy Wright "couldn't believe it." But they accepted his action as "necessary" if the group was to be successful inside the party. They agreed that it was expediency, but they also believed that it was practical. Grant told them:

> If we're going to get anywhere in this party, we have to put aside our personal feelings and just go up and do it.

Grant carried this through all of his party activities, at Council meetings, and with other groups. He was always conciliatory, seeking to "keep peace," as Kathy Wright put it.

Was this for personal reasons? Was he simply trying to further his own career at this point? When asked about this his contemporary associates unanimously say no. They never perceived Grant as using them or the club for personal gain. He had managed to wed his own personal goals with theirs to a degree that made them inseparable. In his associates' perception, he was working to further their collective goals, not his personal career. In so doing he deflected criticism about personal ambition. Interestingly, the goals, the collective directions, were always organizational, not ideological or policy centered. Specific issues were important, and fought over, but in the end the role of the group in the party, and the party in society, were paramount.

Grant's sense of timing about political action, about the wisdom and timing of moves, seems to have been well developed. In 1959/60 the University of Alberta began to experience overcrowding. Residences were full, and projections were for larger enrolments. Students became active on the issue and finally a protest was suggested. Dan de Vlieger and Joe Clark were the original organizers, but they soon brought in people like Jim Coutts and Grant Notley. Four to five hundred students marched across the High Level Bridge from the university to the Legislature Building. At first the doors were locked to keep them out, but eventually they were allowed in. Although Grant was not one of the original leaders, by the time A. Hinman, then Provincial Treasurer in Alberta, appeared to speak to the students, Grant was up front with Jim

Coutts and Joe Clark. As Keith Wright put it, they made sure the CCF was front and centre.

Within the party Grant decided to run for an Executive position. At the 1960 convention of the CCF, held at the Union Hall on June 24 and 25, he let his name stand for First Vice-President. He was defeated but, as the youth members recalled, this did not deter him. He let his name stand for General Vice-President, and was elected. It was a significant convention. Bill Irvine, who had contracted cancer, stepped down as President. He was replaced by Robert Carlyle, but given an honourary presidency for one year, and a life-time membership on the Executive. Just over two years later he died.

In the spring of 1960, Grant graduated with a Bachelor of Arts in History. He decided to go to law school, and enrolled for the term beginning in the Fall of 1960. It is not clear what prompted him to do so. When he was interviewed over twenty years later, he indicated that in 1960/61 he did not see himself primarily as an elected politician. He thought that politics, and the CCF/NDP, would be an important part of his life, as it would with all members of the youth group, but he thought that he would become a lawyer. Perhaps it was simply the lack of attractive choices for a graduate with a Bachelor's degree in History that prompted Grant to contemplate Law. Whatever the motivation, he quickly took a dislike to the training programme. Kathy Wright, who typed his term papers in exchange for free babysitting, remembered in particular a paper on the theft of a broach which Grant thought was just silly. He said to the Wrights later on, ''This [law school] isn't what I thought it would be.'' In the spring of 1961, when he was offered the job of organizer for the New Party in Alberta, he left Law School and the University of Alberta for good.

It is difficult to underestimate the importance of this period in Grant's life. His university years established the main directions of his beliefs, and his personality. Foremost in importance was his devotion to politics, and in particular CCF/NDP politics. But his attitude to politics was curiously ambivalent. He wanted to lead, wanted to be recognized by others, and wanted his voice to be heard. But he also placed limits on how he reached that goal. For him leadership had to have a purpose, and as such that purpose became the outline, the boundary of his ambition. If he failed to achieve recognition, that was acceptable. If he failed because he had misjudged an opportunity or failed to exert enough effort, that was unacceptable. He was a blend of personal ambition and principles, a blend so well mixed that he generally escaped condemnation for personal ambition. He successfully fused his own goals with the goals of principle sought by his colleagues. Such a blend is necessary for any political leader, but it is paramount in nonpragmatic parties of principle like the CCF/NDP.

Grant had many natural advantages. He was bright, had an excellent memory, and an aptitude for analysis of social and political activities. He was generally unafraid of being put out front. However, he was not a natural orator, was not a dominating physical person, and he tended to be awkward in some social situations. As a consequence hard work was necessary to guarantee success. As several of his university friends commented, he simply outworked everyone else. In so doing he guaranteed himself a prominent position.

A corollary of his penchant for work was his preference for action rather than contemplation. He was always more interested in the race itself than the reasons for the race. As a consequence he was attracted to those in the party who wanted electoral success, who wanted to gain and wield power. In the struggle between the "ivory tower" and "electoral" functions, he displayed a distinct preference for the latter. He argued points of policy from general positions, and not from well thought out or finely articulated premises. He tended to want to compromise, to conciliate, to ensure maximum effort, avoiding the clash of ideas. As a "doer" he was loath to allow discussions of principle to reach the point where they disrupted the "doing."

Such an approach influenced his leadership style, making him a leader who sought to conciliate and compromise, or as some would say to homogenize. And yet, no one ever accused him of being unprincipled, or lacking in commitment. Even Floyd Johnson Jr., son of Floyd Johnson the CCF leader until 1961, remembered Grant as someone who was not a socialist, did not like discussion, and yet who was very sincere, and inspired great personal loyalty.

This latter point is perhaps most important about Grant. The combination of hard work, ability, sincerity, and single mindedness inspired loyalty in other people. They identified him with their goals, and he in turn modified his own goals to accommodate them. More than anything else, his university years demonstrated that he could be a leader.

3 THE EARLY NDP

MAJOR DECISIONS in a person's life are usually predictable. What seems at the time to be an agonizing choice is most often decided by a cluster of previous circumstances and attitudes. Some of these are only vaguely understood at the time and some not even recognized. Grant Notley was no different than any of us in this sense. It is understandable why he chose to leave law school and become a temporary organizer for the National Committee of the New Party, a choice which Roy Jahma, a CCF activist, trade unionist, and friend of Grant, later described as "very unfortunate."

There is a tendency now to idealize that choice, to emphasize Grant's commitment to the movement, to social justice, and to the ideals of the CCF. All of this is true in part. Grant was certainly motivated by a commitment to these abstractions. But he was more committed to the organization, the success of the organization, and to his own role in that organization.

This commitment was generated in part from Grant's university experience and his association with the CCF. For the first time in his life he had belonged to a group. He was part of something. Even more, he had become the leader of that group, satisfying both his need to belong and his need to be heard. In four years this shy, socially inept young man, had forged a set of satisfying personal relationships that he was reluctant to abandon. To be sure, he could have continued in law school, but by 1961 it was clear that his role at the university was over. There were new people, as well as a new leader: Irwin Weeks.[1] To use a cliche, it was time to move on to something else.

35

That "something else" could have been fulfilled in law school. But there were disadvantages. It was expensive and required considerable personal resources to finish. He had already been in university for four years. This was still the period before adequate student assistance programs, leaving people like Grant few financial options. Three years in law school would also have kept him removed from the New Party, with little opportunity to be near the centre of the action. As well, he was bored with the studies involved in law. Law and the culture of the law school seemed stultifying and oppressive. Finally, there was excitement about the New Party and its chances in the future. Grant was caught up in this excitement and, as he confided to Myrna Glass in the spring of 1961, he welcomed the opportunity to be in on the "ground floor" of the New Party.

Considering these circumstances, Grant's decision to accept the position as organizer becomes understandable, even inevitable. The "logical" course of staying in law school never really was an option. But his motivation was largely personal, not ideological, or idealistic. The party satisfied his social need, his need to be close to politics, his need for employment, and his personal ideals. It was the perfect compromise. In other words, he became a social democratic politician not out of an overwhelming sense of injustice, or a need to serve his fellow man, but for the more mundane reasons that affect us all, that craft our place and reason in life. This does not discredit him, or even diminish him. It simply makes him more understandable and real.

His decision to join the party staff came at an exciting time within the CCF. The long gestation period for the New Party was about over. The founding convention was slated for the summer of 1961. Stanley Knowles described this period in his book on the New Party:

> Difficulties to face, hurdles to get over, roadblocks to remove? Of course, the New Party is prepared for these things, prepared to meet them. They only tell us that we are making headway . . . . The momentum the New Party has picked up has its origins long ago, back in the life history of this country and its people. The New Party in full dedication to the ideals for which it stands will forge ahead and do a job for Canada.[2]

There was a sense of inevitability in 1961, a feeling that something important would be born, that the political system would be changed forever and that they would build a new Canada as well as a new party.

But who will build a Canada where people come first? Who is going to establish the economic planning, the programs of development, the health care and complete social security, the assistance to education, the opportunities for creative expression and human enrichment that are so long overdue? Not those who have failed to do so . . . . All they have done is to make clear that it is up to the ordinary people of this country . . . to those who believe in social progress through the democratic system, to form their own party and get ready to do the job. The New Party accepts that challenge.[3]

Heady times that were even more intoxicating for those who believed that the final realignment of political parties in Canada was about to begin. But, as this movement came to fruition nationally, with its general feeling of a new beginning, in Alberta it was greeted with suspicion and distrust by the leaders of the provincial CCF.

The roots of that ambivalence ran deep in the Alberta party. There had always been a group in the Alberta CCF which wanted a more "electoral" orientation. These included Elmer Roper, Ivor Dent, and Henry Thomaschuk (from the Packinghouse workers), Roy Jahma from the Oil, Chemical and Atomic Workers Union, and others. They were mainly urban trade unionists, and always a minority within the party. On the other side were Bill Irvine, Nellie Peterson, Floyd Johnson, Tony and Betty Mardiros, as well as most of the rural members of the party. As long as the CCF was small, with a large rural component, the "electoral opportunists" were kept at bay. Even the young activists at the University of Alberta were not enough to tip the scales. Ostensibly this internal conflict had been about how "socialist" each group was, or how "organizationally inclined," individuals were. However, these were simply code words for a power struggle between the two groups.

The national decision to create a new party upset the status quo in Alberta. It generated an opportunity for some to break the grip of the existing CCF leadership. The new party initiative was warmly received by the "organizational" group within the CCF. But, as Tony Mardiros recalled, some were less than enthusiastic when the whole matter was discussed at the provincial convention of the Alberta CCF in Edmonton on January 23 and 24, 1961.

The shadow of the new party hung heavy over the convention and its formation dominated discussion. Guest speakers were Hazen

Argue, . . . and William Mahoney, Canadian Director of the United Steelworkers of America . . . . He [Mahoney] maintained that "doctrinaire socialism" was no more an answer than Diefenbaker's "doctrinaire conservatism." His remarks, understandably, were politely but not warmly received.[4]

Bill Irvine, now sick and dying, was of "two minds"[5] about the new party. His followers were not. They saw it as a retrograde step, and were determined that it ought to be changed or rejected. The stage, was set for a battle in Alberta over the formation of the new party, the role of the CCF in it, and the eventual orientation and direction of a new provincial organization. For the leadership of the CCF the role and representation of the three groups, the (CCF, the labour movement, and the New Party Clubs), was critical. A party packed with "non-socialists" was simply unacceptable to the existing CCF leadership.

The battle over representation was fought throughout 1961, at the very time that Grant became an organizer for the National Committee of the New Party (NCNP). He was among five who applied for the position. Two were trade unionists. The original proposal included sharing the appointment with an urban trade union organizer, but eventually Grant was hired to work in both city and country. His task was immense. Although there had been some work done the previous year, and there was an Alberta Committee for the New Party (ACNP) which had been active, not a great deal had been accomplished. This was in part because of friction between the ACNP and the NCNP, but also because the "political ground" was not as fertile as in other provinces.

Grant set about the task in what was to become the typical "Notley approach" to organizing. He got into his car and began to drive to every area of party support in search of new members. He was used to hard work, and was keen to make a success of the project. His twin goals were to found party clubs and to ensure a large delegation to the founding convention in Ottawa in the summer. He was successful in both.

Grant's new employment brought with it new challenges and new people. He had invested considerable time in ensuring that he had good contacts with senior party members like Ivor Dent, Bill Irvine, Nellie Peterson and others. As a result of the change to the New Party in 1961/62, however, the leadership of the progressive movement in Alberta underwent a complete change. Heading the new group was a man named Neil Reimer. His attitudes toward organizational politics,

Social Credit, energy issues, and political parties shaped the early Alberta NDP, and profoundly influenced Grant's attitudes on these issues.

Neil Reimer was born in the Ukraine in 1927 on the Gnelper River. His father had been a minor official in the area, a mayor, who knew both Lenin and Trotsky. However, he was a Social Democrat, and would not have survived the Stalinist period had he remained. The family emigrated to Canada via Britain when Neil was quite young. Neil remembered the trip specifically, because his sister, who joined them again later, was forced to stay in Britain with an eye infection. The family came to Milden, Saskatchewan, by train and eventually farmed at Snipe Lake Valley near Kindersley.

Neil spoke no English when they arrived, and like other immigrant children, was forced to work hard to keep up. He suffered the typical problems associated with prevailing discriminatory attitudes toward eastern Europeans. His family was adamant about education, insisting that it was something that no government could ever take away from him. For his part Neil always felt caught between the two cultures, defending each to the other. He finished high school in 1937, and started university a year later.

While at the University of Saskatchewan Neil met Hazen Argue, who at that time was a brash, eager, aspiring politician. Together with Hazen and others he started a debating club in the College of Agriculture. But Neil was not to stay with agriculture. Instead he went to Regina where the first cooperative refinery was being constructed, and became active in forming the first Oil, Chemical and Atomic Workers (OCAW) local in Saskatchewan. He was also amongst those active in the Sherwood Coop, and recalls that the Sherwood Credit Union was so small at the time that (as the Secretary-Treasurer) he carried the money in his hip pocket.

In 1950 Neil moved to Alberta. He was set the task of organizing the oil workers in the province into the OCAW. There were no locals, no members, and he knew no one. But he brought with him a strong work ethic, a belief in the cooperative movement, and a strong belief in the worth of the trade union movement. He joined the Alberta CCF in 1950, but was not active until later in the decade. His attention was almost entirely taken up by the task of union organizing. In 1954 he was appointed Director of the OCAW in Western Canada.

His early impression of the CCF was that party members were more interested in discussion than election. Indeed, he recalled that, "organization was distasteful to them," or at least it appeared to be:

They were of the view that as long as there was an atomic bomb around, and as long as there was a hatred toward Russia, that was the thing to address. Everything else paled into insignificance. I think that they were quite genuine about it, but not very practical as far as establishing a political party.

As a result Neil tended to keep his party involvement at the national level. This was especially true after Elmer Roper was defeated in 1955, and Floyd Johnson became provincial leader. From 1956 to 1961 Neil served on the national CCF executive. He assigned his staff people like Roy Jahma to monitor the provincial scene. Neil was also on the Congress of Labour Executive, where he pushed hard in 1956 for the creation on the New Party. Thus, as a result of his background, the strong involvement of the OCAW in the New Party, and the opportunity to form the New Party in Alberta, Neil Reimer decided to play a significant part in the events of 1960-1963.

At the CCF convention of January 23-24, of 1961 the members were clearly of two minds about the New Party. Dominated by Nellie Peterson and Floyd Johnson, the provincial convention decided to hold a special meeting to study the whole proposal before the national founding convention that summer. During the winter and spring relations between the NCNP and the Alberta CCF were characterized by considerable friction. Peterson and others were very worried about who would be involved in the New Party. They were concerned that the New Party clubs were recruiting people with no commitment to socialism or its ideals. They believed that the whole effort smacked of political expediency, the kind of expediency that had been put forward before by the Roper-Dent group in the CCF, and rejected. For them, it was not a question of power, or control, but a question of purpose, of meaning.

On the other side there was tremendous impatience. People like Henry Thomaschuk, Ivor Dent, Neil Reimer and others directly blamed the leadership of the CCF for its failure during the 1950s. They not only rejected the arguments about the motivation of new members, but went on to characterize these arguments as the transparent rationalizations of those who wanted to hold on to power. Even more, they ridiculed the leadership of the CCF for its laziness, accusing them of keeping the membership and organization small in order to perpetuate their own control. Far from viewing the CCF leadership as guardians of traditional CCF socialism, the New Party proponents saw them as inept, incompetent, and destructive. Predictably there was not only vigorous disagreement between the two groups, but also considerable bitterness.

For his part Grant supported the Reimer-Dent group almost completely. Although he had respect for Nellie and Bill, he believed that they, and their lack of practical hard work, were responsible for the decline of the CCF in Alberta. As organizer, he became a target for their disaffection.

After his appointment Grant worked very hard at recruiting delegates to the founding convention, and in starting New Party Clubs. He was also active in setting out speaking engagements for leadership candidates, Hazen Argue especially. His tenuous position in the New Party is evident in some of the early correspondence. Writing to the Reverend Ken Iwaasa in Blairmore Grant was almost apologetic in asking permission for Hazen Argue to speak to a meeting in Blairmore on June 22, 1961. On August 11, 1961, after the national convention, he wrote Iwaasa again, seeking to clear up any "misunderstanding about his responsibility to the CCF."[6] There were obviously rough spots.

However, his efforts at recruitment were quite successful. Alberta sent 131 delegates to Ottawa, 71 of them were New Party Club delegates, 21 from labour, and 38 from the CCF, as well as two National Councillors.

Judith Gorman (then Judith Johnson) recalled the trip to Ottawa for the founding convention.

> There were four of us [all youth group] went down in the same vehicle. [It was] very exciting. I was the only one who could read Grant's handwriting, so I had to go. I left my husband behind, he had to work, so away I went. As I recall I was the Treasurer of the group, [because she worked at a bank] I had all the money.

> [It was a] very tiring trip, we were driving night and day. [We] did stop one night because we just became so exhausted that we had to. I didn't see much of Grant . . . because he was in meetings almost constantly and of course we were all working very hard. It was unbearably hot and humid but we all stuck it out. There was still partying of course, but less than other conventions. We all knew that we were doing something history-making, something that was really important and valid, and it required a lot of thought, and a lot of work.

Others, of course, had a different view of the convention. Nellie Peterson was very distraught at the results and according to some cried all the way home from the convention. Betty Mardiros, part of the leadership of the Alberta CCF in 1961, was deeply ambivilent, torn between support for the goal and distaste for the process:

> When it [formation of the New Party] started . . . I thought that it was a good thing. Bill [Irvine] thought that it was a good thing. I supported it. It was handled not very well, in terms of Saskatchewan and Alberta. I think that the prairie provinces were not consulted nearly enough. I thought that the decision was made too much on the top level. However, following the founding convention I had very serious doubts . . . . Not that it was not a good thing, but whether or not it was premature. I thought that labour was not ready for a political party and certainly the level of discussion at that founding convention, largely from organized labour groups . . . was at an incredibly low political level.

She recalled the debates at convention, especially on the party policy on NATO, as far too influenced by the leadership. In order to control discussion on the issue it was decided that four speakers on both sides would speak from the podium, and then the vote would be taken. On the pro-NATO side were people like Coldwell, David Lewis and Tommy Douglas, heavily influencing the outcome. Desmond Morton describes the process used to prevent a "pacifist" victory.

> Only in two areas was there bitter debate. By the 1960s, the Canadian democratic Left was withdrawing from even its reluctant acquiescence in the Cold War and collective security. The well-advertised horrors of nuclear weapons led to demands for unilateral disarmament, first in Britain, and later, in the United States and Canada. Nuclear disarmament buttons proliferated at the convention, forming one of the few common bonds between many New Party club members and the CCF left wing. The draft programme called for Canada to abandon NORAD but to stay in NATO. It was, frankly, a compromise and it was soon subjected to a bitter, emotional attack from the floor. As they had done in so many CCF conventions, Coldwell, Douglas and Lewis came to the microphones to hammer back the unilateralists. Whatever they may privately have felt, the successors of Woodsworth would not allow the new party to go back to his isolationist pacifism.[7]

Controversy also surrounded the debate on the issue of Quebec, and of course, on the choice of Douglas as leader. The result was viewed by the Alberta CCF leadership as, "a major setback for socialists in the movement." Disappointment, disillusionment, and in some cases confirmation of their worst fears produced different reactions in different people.

The stage was set in Alberta, therefore, for a decisive split on the formation of the New Party. Friction between the two groups continued throughout the Fall. For his part, Grant stayed on in his capacity as Provincial Organizer, charged with the responsibility of organizing for the founding provincial convention. His main activity consisted of selling memberships, and forming New Party Clubs, but he was also involved in seeking out people for leadership positions. In another letter to Rev. Ken Iwaasa in Blairmore on November 9, 1961, he explains that a certain Rev. Mullen would not be seeking the leadership of the Alberta New Party. He goes on to say, "his decision comes as a disappointment to many of us." However, by this time Grant fully supported Neil Reimer, and so his "disappointment" was likely more restrained than that of Rev. Iwaasa. Also in early November Grant wrote for, and received, the details of transition documents and procedures from Saskatchewan. As in so many things before, and after, Grant looked to Saskatchewan for leadership and ideas.

On November 5, 1961, a formal meeting of the Alberta Council for the New Party was held in the Savoy Plaza Hotel in Edmonton. The CCF was represented by Floyd Johnson, and Earl Toane as well as Doug Trace and Andrew Beryl who were sitting in for Nellie Peterson and Betty Mardiros. For Labour, Roy Jahma (Chairman), Jack Hampton and Henry Thomaschuk attended. Representing the New Party clubs were Joanne Cocklin, Verne Hardman, and Pat Ryan. Ryan would become quite active in the New Party in the 1960s. He was already Secretary-Treasurer. It was agreed that the founding convention should be held in Edmonton at the MacDonald Hotel on January 20 and 21, 1962. The meeting also dealt with representation, resolutions and other related business. Grant presented his report which included information that 60 New Party Clubs had been established and that the number would be closer to 80 by convention. He also pointed out that the Medicine Hat Tripartite Committee (all three founding organizations) had arranged for a federal nominating convention for November 18, 1961. Others, he said, were considering rallies.[8]

Despite the apparent progress, however, the bitter fight brewing between the organizers of the New Party and the CCF continued. The hostility toward the New Party which had seethed at the national founding convention broke into the open when the CCF held its final convention on November 25, 1961, in Edmonton. In other provinces the CCF associations had simply dissolved and transferred their assets to the New Party. Such was not to be the case in Alberta. The anti-New Party feeling was quite strong, and the Executive Board proposed three alternatives to the convention.

1) The CCF dissolves as a separate political entity upon the founding of the Alberta section of the NDP;
2) The CCF applies for affiliation with the NDP and retains CCF identity as an association of like minded people within the framework of the NDP;
3) The CCF, before dissolving as a political party and merging with the NDP, will make provision for the setting up of a democratic socialist association for the purpose of education and study, and further, that it be recommended to the New Democratic party that this association be granted the same privilege as the NDP national executive now grants to the Canadian Labour Congress, namely that of appointing a small advising Committee from the association to the provincial executive committee of the New Democratic Party.[9]

Missing, of course, was a simple resolution for merger and transfer of assets to the New Democratic Party. After much debate, in which both Elmer Roper and Bill Irvine spoke for alternative number two, a modified version of number three was passed which simply brought about the dissolution of the CCF and created the Woodsworth-Irvine Fellowship. In one last act of defiance the "armchair socialists" had denied the proponents of organizational politics the assets of the CCF.

Since Grant was still an officer of the CCF he was present when the assets of the CCF were decided upon. While Grant never recorded his own recollections on this night, Dan de Vlieger recalls that it was not a very "principled" exercise.

The transition, then, was not amicable. The CCF had owned a house, and other assets which were denied to the NDP. This caused more ill feeling. When the Woodsworth-Irvine Fellowship was formed (as the organization was referred to in the final option before the CCF Convention), and applied for affiliation, Neil Reimer moved to ensure that this affiliation was blocked at the national level, effectively denying the Fellowship representation at the founding convention. Neil also recalled years later that obstructionism against Grant's organizational activities reached such a level that he agreed to speak to Floyd Johnson about it. When Floyd arrived, Reimer "reamed him out" for the attitude and activities of the CCF. Grant, Reimer said, was duly impressed with this support.

Despite the problems with the CCF, the founding convention was a success. Three hundred and seventy-nine people attended, 172 from labour, 93 from New Party clubs, 85 from the CCF, 19 youth and 10 from Provincial Committees. This was the largest convention that the progressive movement had held in Alberta in many years, and Grant as the organizer was understandably pleased. The convention did a number of things, including passing a constitution, a programme, and electing officers. It was addressed by Mr. James Murray, a Labour M.P. from Great Britain, and Tommy Douglas, the new leader of the national NDP.

One thing that the convention did not do was to elect a leader. The Minutes say that this was because there was a "lack of organization, and a lack of capable people who would be available *at this time*." [Emphasis in original.] Several people wanted Ivor Dent to run, but he was in the United States, finishing his education and was unavailable. It is also clear from interviews that the party was not well enough organized at the time to mount a credible leadership effort. There were virtually no provincial constituency organizations, the membership base was small, and many CCFers were apathetic, if not hostile, to the New Party. When considered together with the fact that a federal election was imminent, it is not surprising that the decision was made to wait on selecting a leader.

The convention itself was a lively affair, with good debate on policy. CCF'ers like Doug Trace were upset with new rules which they felt inhibited debate. For example, resolutions could no longer be amended directly from the Convention floor, but had to be referred back to the Resolutions Committee, something which he believed was simply a device for control by the Executive. However, this did not prevent Nellie Peterson and others from trying to ensure that the socialist content of the New Party program would not be diminished.

Many new members participated in their first convention. One such person was Gordon Wright, a Jamaican-born lawyer, who later became a leadership candidate and subsequently President of the Alberta NDP. Gordon had been persuaded to join a New Party Fabian Club by

his friend and activist Philip Ketchum. Although Gordon took no leading role in the convention, he does remember what he termed the
"passionate" exchanges between CCF and New Party people on matters
of policy and organization. He remembered also meeting Grant Notley
for the first time. His single impression was that Grant was "very young."

The New Party founding convention received very little press coverage in Alberta. The Edmonton *Journal* ran an editorial which chided
the "socialists" and lectured the delegates on their role.

> Delegates in Edmonton will be expected to contribute to a sensible
> discussion of public affairs, not detract from it.[10]

The newspaper thought the chances for success by the New Party were
"highly doubtful."[11] A rally of 1500 people was held in Edmonton to
hear Tommy Douglas speak the night before the convention. The
Journal buried its coverage of the rally in a small article on page 27.
However, on page 28 there was a somewhat larger article on the convention, with a picture of Judith Johnson.[12] On Monday, January 22,
there were three small articles describing discussion.[13] The other political parties also reacted to the convention.

When the convention concluded, the organizational group was
securely in control of the party. Neil Reimer was President, Pat Lenihan,
a trade unionist from Calgary was Vice-President, Norman Riches was
Researcher, and Roy Jahma had been appointed Executive Assistant to
Neil Reimer. Nellie Peterson was the only prominent holdover from the
CCF executive. There had been a concerted effort to purge the old CCF
and put a "new face" on the New Democratic Party. As Betty Mardiros
put it, "we were considered to be an albatross around their neck."
Although Nellie was elected she too recalled later that she did not feel
terribly wanted, and retired the next year. The ill will which had been
generated between the two groups would never be healed. Even years
later when asked about Neil Reimer's leadership Betty Mardiros described
him as a "disaster." Others from the Woodsworth-Irvine Fellowship
were more charitable, but placed Neil at the bottom of the list of past
leaders in ability and success. For his part, Reimer is inclined to view
the old CCF less harshly. He concedes that they operated out of principle, but also believes that they were basically a dilettante group of armchair socialists. Later on, when he was leader, Grant made a major effort
to reincorporate the Woodsworth group. People like Betty and Tony

Mardiros became his enthusiastic supporters. However, in 1962 he was ecstatic that they had been purged, viewing them as blocks on the road to progress.

There is now much debate about the significance of the creation of the New Democratic Party. The Reimer era brought with it substantial change to the party: a new style, new people, and new resources. Without this change it is likely that the CCF would have continued to stagnate. Whatever the assessment, it is clear that it laid the organizational foundation for later gains.

For Grant it was another major turning point. Although he had left law school, he had not yet abandoned it forever. Neil Reimer recalled their conversations on this matter.

> I don't think that he ever completely excluded the thought of not going back [to law school], because I don't think that he felt that he was going to be as successful once he was in it . . . or as important in the movement as it turned out to be.

Neil also thought that Grant had a focus on politics, power, and public office and, in particular that he had a fascination with elected people. This meant that to a certain extent Grant was swept away by the events of 1961-63, and stayed on with the party because of the excitement and opportunity. Reimer described it this way:

> Once you get involved in politics it's hard to get out. Its not easy. You create your own swirl if you like. You create your own momentum, in a political party. There are few other areas, except maybe the trade union movement where you can create your own momentum in a personal sense. There is very much a personal feel to politics. You know what you've done, and you know where you were. There is a sense of accomplishment in politics. If there wasn't that, I don't imagine it would be worth it.

In retrospect it is obvious that Grant was creating that momentum, marking his own "swirl." How far it would take him was unclear at the time, but as he said years later, he always knew that the party would be a major part of what he could do in life.

While Reimer and Notley were busy forming the New Democratic Party, the outside world had been taking some notice. A year before, just prior to a by-election in Medicine Hat, Premier Manning had levelled his guns at the proposal for a New Party. He called it "the greatest threat facing this nation today." Later in the same speech he warned that the New Party was, "the old socialist CCF, masquerading behind the mask of a new home."[14] Manning knew a good whipping boy when he saw one. On the day of the by-election, January 19, 1961, the New Party did surprisingly well. Social Credit won with 4573 votes, but the New Party Candidate got 1326 votes and ran third ahead of the PC candidate who got only 1000 votes.[15]

The creation of the New Democratic Party also caused some consternation for the Liberal party. They attempted to counter its influence by adopting policies designed to outflank the New Democrats, to drive them further to the left. In particular the Liberals proposed nationalizing Calgary Power, and creating a public power agency. In mid-January of 1962, just prior to the New Party Convention, provincial Liberals met to discuss this matter at a convention with the theme "work and win."[16] The proposal for public power was put forward by the Three Hills Liberal Constituency organization, but rather than having the effect of causing trouble for the New Democrats, it split the Liberal Party at the very time that they were selecting a new Leader, Dave Hunter from Athabasca. Keynote speaker for the convention was Ross Thatcher, then leader of the Liberal opposition in Saskatchewan, who reiterated Manning's attack on the NDP, saying, "there is nothing new in it."[17] The convention received considerable coverage in the media.

Gordon Taylor, then Social Credit Minister of Highways, and later a Conservative, attacked left-wing parties, saying that he would prefer atomic war to being Communist, because Communism was a "living death," while he could "hope to survive atomic war."[18] Although it was a New Party, in Alberta the NDP continued to suffer the same old attacks.

There was little time for Grant to contemplate these matters, however. He was appointed Provincial Secretary of the New Party, and took up his duties immediately. Reporting to the Provincial Council after the convention Grant outlined the financial and membership figures. The total membership in the New Party was 195. This did not include affiliates, or CCF. Neil Reimer recalled that the CCF turned over a membership list of less than 300 to the New Party. The Council also set up several committees, dealt with matters like bonding, finances, and the *Commonwealth* (a Saskatchewan party newspaper), and outlined a budget (which Grant had prepared). Sparks flew at the meeting when Nellie Peterson questioned the appointment of Roy Jahma as Executive Assistant to Neil Reimer. She was opposed to such an appointment. Reimer defended the appointment as normal practice in trade unions, and assured the Executive that the President would remain responsible for any actions by Mr. Jahma. While Roy would have a voice at meetings, he would have no vote. This was the first of several conflicts which led to Nellie's defeat at the next convention.

The 1962 convention marked the transition of the CCF to the NDP, the transfer of control of progressive politics from a rural, intellectual group, to an urban/trade union group. That transfer had dramatic effects. The new leadership, which included Grant, was intent on establishing a winning electoral machine. Their interests were organizational, their approach competitive, and their focus provincial. There was little time for philosophical debate about policies and issues, an approach which dismayed many in the old CCF. Instead there was a deliberate concentration on short-term tactics, the advantage of position on immediate issues, and a new policy of direct attack on E.C. Manning and Social Credit. In the mind of Neil Reimer it was not possible to defeat Social Credit without discrediting the Premier. Reimer believed that the combination of religion and politics which Manning had fused together in Alberta was unassailable until Manning had been shown to have feet of clay. There was, therefore, a deliberate effort made to dig up and expose scandal in the Manning government, a tactic that the CCF leadership had deplored as gutter politics.

In all of this Grant was an enthusiastic supporter. He threw himself into the position of Secretary with his usual hard work. His first task was to set up an office at 9629-111th Avenue in Edmonton. The Council authorized $1500 for office equipment. Money was to come from the New Party fund (now transferred to the New Democratic Party), donations, trade union donations, and an anticipated federal subvention. In the latter case the initial request was for $9000.[19] Elizabeth Gilroy, a party activist from Edmonton, was hired as office manager, and the task of organizing the office began. By May 1, they had spent over $8000, sent out 100 membership cards, mailed over 3600 notices, organized a Victory Fund, and coped with the demands of the federal election in Alberta. Many volunteers were recruited, including Alice Jahma, wife of Roy Jahma, and Vern Hardman who was later to replace Mrs. Gilroy.[20]

For his part Grant was busy organizing both federal and provincial constituencies. He called upon the former members of his youth club for help, including Lawrence Radcliff and Dan de Vlieger. Radcliff travelled with Grant often, while de Vlieger was appointed organizer in southern Alberta for the election campaign. Such "recalls" to duty were to happen to Notley loyalists several times over the next years.

Organization in Alberta took many forms. The most immediate need was to secure candidates for the federal election, and to ensure funding for the provincial office. There was little help from the federal party. The provincial party had inherited few assets and many problems from the CCF. Throughout the Fall of 1961 it had struggled to keep afloat, while attempting to weld New Party clubs, trade unions, and CCF constituencies together. Outside events did not always help. In Saskatchewan, the CCF lost the seat of Weyburn, Tommy Douglas's constituency. On February 18, 1962, Hazen Argue defected to the Liberals, delivering a crippling blow to NDP morale in the already weak Alberta organization. In view of this, Grant's ability to field a full slate of candidates was testimony to his determination. In Calgary on February 19, 1962 he set up a coordinating committee and tried to organize membership activity. In other areas he concentrated on candidate search and founding conventions. At each one of them Grant gave a speech on organization and funding, or on the New Party. Most often, he would travel with an associate like Henry Thomaschuk, who would alternate with him on speeches. His schedule always included several stops, like Lethbridge, Calgary, Blairmore, Vulcan and Fort MacLeod. While he was enthusiastic about the federal campaign, Grant never lost sight of the fact that the federal campaign should be used for provincial purposes. As organizers went through on federal party matters, Grant also asked them to bolster provincial organizations, and look for possible candidates:

> I suggest that, as we have a number of contacts in MacLeod, it might be wise if we organized a meeting of the Executive. Lawrence [Radcliff] could take the first steps in organizing a New Party Club in the Vulcan area.
>
> I have the name of a contact who might be very valuable—his name is Garth Turcott, and he is a lawyer in Pincher Creek . . . .
>
> The second thing I wish to raise with you is something that I have discussed with you many times before, that is my strong feeling that you would make the best candidate in that constituency. While I realize your hesitation . . . I hope that you will reconsider . . . . [21]

Things went relatively well for the NDP in Alberta, although financial problems plagued the fledgling organization. On April 6, 1962 Mrs. Gilroy sent a letter and a cheque to the landlord for the rent, with apologies for the "oversight" in not sending it earlier. Such "oversights" were to be a common thing in the NDP of the 1960s.[22] On May 2, Tommy Douglas spoke in Lethbridge to a good meeting, and visited other towns in the area. Throughout, Grant coordinated the media for the party in the province, both free-time and paid media. In total the party spent $3836. One of the "star" candidates in the election was Ivor Dent, who appeared in many of the television spots in March and early April. Another candidate, in the Vegreville riding, was Ted Chudyk, later to become an organizer for Grant, and eventually a top official with the Manitoba NDP.

The results of the June 18 federal election were disappointing, but expected in Alberta. In a lengthy 12 page analysis of the election, Dan de Vlieger outlined some of the positive results. He especially noted that the total vote for the party in Alberta had gone up by 23,227, a 100% increase. Trying to put the best face on it he ended his report by saying, "My opinions may be wrong, but the facts are not."[23]

On June 4, 1962 at an Executive meeting held in Edmonton, plans had been drafted for the future. It was decided that the party should go ahead with its leadership convention in Edmonton the following January. Grant was charged with the responsibility for details. It was also agreed that Grant should organize a Victory Fund Drive, to begin October, 1962.[24] He completed a plan of action which he presented on July 27, 1962. It emphasized the success of his efforts in the spring, noted that a minority government in Ottawa might mean another federal election could come at any time, and anticipated that in any event a provincial election would come in 1963. Funds collected were to be distributed 45% to provincial constituencies, 40% to the provincial office, and 25% to the federal party. However, a sliding scale ensured that the provincial office received 80% of the first money that came to the party. The scheme had a target of $60,000, with an elaborate global system.[25] Attached was a membership list, which totalled 2,389 members. Constituencies ranged from lows of 0 in Three Hills, 1 in Athabasca, and 2 in three other constituencies, to 116 in Edmonton East, and 144 in Spirit River.[26]

While Grant's plans were well thought out, and had detailed objectives, in fact they were completely unrealistic. Indeed, the party was in a financial mess for which Grant was largely responsible. The office manager, Mrs. Gilroy, had been put on part-time through the summer. The party was financially exhausted. More importantly, the office financial records were disorganized and incomplete. After much discussion and suggestions for improvements, a financial statement was accepted. Grant's own reputation was hurt by the mess.

> Incidentally, the fiasco over the financial statement is slowly being forgotten amid the accomplishments of the office during the past several months. Providing nothing else happens, all should go well at the Convention and the Council meeting immediately afterwards. As a matter of fact, my growing self-confidence is but a reflection of a gradual, but growing confidence among the party members as a whole.[27]

As it turned out these words were a bit of bravado. In fact the Fall drive had been disappointing. A series of meetings and nominating conventions had been undertaken throughout August, September, and October. Grant worked hard during this period but the position of the office did not improve. For example, on October 9, Mrs. Gilroy wrote Dan de Vlieger, who was by then in graduate school in Illinois, reminding him that he owed the party $200.00. On November 2, she wrote again, pleading,

> Mr. Notley has asked me to send a reminder to you regarding the $200.00, which he tells me you agreed to turn into the office.
>   We are desperately in need of this money, and he would like to have it by return mail.[28]

When, on October 16, 1962, Irene Dyck, from the Bow River constituency (who was later to give millions of dollars to the Alberta NDP) wrote asking the office to send her 100 signs, Mrs. Gilroy wrote back saying she couldn't. "It's awful to be broke," she concluded.[29] When Dan de Vlieger did send the $200 he owed, Grant wrote back saying:

> We have been able to carry on this Fall, but the $200 will definitely be a help to tide us over December, which would otherwise be a pretty lean month.[30]

At the November 18 meeting of the Executive Grant reported the following:

It was pointed out in the office report that the financial position of the office was precarious, and that special steps over and above the allocation of quotas would have to be taken if the office is to be placed on a solid financial footing.[31]

Despite this the establishment of provincial constituency organizations continued, and plans for the leadership convention were finalized. As well, the first efforts were made at establishing the election platform for a 1963 campaign. Not surprisingly, one of the key areas for Neil Reimer was energy policy. Alberta had boomed on the sale of oil and natural gas rights, royalties, and drilling activity, and any future economic policy had to take account of the oil industry. Given his union's position in the industry, Reimer was doubly sensitive to this need. Neil had come under some criticism from an oil consultant in Calgary named Joe Yanchula (who would later be a party candidate), for his stand on some statements to the Mineral Rights and Justice League.[32] It was clear that proposals in this area needed to be firm and coherent. Later in the fall, Grant wrote to J.H. Brockelbank, a cabinet minister in the Saskatchewan government, asking for the Saskatchewan proposals in the field. He received a reply in October, detailing that policy. As a result the Executive discussed a tentative programme at its November 18 meeting. Reimer proposed a four point program involving:

1. Public development of the Tar Sands;
2. Extension of the cooperative movement into the Petroleum industry;
3. Net royalty lease system;
4. Surcharge on exports.[33]

On the key question of public power Reimer opted for a public corporation which would have the right to purchase and distribute all power in the province, obviating the need to purchase Calgary Power, and avoiding a debate on public ownership of power. This was prompted in part by the desire to exploit divisions within the Liberal party, which had tried to push the NDP to the left by opting for public ownership of the power industry.

On November 27, 1962, Grant wrote to Woodrow Lloyd, then Premier of Saskatchewan, asking him to be the main guest speaker at the January leadership Convention. On December 7, 1962, Lloyd responded, agreeing to Grant's request. Having secured his agreement, Grant, as usual, tried to occupy every possible minute of the Premier's time. He attempted to get Premier Lloyd to address the Campus Club University of Alberta (still keeping his attachments close) one half-hour after the Premier was to arrive in Edmonton, as well as to get him to go to Calgary to help with organizing a campus club there. An obviously annoyed Lloyd telegrammed tersely that he would not be able to take on extra commitments.

As the convention approached, Grant continued his efforts to get constituencies organized and represented at the convention. He was not always very diplomatic and, as Neil Reimer put it, "he made some enemies" around the province. (These people, together with those upset about the financial fiasco of the previous year, were to come back to haunt Grant after the convention.) But, by January 4, 1963 Grant was able to report to the Executive that 46 of 63 constituencies were organized, including 9 of the 10 Edmonton ridings. He expected another 5 to be ready by convention.[34]

Two other important events had happened during Fall of 1962. The first was the death of Bill Irvine on October 27, 1962. Bill Irvine had played little part in the party during the latter months of 1962, but despite that, there was a great outpouring of feeling on his death. He had become the "grand old man" of the progressive movement in Alberta, and his death touched them all. Many years later Grant remembered him fondly as a powerful figure, and a great orator. Even those who had been on the "organizational side" of the CCF, like Henry Thomaschuk, had good memories of Bill. Those in the Woodsworth-Irvine Fellowship especially felt his loss keenly. His death symbolized the passing of the old CCF, at a time when the New Party was about to select its first leader.

Of more lasting importance to Grant was the arrival of Sandra Wilkinson (later Mrs. Grant Notley) in Edmonton in the Fall of 1962. Sandy was born at the Emerson Hospital in Plunkett, Massachusetts, November 1, 1938. Her early life was spent on a poultry farm (which her grandfather owned), with her mother Gertrude Alice and her father Randolph Hyde Wilkinson, who was always called Joe. Sandy's father was a lawyer in general practice in Pittsfield, Massachusetts. Her mother was a housewife. When she was nearly five years old her father was offered the job of legal counsel for a small insurance firm and the family left the ancestral farm to take up residence in Pittsfield. By this time she had two younger siblings, Virginia Gertrude, and Wilkinson Lee.

Except for failing grade one, which she attributes to her young age and being last to read because of her name Wilkinson, Sandy had an unremarkable school career. Her parents were quite active in local politics, and at an early age Sandy went out with her mother knocking on doors for various municipal plebiscites. Her folks were Republicans, but she recalls that they were on the "liberal" side of the party, people who would likely be called red tories in Canada. After high school she went to the Rhode Island School of Design, where she pursued various options.

> I went there to become an architect, so for the first year I was going to become an interior designer. I decided that I didn't like it, so I then decided on graphic design. I didn't like that. So I did my third year in painting . . . .

She eventually completed a degree in Art Education. However, throughout her education her real love was the college paper, of which she was Editor-in-Chief. She was not terribly active in politics, restricting herself to attending a rally in 1960 for John Kennedy. She had no developed sense of radical politics, recalling that in Rhode Island she was generally uninterested in politics, and slightly conservative.

After four years at the School of Design she was convinced that she wanted to be a journalist and enrolled in Political Science at Boston University in 1961. She soon changed her attitude toward politics. Becoming part of the radical campus movement which was growing at that time, she travelled to Washington for a "ban the bomb" demonstration and went down to Maryland to try and desegregate southern facilities. She became involved with Abbie Hoffman and others, and wound up working in the campaign of a local professor, Stewart Hughes, who was running an anti-nuclear-weapons campaign. She had taken the semester off to do this, and when the campaign was over in November, she decided to come to Alberta to visit her friend Judith Johnson (later Gorman). She fully intended to return in February, but because Judith was heavily involved in the New Party, Sandy was pressed into service as well. She volunteered to help in the office, and met Grant Notley.

> . . . the first conversation I can ever remember having with Grant was one day he brought stuff into the office and asked me to type it. He asked me to type the complete text of a speech which he was going

to send out to the media . . . I said, "Grant, this is not how you write
a press release. You take two or three key sentences and say, blah,
blah, Grant Notley said at the Edmonton nominating meeting last
night, and then you have a few other key sentences, and then you send
them about two pages, double-spaced" . . . . He said, "ok, rewrite
it." So from then on, I was doing press releases.

Grant did not pay Sandy much attention, but she noticed him at once,
especially at the leadership convention.

But, I can tell you when I decided to marry him. I decided to marry
him at the provincial convention in the last week of January,
[1963] . . . . He was using his talents instead of being the shy young
man who politely asked his secretary would she mind typing something, and not really powerful in terms of staff direction. But when
I saw him operating at the convention, I said, I'm going to marry him.

Things took a bit longer than Sandy anticipated before there was any
talk of marriage.

As the 1963 Convention approached, the question of the provincial
leadership became paramount. One of the reasons for delay in 1962 had
been the lack of alternatives to the CCF leader Floyd Johnson. As President, Neil Reimer had become *de facto* leader during the period between
January 1962 and January 1963. By late 1962 Ivor Dent had returned,
and had decided to run for the leadership.

This was still the era of cold war politics. The residue of McCarthyism ran strong in the United States, with its inevitable consequences in
Canada. It was a period when anyone who was a Communist or a suspected Communist was under surveillance by the RCMP. This was especially true in the trade union movement, during what Neil Reimer
describes as a "shameful period" in their history. Prior to the 1963 leadership convention of the New Party the RCMP in Alberta intervened in
the contest. They were concerned that Pat Ryan, a member of the NDP
but also "suspected" of being a Communist, was reported to be considering running for the leadership of the party. One day before the
convention Neil Reimer received a call from a member of the federal
security force who was obviously seeking information. Neil recalls that
the officer said:

You're offering yourself for public service and anybody who offers himself ought to be appraised [sic] and get the protection that is necessary.

He went on to say:

"The Commie forces don't believe that you will be running. That you're playing a game. That you'll be stepping down and throwing your weight to Ivor Dent." I [Reimer] said, "if you're phoning me to find out if that is true, I'm telling you that there is no truth to that." Well he [the security officer] said, "we don't think so, but they have chosen Pat Ryan to run as leader, in case you do that."

The strategy, according to the security service officer, was for the Communists to attach themselves to Reimer, and if he decided not to run, to attempt to transfer that support to Ryan.

Reimer decided to test this information and confronted Pat Ryan with the matter at the MacDonald Hotel the day before the convention. When he asked Ryan about the rumour Ryan replied, "who told you" rather than denying the story, supporting Reimer's suspicion.

Such RCMP scrutiny of a legal political party as late as the 1960s in Canada raises a number of unanswered questions, not the least of which is what other activities of the NDP had been scrutinized by the federal government.

Although the main objective of the 1963 convention was to elect a leader, there were also a number of secondary objectives. One of them was to completely erase the influence of the remaining CCF executive members. Throughout 1962 Nellie Peterson and others had continued to fight a rearguard action in favour of their view of what a socialist party should look like. To Neil, Grant, and others, this looked like sour grapes and obstructionism. Much of this rearguard action centred on Grant, since critics were unwilling to confront Neil directly. Neil Reimer remembers that he could almost set his watch on return from an out of town trip.

They knew exactly how long it took for me to get from the airport to my house. Then either Nellie or Grant would call me.

Finally, Neil told Grant to quit calling him. He pledged that he would "protect his back" as long as he was out there trying to build the party.

One of the people who ran for office at the 1963 convention was a man named Ted Chudyk, a young farmer from Vegreville. Ted would become a life-long friend of Grant's, and one of the people who would manage winning campaigns in Spirit River-Fairview. Their initial contacts were not extremely friendly, however.

Ted was born in the Mundare area of Alberta, in 1933. Initially Grant did not trust him. He suspected him of being a Communist sympathizer, an opinion which Grant passed on to the national NDP headquarters.[35] Ted always felt aggrieved at this opinion, since he adamantly asserted that he knew too much about Communism to ever become a card-carrying member. For him, the mixture of social justice and individual freedom to be found in democratic socialism was the perfect compromise between capitalism and communism. More importantly for their future friendship, both Chudyk and Notley were attracted to the excitement of politics. They both enjoyed organizational work, and the electoral side of the exercise. As a result, despite early misgivings, Grant and Ted became life-long friends and colleagues.

Ted Chudyk's first impressions of Grant were consistent with those of others. In particular he thought that Grant looked very "young," and dressed terribly.

> I had to beat out of him almost, that his tailor should be the Army and Navy. He was god-awful, and he didn't care about his appearance . . . Grant was too cheap. I would tell him that what you're doing requires you to be, to present some presence. [His reaction would be] "but the money": He would never wash his car because it would cost a quarter or whatever.

As well, Ted recalls, in some ways Grant was one of the most naive people he had ever seen. He did not smoke, drink, swear, or carouse. Ted invested considerable time in trying to "humanize" Grant, with only limited success.

Initially, Ted recalls, Grant was not interested in people as people. He saw them only as sources of funds, or candidacies, or work for the party. There was no genuine interest in the people themselves. Ted described this as the "shallow" part of Grant, something that he never lost, although later Ted believed that Grant came to care genuinely for people and their problems. However, in 1963, it was plain to Ted that Grant was involved in politics for himself. And yet, he was able to keep

Ted's loyalty, and the loyalty of others, through his own urgency and enthusiasm. He left people thinking that they were important.

> He used people, but you never felt used. It wasn't for his own personal usage. He would risk his reputation to push you as far as he could.

What remains mystifying about this assessment is Ted's conclusion that Grant could be absolutely hard when he felt opposed.

> If Grant ever felt threatened by, or not total cooperation from any of the members, he just had them replaced along the way.
>
> It's not that ruthless, why wouldn't he? If he had the ability to do it? He would search half of a year to find somebody more harmonious. That party was being built, along with Neil Reimer's image, it was being built in Grant's image too.
>
> He never forgave. He would work with you very happily . . . but boy the time would come . . . There would be people who voted against his wishes, so he would work along with you in a friendly sort of way, but as soon as he could dump you, he'd dump you.

This attitude was especially evident toward Nellie Peterson and the remainder of the CCF in the NDP at the 1963 convention. Ted recalls that Grant worked to purge these people. They were a threat to him and his future. Therefore they had to be removed from the Executive. Ted was used to ensure that Nellie was defeated. He did not know it at the time, he claims, but realized it later. He was not asked to run for Vice-President; he was told by Grant.

> I was just told by Grant. I had a great deal of respect [for Grant] and took my direction from him. I didn't even ask why. I felt good about it. I had an ego as big as all outdoors. I was very flattered, and accepted it . . . . It was later that Grant confided to me that he thought that I was the only one who could knock off Nellie Peterson.

The Convention was successful. Grant commandeered his university "crew" to help with the arrangements. They spent the entire night decorating the main hall, finishing at 8:00 a.m. The leadership contest itself was a foregone conclusion. Neil Reimer was elected.

After the Convention the new Executive met to deal with immediate business. First on the agenda was appointment of the Provincial Secretary. For many, this also seemed like a foregone conclusion. But it was not. Indeed there was a maneuver resulting from the leadership contest which sought to put Pat Ryan in place as Provincial Secretary. For a variety of reasons this was almost successful. At the time Grant was not secure with the Executive. Neil Reimer explained it this way:

> Grant, with his immaturity, and doing the kind of things that were necessary to be done, he made enemies and sometimes he was a little, you know, didn't quite produce all of the things that he wanted to produce. He would say to a constituency, maybe he wanted to do something, but coming back home just didn't have the wherewithal yet to do very much, and it didn't make him look very good. But, I would feel that people like Pat Ryan, . . . with a lot of organizational experience shouldn't take advantage of that kind of thing. We were just in the growing stages, and a lot of people didn't get the policies that they wanted, that was obvious. They had a habit then of attacking Grant on a lot of things where they really should have been attacking me. But he was more vulnerable.

After the Executive assembled, the question of appointment of the Secretary was raised. Immediately Pat Ryan's name was put in nomination. As Neil Reimer recalls, he had just been elected leader, and "didn't suspect anything yet." It became apparent to him that he didn't have the votes to elect Grant. He decided to delay, and to force the Executive to choose Grant. As Henry Thomaschuk later said, "he became the Union director for a day." Indeed, Neil told the Executive that if Grant was not appointed, they would have to call another leadership convention immediately. He was prepared to resign over the matter. Ted Chudyk, newly elected Vice President, having defeated Nellie Peterson recalls that there was then a recess, during which he was subjected to a lot of pressure. He was in favour of Grant, but because of Ted's rural background, and supposed association with the Communist Party, he was suspect. When the recess ended, Grant was appointed by a narrow margin.

It was another one of those crucial turning points in Grant's life. Had he been defeated by Ryan it would have meant seeking a livelihood elsewhere, or a return to law school. Undoubtedly he would have remained active in the NDP, but certainly in a different role, and with a different outcome. Of course, Reimer's strong support for Grant meant that Grant was linked inextricably to Reimer, and indeed he showed complete loyalty during the time that Neil was leader. Only after Neil stepped down did any crack in that relationship appear.

Neil's strong support of Grant was undoubtedly based on two considerations. First, he looked upon Grant as his own protege in the party. By supporting Grant he tightened that relationship considerably. Second, he was vigorously opposed to any Communist "infiltration" of the NDP. Although he was tolerant of the right of any individual to choose to become a Communist, he was absolutely opposed to their organized involvement in the NDP. In his mind, one could not support both causes, and he viewed anyone who tried as an infiltrator. Such a harsh view was born of his trade union connection, and meant that Ryan's candidacy was totally unacceptable to Neil. Had the Executive decided to nominate Ryan, there is little doubt that Neil Reimer would have resigned as leader.

Grant's re-election as Provincial Secretary ensured his future in the Alberta NDP. It also ensured that his own life would be totally dedicated to politics. Other options were derailed by the fact that during the next five years he was involved in three federal elections, two provincial elections, and several key by-elections. It was an exciting decade in the NDP and in Canada, and Grant found himself swept away by the pace of events both inside and outside Alberta.

4 PROVINCIAL SECRETARY

ANY HOPE OF a respite between hectic events was dashed for Grant when the Diefenbaker government was defeated in the House of Commons. In 1962, after one term in government, with the largest majority in Canadian history, the Progressive Conservative government was reduced to a minority status. Worse, their best asset, John Diefenbaker, had proven to be a big disappointment, and internal dissatisfaction reached the point where talk of his removal could not be ignored. The result was that on February 7, 1963 the government was defeated in the House of Commons. However, instead of stepping down as Prime Minister, John Diefenbaker led his party into an election.

For the federal NDP, such an election was unfortunate, to say the least, and potentially disastrous at worst. The party had very little in the way of resources to muster. It had not recovered financially from the election of the previous year, which had come too soon after the founding convention. As well, some of the euphoria and expectation had worn off as a result of the poor showing in 1962. Many were now more pessimistic about a polarization and breakthrough than they had been in 1961.

In Alberta the timing for the federal campaign could not have been worse. It occurred at the precise time that the provincial party ought to have been concentrating on the run-up to the expected spring provincial campaign. There was little hope of electing anyone federally in the province, and a great fear that the meagre available resources of the party would be squandered on a fruitless federal campaign. When the

63

Executive met in Red Deer on February 9, 1963, it was to discuss how the party would cope with this situation.

Grant gave an organizational report which indicated that six federal candidates were nominated or had nominations scheduled, including Ivor Dent in Edmonton East. He urged that both federal and provincial nominating conventions take place during the federal campaign, and that funds for both campaigns be accumulated while interest in the party was high. Neil Reimer also urged that a full slate of federal candidates be nominated with close coordination between the federal and provincial campaigns. The Executive agreed. Grant was delegated the task of coordinating advertising, including television. It was decided that several short spots featuring Ivor Dent should be used. (As it turned out these were produced by Sandy Notley, who also helped produce five "talking head" spots for Neil Reimer later on, which she described as "appallingly bad."[1])

The federal campaign in Alberta started badly with a dispute between the three Calgary ridings. It had been decided on February 8, 1963, at a coordinating committee meeting, that there would be one committee room for all three area ridings. At a meeting on February 19, strong objections to this plan were raised. Passions ran quite high and as Grant described it to Ivor Dent in a report, "the meeting was very tense," and "almost came to blows."[2] Grant was forced to stay over in Calgary and mediate the next day. Finally it was decided to have two committee rooms, one north and one south. Donations and campaign publicity were to be divided equitably.[3] The agreement did not bring much more cooperation.

Steven Galen was one of the activists in Calgary at this time. A young man of Ukrainian descent, he became politically active as a result of RCMP harassment of the Shevkenko Dancers, a Ukrainian dance group, with which he was associated. That political activism took concrete form in the early 1960s when, together with Mort and Helen Freeman, he organized the New Party Club in Calgary Northwest. He became the major organizer for the Metro-Calgary area, and assisted Bill Steemson and Gary Storey in forming a Youth Club at the University of Alberta, Calgary campus. Steven attended the national founding convention in 1961, and came away with mixed feelings. He was especially upset with the Hazen Argue forces at the convention, whom he thought to be too overpowering. At the 1962 provincial convention, he supported Neil Reimer for President, but in 1963, he supported Ivor Dent.

During the federal campaign of 1963, Grant often stopped at Galen's home, sometimes quite late at night. They would talk "politics" as Steve recalled, never anything else. Eventually Steve gave Grant a house key, so that he could let himself in at anytime. It was the beginning of close relationships with several key Calgary New Democrats, who delivered the Calgary vote to Grant at the leadership convention in 1968.

During the campaign Sandy was responsible for contacting media stations, candidates, newspapers, and TV stations. It was obviously a heavy work-load. However, she coped quite well, and despite the abrupt and sometimes abrasive manner of her correspondence, managed to get results. Although there were good turnouts for meetings, such as the Tommy Douglas rally in Calgary in February, press coverage for the NDP continued to be negative. On February 28, 1963 Grant wrote to the Calgary *Herald* complaining about coverage of the Douglas meeting, disputing their assertions that it was a "luke-warm address," and that Douglas received "no standing ovations."[4]

Nationally the NDP was in disastrous shape. The party had only about $70,000 for the national campaign, and little help from some of the provincial sections. Despite this the NDP gained momentum, and wound up a series of successful meetings with a Toronto rally in Maple Leaf Gardens that drew over 15,000 people. However, the cries for "stable" government cut into NDP support, and on election day the party gained almost exactly the same number of votes as it had the year before. The big losers were the Liberals, who had started well ahead in the campaign, but declined steadily until a majority government fell from their grasp. Remarkably, Diefenbaker was able to recover sufficiently to stop the Liberal rush, and to save his own leadership for at least one more election. Despite Grant's best efforts, and a full slate of candidates, no one was elected for the NDP in Alberta. In Edmonton East, where Ivor Dent had run, the party showed well, but was nowhere near a win. The NDP dropped from 8% to 5% overall, far behind the Conservatives and Liberals, and 20% behind Social Credit in Alberta. The election confirmed, however, that Social Credit with its two seats would never again recover its previously dominant position in Alberta federal politics. For the next 30 years the Conservatives could count on Alberta for solid support. That this would inevitably have provincial consequences for the Social Credit government was not at the time foreseen.

In his organization report to the Executive meeting of April 21, 1963 Grant called the federal election in Alberta a "disappointment to all of us."[5] He noted especially that rural support had dropped back to 1958 levels. Most of Grant's report was self-serving hearsay, designed to put the best face on what was really a serious setback. He went on to assess the implications for the provincial election in the following manner.

My main criticism of the campaign lay in the fact that while this was to be a building campaign for the provincial election, the federal campaign occupied the forefront to such an extent that the provincial scene was all but forgotten . . . this makes our job all the more difficult in the succeeding weeks.[6]

It was one of Grant's endearing qualities that, like a bulldog, once set on a course of action he never varied. His view of the federal NDP, and federal elections, was that they were to be used for provincial purposes, and never to be taken seriously in their own right. After all, he would say, we will never elect any federal MPs here anyway.[7]

Grant also reported that despite the federal campaign, 17 provincial candidates were nominated, with only 10 constituencies doubtful of ever fielding a candidate. He also outlined a detailed leader's itinerary which provided for a full scale leader's tour, something that had not happened in many years for the CCF.

Not included in Grant's report was a description of his efforts to lay out research and background in several policy areas. In one area he was singularly unsuccessful. On March 21, 1963 he had written to Professor John MacDonald in the Faculty of Education, at the University of Alberta, asking him to get a group of people together to formulate an educational policy for the provincial campaign. He was careful to include a body of resolutions and former policy stands on the issue. He subsequently wrote again reminding Professor MacDonald of his request. He received a blistering reply which said in part:

I have talked to some of my colleagues . . . . We are in very firm agreement on the following points.

1) An educational policy . . . is not set down in a week or two, but requires careful study over a much longer period. It may be part of the tradition of the other Canadian political parties that policies are not carefully thought out before presentation to the electorate (but jotted down on the backs of envelopes in smoke

filled rooms); we do not think that this ought to be true of the NDP.

2) We do not wish to be relegated to the status of "boffins" or back room boys, or to be seen as experts or "eggheads" whose task it is to present briefs to "practical men" who use them as they see fit . . . . We feel that the kind of proposal set out in your letter has the effect of cutting us off from the party.[8]

There is no record of a reply to Professor MacDonald from Grant, but one could conceive of Grant writing back and saying, "so what's your point?"

In fact, a campaign platform was discussed and passed by the Executive at its April meeting. It was a 13 point programme which included:

1. A new economic balance;
2. A 5% reduction in gasoline prices by supporting co-op refineries;
3. Public power and gas at cost;
4. Open Government;
5. Medicine;
6. Public Auto insurance;
7. A Department of Cooperatives;
8. Labour act reform;
9. A crown corporation to develop the tar sands;
10. Free direct dialing inside Alberta.[9]

Neil Reimer also informed the Executive that he had gone on "full-time status as leader" on March 1, and that his expenses would be picked up by the OCAW. The Executive also agreed to co-sign a $5000 loan to enable the party to start organizing immediately.

The election was called in May, 1963. Grant had a dual role. He was both campaign chairman and a candidate in Edmonton Northwest. In his former role Neil Reimer recalls that Grant's main job was to get candidates, and in that effort they travelled together extensively.

We were in Medicine Hat. We had a reasonable meeting. The next evening we were supposed to be in Grande Prairie. We had something else to do during the day. This was the first time that I realized that youth had something to say for itself, you know, because he made me feel old sometimes the way he carried on with his car. Of course he was in love with his car. It was his first love. He had a Plymouth and I think that he must have driven it nearly 300,000 miles. It was surprising how that motor stood up, but he just loved that car. He lived in it.

So we take off at night. Whatever we're going to do, with that schedule we're going to have to drive all night. That was his answer to the problem. So we did arrive there [at Grande Prairie] on time and by golly for us in those days it was a big meeting. We had nearly 50 people out. They weren't that interested in nominating, but this was a nominating meeting. So I spoke on the importance of nominating . . . . So they nominated three people. The Chairman, a well known NDPer up there, was nominated last. And because he was nominated last, it went through my mind that I better take over the chair. So I said, we'll ask the people . . . whether they'll stand. I did that. So the first guy declines, the second guy declines. Charlie [the chairman] says, "well . . . I don't think so." So I said, seeing as so and so declined and so and so declined, but Charlie only says he doesn't think so, I declare him elected.

Finding candidates was a tough job for the NDP in 1963. Although there was enthusiasm about the New Party, there was little money, and even less organization in the country. Years of organizational neglect had atrophied the old CCF organization, leaving Grant the painstaking job of rebuilding it.

In the Provincial Office Verne Hardman, who had volunteered for several positions in the period 1961-1963, and headed the Constitution Committee at the 1962 provincial convention, took over as Office Manager. She was recruited by Neil and Grant. She did not know Neil very well, but agreed to take the job.

Verne had moved to Edmonton with her husband Dave in 1953. Both of them had a strong sense of fairness, generated by their experience in the Depression. They became active with the CCF, and eventually Dave became a candidate. Verne volunteered to help in the old Woodsworth House organization, where she got to know people like Alice Jahma and Ivor Dent. When the CCF dissolved in 1961, both she and Dave became solid supporters of the NDP.

She met Grant for the first time in 1958. She was immediately impressed with him, describing him as a born leader. Since she already had some experience, and knew Grant, she was agreeable to taking the position as Office Manager. She recruited other people to help in the office, including Sandy. She recalls that Grant was singleminded about his passion for politics. He never seemed interested in anything else, including dating, unless it involved the party.

During the campaign this passion, together with the enormous difficulties in the campaign, led him to express great frustration. Verne remembered Grant as both a public and private person. In private he would get so frustrated that he would blow up. He would, as Verne put it, "rant and rave." At this point Verne said, she would, "go for coffee." In public he was completely under control, and able to perform both as an organizer and as a candidate.

As the deadline for nomination day approached in June of 1963, the scramble for candidates became even more intense. On nomination day, June 3, 1963, there was still several uncovered ridings. Grant went to St. Paul to ensure that the candidate there was properly nominated. One of the ridings still vacant was Calgary Glenmore. Sandy, who by this time was planning for the future, offered to try and find a candidate by 2:00 p.m. that day. Grant was more than a bit skeptical, indicating that he had been trying for eight weeks to get a candidate. Sandy then offered to make a deal with Grant, obliging him to drive her to her home in Massachusetts if she could produce a candidate. He agreed. Later that day she got Steve Galen to run, and Grant was forced to drive her home.

On nomination day the NDP had 53 candidates. The Liberals had 55, and the Conservatives had 33. Only the Social Credit had a full slate of 63. The Premier, E.C. Manning, ran in Strathcona East. Dave Hunter, the Liberal leader, ran in Athabasca, while Milt Haradence, the PC leader, ran in Calgary West. Grant ran in Edmonton Northwest (where the Edmonton *Journal* misspelled his name) and Neil Reimer ran in Edmonton Northeast. Despite all of the effort to secure candidates, the party believed it really only had one chance, that being in Neil's riding. Accordingly, they concentrated on it, putting in major resources and people.

This was the first campaign in which the NDP had run provincially, and the first under the leadership of Neil Reimer. Two fundamental principles guided the campaign. The first was that Social Credit could not be defeated until Ernest Manning was discredited. The second was that the NDP had to concentrate more on issues relevant to the electorate, pocket book issues, and less on the kinds of ideological or general issues which had been emphasized by the CCF. Along with these assumptions, it was agreed that the party would now concentrate in the urban areas, more in keeping with the new alliance with labour.

In 1963 the question of Manning's integrity was broached by Reimer through the open government issue.

> I insisted that we address the question of open government. The Legislature here didn't seem to mean very much. We had taken an analysis and a count on Orders-in-Council. Manning ran the province by Order-in-Council. There wasn't much doubt about it. Whoever was in the Opposition . . . there was no real Opposition.

It was a strong attack on Manning's dictatorial style, and the beginning of a different style of leadership than the CCF/NDP had been used to. Ted Chudyk thought this difference was quite important.

> Neil came to the conclusion at sometime in his life that in Alberta, the only way that you could move forward was to destroy Manning . . . so policy became secondary. He didn't think that you could debate your way through Manning. Manning with his pulpit almost mesmerized the people, so he could almost even sell an incorrect or wrong policy, and get away with it. Neil felt that somebody had to bring Manning down, to get through that he was corrupt, discredit him, whatever it took. Even today, Neil feels that Lougheed owes him a great favour. It was because of Neil Reimer that it was possible for Peter Lougheed to form a government.
> As long as we were prepared to let Manning play God, and run around this province with a Bible, and afraid to attack him, we wouldn't succeed.

During the campaign Neil hammered on how closed government led to scandal and patronage. On June 6, 1963 he charged that a pulp mill was being delayed in Edson because of contributions by a rival company to the Social Credit party. He continued his theme of open government on radio, TV, and in his speeches. His attacks so irked Manning that the Premier lashed back in a speech, calling Reimer a "gutter politician," and saying that he had "nothing but utter contempt for rumour and scandal mongers." This tactic, which was controversial in the party, nevertheless seemed to touch a nerve in Social Credit, whose leaders had for so long portrayed themselves as good Christian men.

On the policy side the NDP stuck to its more pragmatic approach, continuing to emphasize those items of the platform that were people oriented. The issue of medicare was especially important. The Alberta government had not yet announced its intentions, and Reimer charged that they were simply playing politics with people's health. The issue was extensively addressed by Saskatchewan Premier Woodrow Lloyd when he spoke on behalf of the Alberta NDP to a meeting of 140 people in Medicine Hat on June 5, 1963. Manning was forced to deny that the election had delayed announcement of a plan. (However, on June 14, three days before the election, Premier Manning announced a full medical care plan for Albertans, just in time to make it the top story for the whole weekend.)

Throughout the campaign the NDP picked away at several other issues: Education, the farm problem, public power, and other important planks were publicized on radio or in the print media, usually late at night on the electronic media because of cost. It was during this time that Sandy Notley produced the series of "appallingly bad" talking heads for TV. It was a time of learning for all.

As a candidate in Edmonton Northwest Grant did not have as much time to devote to campaigning as he would have liked. He did attend forums however, and on June 10, 1963 he spoke to a meeting organized by the OCAW, at which his two opponents, Gerald Amerongen for the Conservatives (who would later become Speaker under the Lougheed government) and Ian Nichol for the Liberals, also spoke. The Socreds did not appear. Grant described the NDP as the only logical alternative to Social Credit, and proposed property tax relief for property owners. But he concentrated mainly on the issue of open government, hitting the Socreds for governing by Cabinet and Boards and usurping the powers of the Legislature.[10] In his own style he followed Neil closely.

Throughout the campaign the NDP enjoyed relatively good press, and a sense of momentum and optimism. A local commentator, Eddie Keen, said in his column:

> The New Democratic Party is waging the most vigorous campaign with its 53 candidates.[11]

On June 9, 1963, the NDP was able to mount a rally of 1500 people at the city auditorium, at which both Reimer and Tommy Douglas spoke. Reimer hit hard at Manning, accusing him of, "stooping to the slimy slanders of McCarthyism."[12] An editorial cartoon in the Edmonton *Journal* the next day showed Reimer and the other party leaders with axes, looking contemplatively at a "Manning Tree." In all, there was a good feeling in the party about the campaign.

By contrast the other opposition parties had not been as successful. The Liberals suffered from a number organizational problems.[13] In the middle of the campaign for example they were forced to move a cocktail party from the MacDonald Hotel to a private home because the serving of liquor at a public function was forbidden during an election campaign. More importantly the proposal for publicly owned power, which had been passed by the Liberals in January, continued to plague the party in the campaign. It finally boiled over in June, with an open split between candidates on the issue.[14] The Conservatives, who had not yet recovered provincially, were only able to muster 33 candidates, making them a marginal force.

On the eve of the election, the NDP seemed to be in relatively good shape, and expectations were high that at least Neil would be elected. Even the Edmonton *Journal* was predicting that there would be more opposition than in 1959.

The results, were, of course, a landslide for Social Credit. The unofficial campaign slogan for the government had been "63 in 63," referring to the 63 seats in the House, and the year 1963. They missed it by only 3, getting 60 seats, along with almost 55% of the vote. The Liberals got 19.8% of the vote and 2 seats, while one independent was elected. The Conservatives got 12.7% of the vote, but no seats. For all of its vigour the campaign only yielded 9.5% for the NDP and no seats. Although this was double the 1959 percentage, it was still well behind the other two opposition parties.

In his own seat Neil Reimer ran second, but lost by 1449 votes. Compared to the provincial average, Grant did quite well, although he ran fourth, and did not win a poll. He received 1313 votes, to 4388 for Social Credit, or about 15.6% of the vote. For a 23 year-old rookie, who was only a part-time candidate, it was a good showing. Despite the lack of a win, the party was pleased. On election night Reimer told the press that the NDP would hold its first meeting the next day for the next election. In private he was pleased that they had doubled the vote, but less pleased with the results in Edmonton. He was particularly incensed at a number of irregularities, which he brought to legal notice later.

In his report to the Executive after the election Grant emphasized the overall gain in popular vote. He pointed out that the gain was real and not the result of simply running more candidates, since the party had improved its standing in 27 of the 32 ridings it had contested in 1959. He also pointed out that coverage was much better in the media, especially in the Edmonton area, and that there had been a far larger number of people participating in each constituency. It was apparent that although the party had not elected anyone, it had taken significant steps toward building for the future. More importantly for Grant personally, he had firmly established himself as Provincial Secretary. Two elections had gone a long way toward dispelling any doubts about his ability to handle the job. Grant was now able to relax somewhat, and contemplate the longer term.

From the time he entered his university career, and through the time that he worked for the New Party, Grant had devoted himself almost completely to politics. To say that it consumed him would certainly qualify for understatement. With little time for anything else, the first casualty of this preoccupation was his social life, or more precisely, any relationship with someone who was not political. When faced with the question of Grant's lack of attention to members of the opposite sex people inevitably would comment that it would be strange for someone else, but not for Grant. As Verne Hardman said:

> He had no time for women. Politics was it. Grant and I were great friends. Grant gave me a big kiss anytime I met him, didn't matter where it was, but that was strictly that we were friends.

Ted Chudyk also remembers that Grant seldom dated, although one or two women had "set their cap for him." He would rather sit down and discuss politics with someone.

Grant did not dislike women. He worked closely with women throughout his life, and generally was respectful of their contribution, but it was always in the context of party work. Indeed, he was so oblivious to this facet of male-female relationships, that occasionally he had to be saved from himself. In one case in particular Verne Hardman recalls that he had "double-booked" himself.

> There was a meeting at Barrhead [Grant had asked both Sandy and another woman to go with him], and they both had every intention of going. Neither one knew that the other was going. Grant didn't realize that this was a problem. I took him in the office and shut the door, and I told him. "Well," he said, "I'm just taking them along to work

on registration desk.'' They thought there was something more to it, but not Grant.

Sandy recalls the incident from her point of view, since Grant called her and cancelled the "date" with her.

So Grant made the obvious decision that I would not have a nervous breakdown or slit my wrists if he told me he wasn't taking me, so I was the one who didn't go.

In an interview 20 years later Grant recalled his first meeting with Sandy in very general terms.

She was in Edmonton. She was also active in the Church; and still is. Her perspective was much more one of Christian activism. Her first political involvement in the United States was in the Hughes campaign for the Senate when Bobby Kennedy was elected.

When I first met her though she had a lot of American views. She was not in favour of medicare. She was left wing in the sense of peace but not very left wing in other social areas.

She came over and volunteered to work in the provincial election campaign of 1963 at our office. I was Secretary at the time, and one thing led to another.

The "one thing and another" was quite hurried as Sandy recalls. They went out to a few parties during the campaign, but usually with other people. On the 24th of May Sandy went with Grant, Lawrence Radcliff, and another girl friend to Jasper. They came back by way of Olds, where Sandy was introduced to Grant's parents.

They were very nice. I like them very much, particularly Grant's Dad . . . . Wally would really have liked to have a daughter, and was really glad he finally had one.

She was not as impressed with living conditions in rural Alberta however.

Because I was from the east and I had never been in a farm house before, I had never been in a house where there wasn't the full complement of plumbing. So often we had to go outside to the bathroom. That surprised me.

During the 1963 provincial campaign Sandy and Grant became closer, and often Sandy was called on to "rescue" Grant from himself or others.

We were in the office one day, and Myrna Glass phones and says, Sandy, Grant's been arrested. You've got to go down to the police station right away and pay his fine. It turned out that he was getting repeated summonses for a $2.00 parking ticket, and Lawrence Radcliff had been throwing them behind the bureau. So one day they came into the committee room when he was campaigning, and arrested him for the $2.00 parking ticket, and threw him in jail for a couple of hours. I went down and paid the $20.00 fine and they let him out.

Bill Glass, who was a campaign manager at the time, was in the office quite often. He thought he saw an instant spark between Sandy and Grant. Most of the old university crowd had paired off by then, leaving only Grant and one other girl. Bill did not think that she was suitable for Grant and was pleased that Grant and Sandy seemed to hit it off.

When I saw him relating to Sandy in a high spirited fashion, I thought obviously this has got to be something better. She can stand toe to toe with him, put up with him, and stand up to him. She was capable, tended to be a little on the bossy side, and rubbed some of us the wrong way, but I got along quite well with Sandy.

When Sandy was due to go back down to the States I sat down with Grant in the office one day, and had a little personal chat with him. I suggested to him that he could do worse. I like to claim. . .that I had prompted him to take some action here. He always claimed that he had already thought of it by then.

Whatever the reason, whether it was because Sandy had made a deal with Grant on the candidate in Calgary, Bill Glass's encouragement, or because he wanted to, Grant decided to drive Sandy back to Massachussets to her parents' home. They went with two other people. In Pittsfield, Massachusetts on the 28th of June, 1963, Grant proposed.

He actually proposed in Pittsfield, walking around the block about 8 times; and when he finally got to it he said, "What would you say if I asked you to marry me?" I said, "I don't think I should answer that question unless I have a 50/50 chance that you would ask me after I told you." He said, "Well you have a 50/50 chance," and I said "as a matter of fact I want a better percentage than that." So we worked the percentages. Anyway it worked out to about 90% and I said, "Ok, if you ask me to marry you I'll say yes." He said, "Will you marry me?" I said, "Yes," and he kissed me.

They returned to Edmonton and were married on July 6, 1963. It threatened to rain that day. Lawrence Radcliff was the best man, and Verne Hardman, whom Sandy had called from Boston, was Matron of Honour. Grant was typically Grant. When all four went to the Minister's office after the ceremony, Grant said, "Thank God that's over."

The Minister said, just a minute Grant, its not quite over. There is a little matter of a few signatures here. Grant looked at me, [Verne Hardman] tugging at his tie and his collar, and said, "Why don't you do it."

The reaction to the marriage from those who knew Grant was predictable. Ted and Anne Chudyk were "astounded." Bill and Myrna Glass were surprised, but delighted. Neil Reimer did not think that Grant was a romantic guy and wondered how it had happened. He wondered who proposed to whom, he was that surprised.

Why Grant got married so suddenly is still a bit of a mystery. Some, like Ted Chudyk, believe that it was just the timing. All of the other members of his group had paired off, and Grant thought that it was time for him to do so also. The combination of his shyness and passion for politics left him little time or inclination for romantic games. Others are less charitable, conceding only that he thought that it was timely for his political career, that he needed a wife and Sandy was available.

Sandy believed Grant to be in love with her, although she concedes that Grant's views of marriage conditioned his love. He had a very dispassionate view of marriage, seeing it through the eyes of duty and responsibility, rather than affection or love. He understood his role as a husband and father to revolve about a duty to provide, a responsibility to his family. He had little time for some of his colleagues whom he perceived to have surrendered this duty to amorous or romantic moments.

Not surprisingly then, as Neil Reimer said, Grant did not allow his new family responsibilities to interfere with his work. Sandy was required to shoulder the burden of family life, to "keep the home fires burning."

Frankly, I don't think that it [the impact of politics on his marriage] ever crossed his mind. His family came second. He was already in politics. I married him on the assumption he was going to be in politics; the family operated on the assumption that he did what he did, and that came first.

Grant thought that political life was very hard on his family.

It's difficult. People in public life, their families pay an enormous price in so many ways. Your father is in the centre of one storm after another. It's not just the being away, it's the being at the centre of things. But it's still a heavy price to pay. It's too big a sacrifice.

But at the time there was no thought of abandoning politics for the quieter family life involved in some other profession.

In his presentation to the Executive on July 4, 1963, two days before his marriage, Grant made no mention of it, which undoubtedly made it more of a surprise for Neil and others later one. The meeting itself was quite upbeat. Grant emphasized the gains in percentage in most seats, and concluded that the NDP had made real progress from where the CCF had stood in 1959. In 1963, victories or defeats were not measured in the winning or losing of seats but in the minutiae of almost imperceptible gains in the popular vote. Not that the goal of winning was excluded, or uncontemplated. It was simply that the party was content to measure itself in terms of "moral victories," the winning of greater numbers of voters from the previous election. It was an attitude which prevailed throughout the 1960s. No one ever dared question the assumption that such small changes might be the result of largely random causes, as opposed to definite and mounting progress in voter acceptance. Indeed, to keep going, it was necessary to emphasize and re-emphasize such gains. This was especially true for the Alberta party, which was attempting to demonstrate the superiority of the new "organizational approach" over the old CCF methods.

The Executive meeting also endorsed a continued campaign against Social Credit during the inter-election period. This reinforced another new article of faith, that the attacks on Manning and Social Credit were the key to any future success by the NDP. Any lessening of this blunt strategy would, it was concluded, prolong the term of the government and put off the final day of victory.

There was also a proposal for leadership and organizational schools in the Fall. These schools were to be accompanied by the production of educational materials, and the formation of discussion groups. Policy was to remain pragmatic, and pocketbook oriented.

Thus the three approaches of the Alberta New Democratic Party in the 1960s were set in place. Attack Social Credit and Manning, work hard on organization, keep policies flexible, pragmatic, and oriented to everyday pocketbook concerns. These approaches became articles of faith during the next five years.

For Grant, the summer of 1963 marked another turning point. A time of substantial testing was over. He had gone through his "electoral baptism of fire," and had been judged successful. He was now firmly entrenched as Provincial Secretary. His life in politics, at least in the near future, was assured. As well, he had married, and "settled down" like the rest of his university group. He now had some stability.

Grant spoke little of this time, but it is obvious from his actions and from the comments of others that he had asserted himself in a way which inspired greater self-confidence. One of his own immediate goals was to get elected, to be an MLA. He was now well positioned for that run. As well, he knew that the leadership would change at some point, although he did not expect it in the near future. Whenever it came however, he would be prepared for that change. In a very pragmatic way Grant did two things to further these goals. First, he remained absolutely loyal to Neil Reimer. He knew well that Neil would not tolerate open ambition, or fundamental disagreement with his own approach. Neil was a strong, opinionated, domineering, and if necessary ruthless person. But he was also bright, allowed a lot of latitude for subordinates, and tended to be loyal in return to those who were his "proteges." Grant never seriously challenged Neil in the next five years. Second, Grant began to alter his own responsibilities away from purely organizational detail to more policy and "leadership" activities, especially in rural areas.

Grant firmly believed that Neil did not understand rural Alberta. He also did not believe that the strategy of concentrating exclusively on urban areas would be enough to take the party to government. Grant was not comfortable with urban union leaders, adding more weight to his own judgement that strong rural areas ought not to be abandoned. He believed that it was more difficult to win one urban seat than a rural one. Urban voters tended to vote en masse, regardless of constituency boundaries, meaning that a single seat probably could not resist a serious trend against the NDP. By contrast a rural seat, especially a more isolated one could be won and held by a strong individual more easily. Rural areas were not homogeneous, and in particular he believed strongly that the rural north would continue to be a source of support for the progressive left in Alberta.

In line with his belief about Neil and his analysis about rural Alberta, Grant deliberately began to fill in what he perceived to be a gap. He travelled extensively to rural constituencies, put rural and agricultural issues forward. He took on the role of guest speaker at meetings, instead of the normal role of speaker on organizational issues. As Ted Chudyk recalls, Grant made sure that someone also was always along to make a financial appeal, or report on organizational matters at a meeting, so that Grant could speak on policy matters.

This accomplished several things. It filled the gap in Reimer's appeal (as Grant perceived it). It gave Grant practice in honing his speaking skills and his policy background. And it accumulated potential support for a future leadership convention. It was a very deliberate, well thought out, long term strategy.

Ted Chudyk recognized Grant's strategy, and did not oppose it. He did disagree however, with Grant's analysis about Neil Reimer's appeal in rural Alberta.

Even while Neil was Leader Grant loved to take on speaking engagements . . . on behalf of the leader. What I observe in hindsight is that Grant was very much disposing of those things which made him less than a statesman.

Grant had some reservations that this labour man wasn't going over in the farm community. He would almost discourage Neil from taking a speaking engagement in Vegreville or wherever, and do it himself because he thought he was more acceptable. Neil on the other hand, felt very comfortable.

Later Grant was accused of having undermined Neil in the rural areas throughout the period 1963 to 1968. For Chudyk's part he believes that Grant had a real worry about Neil's ability to impress rural voters, but he also thinks that perhaps Grant also recognized that ultimately this would benefit him in any future leadership contest.

Secure, self-confident, stable, Grant was ready to help the NDP defeat Social Credit and elect New Democrats to the Alberta legislature at the next opportunity. He was now committed completely to a life in politics.

Despite optimism in the Executive, and the decision to push ahead with organizational and leadership activities, one small nagging matter was unresolved. The party was broke. Worse, it was in serious debt.

At the July 4 Executive meeting Robert Gordon, the Treasurer, reported that the financial position of the party looked better than it actually was. Only one third of the TV commitments had been paid, and there were other outstanding debts. There was also the matter of legal fees should the party decide to go to court to challenge irregularities in Edmonton East. It was decided to increase the membership fee, and to contact the Alberta Federation of Labour, ''clarifying'' their pledge for $5000.00. The financial situation would continue to deteriorate over the next year.

During the Fall of 1963 Grant worked on a four-year strategy for the Alberta NDP, which he put to paper and eventually presented to the Provincial Executive in January of 1964. The document, entitled ''Four Year Plan,'' was a comprehensive attempt to set out organizational goals for the fledgling party between 1963 and 1967. Several things can be said about this document. It was very well written. The level of word usage, continuity of ideas, and paragraph construction are all of the first order. If anything, the document suffers from a certain ''academic bent,'' a proclivity to subordinate clauses and too much punctuation. While organizational in nature, the document has substantial philosophical content, speaking to the problems of participation, world order, and the tendency toward an organizational psychology which the document describes as ''subsistence'' in nature. Finally, there is a genuine attempt to apply the philosophy of the democratic left to its own internal organization, that is, to ensure that the leadership within the NDP did as it prescribed others ought to do. For example:

> We, the party of planning, must convince our membership that, rather than drifting aimlessly, we know where we are going. In other words, we should use the same medicine to heal our internal problems as we rightly prescribe as a curative for the economic ills of the country, namely planning.[15]

The document begins by addressing the right of local involvement and control, and the needs of a strong central office. It states bluntly that, "local leadership must follow the general decisions and objectives of the party. Any other policy would lead to chaos."[16] But it goes on to urge caution, and to encourage maximum leeway for local leaders, warning that too strict a control will induce either rebellion or impotence. However, throughout, the document leaves little room for those stated goals of autonomy.

The Four Year Plan also rehashes the arguments against a CCF style approach to political action.

> . . . we must induce our constituency associations to find a balance between discussion, education, and philosophy on one hand, and the more practical aspects of organization on the other . . . . Endless discussion, or philosophical debate, undisciplined by an accompanying responsibility to actively build and support the party *is dangerous.*

No return to the Peterson, Mardiros style party is the translation of this paragraph. The new NDP must be organizational in outlook, and dedicated to the practical aspects of political work.

> It is unrealistic to live in a dreamer's world, hoping to win elections with the infant organizational base that we have at the present time.

The remainder of the document, which is 11 pages long, is dedicated to proposal for a reorganization of the party. These included:

1. Providing an adequate organizational staff for the Provincial office, including a Director of Research, and field organizers.
2. Raising the provincial office budget from $23,000 per year to $45,000.
3. Establishing a branch office in Calgary.
4. Establishing viable, organized constituencies, with regular offices and meetings.
5. Regular communication networks in the province.
6. Annual membership canvasses.
7. A general strategy for the next election, which included concentrating on key constituencies.

The plan also laid out a timetable for action on a step by step basis.

It is a remarkable document. In his essay on Grant, Larry Pratt described the document as "vintage Notley," and "curiously, is one of the very few actually written by him . . . ."[17] A curious document indeed. In one respect it is a vintage Notley document. It is clearly organizational in character, with no discussion of policy goals, or goals for an eventual NDP government, although he might be forgiven for not speculating on the latter in 1963. Nor is there any answer to the question of why people will become enthusiastic about the NDP. It just assumes that hard work will net the party gains in membership. It accepts the assumption that it is sufficient to aggregate the dissatisfied, rather than to follow the CCF model of providing positive reasons for voting for the alternative. Why would people join Reimer and the NDP? Why not the Liberals or Tories? This question is not answered, and proved fatal in 1967 when Albertans began to tire of E.C. Manning. However, most of the ideas in the document could, with a few exceptions, be Notley ideas.

Two things about the document are not typical of Grant Notley. First, Grant was not inclined to commit himself to this kind of detailed, comprehensive plan. He always preferred to have much more flexibility, to operate in a much more *ad hoc* manner. It was typical of his personality that he was more for the "doing," than for the planning. This did not mean that he did not plan. However, his style of planning was always more precise, less general, and much shorter range. Second, the writing style is definitely not Grant's. Bill Dryden, a long time associate of Grant, who looked at the document, had this to say,

> It's an astonishing document from what I remember of the time, in that it didn't fit what the party was doing organizationally out of the party office. I didn't see any of the elements of it being carried out in any whole-hearted way . . . .
>
> Moreover, aside from how it was received, I don't think that Grant wrote it. I don't doubt that Grant delivered it, the records say that he did, but he was not that precise a writer. It also has contradictions to what he himself thought constituencies should do . . . you might as well be saying something in moon language as have that purported to come from Grant Notley. It just doesn't fit.

Indeed, Verne Hardman recalls that there were several meetings about this document, with former university colleagues like Bob Gordon,

Robin Hunter and others. She agrees that probably one of them actually wrote the document, and that it was a composite of collective ideas. Whatever the authorship, it has become associated with Grant, since he presented it to the Executive and the 1964 convention.

The reasons for its production are probably clearer. For his part Grant was now in control of the Secretaryship, but continued to need to solidify his position in the party. This document served a variety of personal purposes for him. As well, there was considerable optimism about the future, couched in an understanding that it would only come about through careful planning and hard work, the kind advocated in the document.

Unfortunately, the document was soon forgotten, with only the goals of raising money and hiring organizers fulfilled. In the NDP at this stage, the trouble with long-term planning was the lack of permanent long-term resources. The party lived on the edge of financial disaster at the best of times, and was forced to close down at the worst. In that atmosphere, much can be forgotten quickly.

Throughout the Fall of 1963 Grant continued his preparation for 1964. As Verne Hardman noted, his marriage did not interfere with his duty to the party. In some ways it even enhanced it. Even when it came to the traditional male responsibilities around the home, Grant was an able delegator. On his first visit to the Notley household Bill Dryden noted that one of the legs on the bed frame was broken, to which Grant replied, that Sandy "just couldn't fix anything." He remained absolutely single-minded during this period.

For her part Sandy Notley was beginning the process of integrating into the Notley family, and adjusting to married life with Grant. Sandy's parents played little part in their life. Grant was not terribly well disposed toward them, and over the years they grew to dislike him. Given the distance between them, both geographical, and ideological, this is perhaps understandable. For her part, Sandy felt increasingly comfortable with Grant's parents, although she recalls that their lack of passion mystified her. She realized early on that Grant had inherited his dispassionate, insular nature from his parents. Nothing seemed to perturb them.

One of the things that really amazed me, before I realized about farming in Alberta, there was 90 seconds of hail one noon hour, and it wiped out what Dad [Grant's father] had, greenfeed, barley and stuff for the cattle. When it stopped hailing everyone went back and finished lunch. They took it very casually.

She recalls as well that Grant's father was the more talkative of the two. Grant and his father would talk about provincial issues, what people were saying on open line programmes, and about Manning and the Social Credit. With his mother Grant would always "catch up" on the latest area gossip, something which irked Sandy considerably.

> I can remember exactly when Grant went home, he spent hours pumping his parents about all of the gossip in the neighbourhood . . . .
> There was always some gossip. Grant kept digging; if Grant ran out of new gossip, he would ask his mother to rerun things from several years ago.

For those who knew Grant, it was clear that his penchant for gossip was not restricted to Olds. He invariably wanted to know everything about everyone.

Sandy realized that Grant's parents were better educated than most in the area, one thing which undoubtedly allowed her to accept them better than if they were less aware of issues and history. It was obvious to her that Grant's parents were proud of him, and most importantly, they accepted Sandy.

The Fall was also occupied with several matters other than the family and the Four Year Plan. These included, as always, fund raising, preparation for convention, and leadership schools. The NDP agreed to send $1500.00 to the BC NDP for the election, and set the date for the next convention in Calgary for February 8 and 9, 1964. It was decided to circulate a petition on Auto Insurance in the province to keep the party active on the issue. Ted Chudyk, then First Vice-President, also raised the problem of communication with farmers. He believed that there was a problem that needed to be addressed. It was decided that a committee of table officers, chaired by Chudyk, should be set up to investigate the problem.

In early 1964 it became obvious that enthusiasm for the NDP was waning. The effect of the 1963 election had, predictably, run its course. One of the difficulties of running a political party is that the event you are organized to contest happens only once every four years. Parties tend to follow cycles, especially if they are in opposition. There is great enthusiasm just before election time, and during the campaign itself. If the party does reasonably well, that enthusiasm continues for a period after the election. By the time a year has passed, however, it becomes very difficult for party leaders to generate activity and money. One of the ways that parties try to combat this is by holding yearly meetings or conventions, at which they discuss party business. The NDP in Alberta in particular used annual Conventions to make money.

The February, 1964 Convention was no exception. It was geared as a fund-raising event. In the final analysis, it made $1,730.88, or about 10% of the annual revenue of the party. The convention was carefully orchestrated, ensuring that provincial issues were given priority over national or international issues. As well, Grant's "Four Year Plan" was presented to the convention. However, Ivor Dent, then Provincial President, wanted the idea of target ridings taken out of the plan so as not to give the impression that the NDP was only capable of winning 5 or 6 ridings.[18]

Despite the best efforts of the office, general activity continued to decline. Some ridings in Edmonton were unable to send delegates, or could only send partial slates to the convention. Quotas for the constituencies were not filled, and many members were in arrears. The Executive meeting in February of 1964 was dominated by discussion of financial matters, and plans for financial drives. As Verne Hardman recalled, "We were short of money. We were always short of money."

It was also clear that there were problems in the office. The Executive decided to set up an "Office Advisory Committee," to "advise and make suggestions for more efficiency in provincial office."[19] From Verne's recollection of events, Neil Reimer and Ivor Dent were not satisfied with her position as office manager. They were concerned that she was too close to Pat Ryan, who had run against Grant for the position of Secretary, and whom the RCMP had brought to Neil's attention. Verne's husband Dave and Pat were good friends, which put her under suspicion. As well, Neil and Ivor wanted one of their own people in the office to keep track of things. Verne says she was asked by them to report to them directly on office activities, but declined to do so, which also contributed to critical comments about her performance.

Despite Grant's best efforts, many things remained beyond his control. Virtually nothing important politically was happening in Alberta at this time. Social Credit was into the second year of its mandate, with virtually no opposition in the Legislature. While the local media decried the situation, there was little to organize around.

Even worse, events outside Alberta contributed to a deepening sense of electoral gloom. The 1963 federal election had not produced a breakthrough, despite the able leadership of Tommy Douglas. In Saskatche-wan the NDP government had carried on under the able leadership of Woodrow Lloyd. In March of 1964 Lloyd decided to seek a new man-date, the first under his leadership. He called the election for April. It was a mistake, and the government went down to defeat for the first time in twenty years.

Grant had gone to work in the election, helping out as best he could. While he was away Sandy delivered their first child, Rachel. Lawrence Radcliff, best man at their wedding, took Sandy to the hospital, and tried to contact Grant. The birth was difficult, and ultimately the baby was delivered by caesarian section. Finally, over a day later, Grant was tracked down by Les Benjamin, then Provincial Secretary for the NDP in Saskatchewan and later an MP for Regina. At a rally he approached Grant and congratulated him. Grant looked at him in surprise, and asked, "what for?" Les told him he was a new father, the first Grant had heard of it. As it turned out, Grant would be away on party business for the birth of their next child, Paul. Sandy joked:

> When Paul was born Grant was out in Edson . . . organizing . . . .
> He was leader, speaking or something. Bill Glass took me to the hospital to have him, and I said I was going to keep having children until he was there for one. He wouldn't have been there for Stephen either, except Stephen was a week late . . . . He did finally manage to take me to the hospital to have Stephen.

Grant was on the road constantly during this period. The loss in Saskatchewan meant that the NDP was about to enter a five-year drought in Canada, broken only by the election of the Schreyer govern-ment in Manitoba in 1969. It became more and more difficult to raise funds, despite long hours in the country, with Henry Thomaschuk, or Roy Jahma. Roy, who later became Provincial Treasurer for the party remembers travelling in the famous Plymouth. He specifically remembers that Grant had a very "heavy foot." One time on icy roads Grant was slipping and sliding so badly that Jahma was "scared to death." But he and others continued on with him, trying to keep the organization going.

In June of 1964, the party hit a low ebb. There was simply no money to keep the office open in Edmonton. It was closed and Verne Hardman was fired. While there were savings from this it also meant that the normal work of the party could not go on. For the next year Sandy Notley took on the job of keeping the administrative work up to date. This meant long hours at home, typing memberships ("greenies" as they were called) and sending out receipts. For his part, Grant spent longer hours away, travelling on the road for two cents per mile and $300.00 per month. There appeared to be little chance that the party would soon meet the financial objectives outlined by the "Four Year Plan" submitted only six months before.

In order to breathe life into the party the Executive agreed to a number of initiatives in September of 1964. Those included trying to get the trade union movement to contribute to a TV fund, and agreement that Reimer, Dent, and Notley should begin a strategy for the next provincial election. To supplement this Grant was given the task of organizing a series of policy seminars. At the same meeting the Executive heard a submission from a Mr. Thomas O'Duire, an Edmonton land developer. He outlined some charges of impropriety against the provincial government. The results, or details, of these charges are not known. What is clear is that Neil Reimer and the NDP were still searching for those essential elements of corruption which they believed existed and could be used to bring down the Socred government. This search would ultimately lead to charges in 1966 against Alf Hooke and the Premier.

The policy seminars were discussed with several people at the University of Alberta, including a political science professor named Tom Pocklington, who would later be on the Provincial Executive, and a political science student named Bill Dryden. Both Bill and his wife Anne would become close associates and friends of Grant's for the rest of his life.

Bill was born in Calder in 1934, on "the wrong side of the tracks," as he put it. His father was from Moncton, New Brunswick and his mother from Fredericton. His family was a railroad family primarily, although his own father had become a fairly successful entrepreneur. Bill has strong memories of his mother's interest in politics, and particularly the CCF, which Bill probably correctly concludes she passed on to him. In Alberta she attended CCF meetings with Bill Irvine and Nellie Peterson, and generally worked at matters in the office in her spare time. Often she took Bill with her.

As with most young adults, Bill at first rebelled against this, leaving high school in Grade 10, going to work for the railroad in the early fifties, and continuing his activities in union politics. In 1956 he met Anne, a young woman from Texas, and they were married shortly thereafter, but later divorced in 1974. Their three children were born in the three succeeding years. Bill decided to finish his high school education and go to university.

He remained inactive politically until 1962 when his interest in the left was rekindled by the creation of the New Party. He was an admirer of Neil Reimer, and worked to try and get his own railway union to support the New Party. By 1963 he was at the University of Alberta, and used to attend the noon-time meetings, some of which featured Grant as the speaker.

At first Bill did not like Grant. When Grant came to the university Bill thought that he looked "bored," things there now seemed to be *passe* for Grant. Indeed, Bill did not think that Grant was much of a natural leader, and was even a trifle arrogant. More importantly, he thought Grant to be too provincial, not radical enough. Bill observed that Grant had a public and private persona. In private, at the office he was a different person.

> [At the university] he acted like some kind of commerce student, or a law student, . . . he was coming there to deliver some doc-trinaire . . . message to people. He was speaking in a sophisticated labour language around there . . . . It didn't fit the radical politics of the university at that time . . . . He was marching to a totally differ-ent drum. He knew something that I didn't know. Grant always worked on a practical basis. [At the office] he was quite different, now you were on his turf and he'd come up and greet you.

Despite this rather disapproving beginning, Grant was able to win Bill over, and Bill found himself coming to the office quite often to help out. There were little "work bees" as Bill recalls, which Grant was very adept at getting people involved in.

Bill remembers the 1964 policy committees at the university as hav-ing two functions. The first function was to get people involved. Several people participated, although Bill did not. The second was to cultivate some policy contacts for Grant.

> He always knew that he would eventually require some linkage with academics, particularly with the university, that could produce some philosophical material, because Grant wasn't capable of doing that. He put all of his energy into the organizational side.

Once again, however, the results seem not to have been spectacular, since the matter was not discussed again by the Executive. For his part, Bill Dryden believed that policy was not Grant's forte at this point in his life, that this ability came later, something that his ex-wife Anne agrees with.

The first small glimmer of a turnaround for the party began in October of 1964. In the civic election in Edmonton Ivor Dent and Joyce Kurrie, who would later become the office Secretary, both ran for City Council. Ivor won, and began a career in civic politics which would lead him to the Mayor's chair for two terms. New Democrats had been elected to civic posts before, most notably Elmer Roper as Mayor of Edmonton, but Ivor was President of the NDP, a very high profile person, which meant that it had not deterred the voters. Most New Democrats saw this as a hopeful sign.

It was countered, however, by the continuing dismal financial situation. At the Executive meeting of October 25, 1964 a special committee was struck to try and deal with the situation. At the same meeting it was recommended by Neil Reimer that the party consider nominating 12 prominent candidates who would become *de facto* spokesmen for the party. This latter suggestion was contradictory to the recommendation in the "Four Year Plan," which contemplated only five or six key constituencies.[20] It appears never to have been implemented.

By January of 1965 it became apparent that there might soon be a federal election. The Pearson government had been in a minority situation since 1963, and Liberal party advisors were urging an election to try and get a majority. Federal NDP officials wanted the Alberta party to nominate in all ridings and to prepare for the federal party convention in July of 1965. On the provincial scene the NDP began to take up a number of issues, the most important of which was the energy question and development of the huge Athabasca tar sands deposit. Neil's involvement with the OCAW made this a natural issue for the party and it was believed that the public would also see it as important. Passing almost unnoticed by the NDP was the fact that the provincial Progressive Conservative party had begun to reorganize, under the guidance of an energetic and youthful Peter Lougheed. The attention of the Alberta NDP was still on the Social Credit.

The provincial convention was a lively one, with several policy panels, and a major discussion of international affairs. The elections were uneventful, with Neil Reimer and Ivor Dent re-elected by acclamation.

The contests came mainly in the election of Vice-Presidents. As usual, the convention made money.

Prior to the convention, on February 29, a special meeting of the Executive had been held in Edson, Alberta. The Social Credit MLA for Edson, N.A. Willmore, had died, and a by-election was going to be held. The wisdom of the leader running in the by-election was the subject of the discussion. The meeting was called "informal," and discussion was supposed to be "frank." The meeting was held in the office of Dr. Peter Cohen, a member of the provincial executive and resident of Edson. Present were Ivor Dent, Neil Reimer, Roy Jahma, Henry Thomschuk, Bob Douglas, Ted Takas and Grant Notley. The minutes of the meeting were handwritten by Grant. After considerable discussion, it was the "informal" consensus that Reimer should run.

Initially Neil resisted the idea of running in Edson. He believed fundamentally that the party needed to stick with its urban strategy, and an Edson candidacy was a serious deviation from that goal. Neil now says that he ought not to have listened to the Executive. But at the time he believed, having been a trade unionist all his life, that he should listen to his council and membership. With a tinge of bitterness he explained in an interview:

> When your membership has spoken, your membership has spoken, and that's final. I resisted going into Hinton, but people like Henry Thomschuk convinced me. There were people there like railroaders, in Jasper, the miners, the cement plant, . . . and pulp and paper workers. There was a strong trade union presence there.
>
> I later realized that people like Tommy Douglas and David Lewis and what not, they really didn't give a shit what convention said or did when it came to their own personal career. I didn't feel that way.

Clearly Neil believed the decision was a bad one because it locked him into running in Edson again in 1967, something that he did not want to do. As well, Neil realized that he would be an outsider, and subject to charges of opportunism.

It was a tough campaign. Initially there was not great enthusiasm. But as the campaign went on enthusiasm mounted. Soon Neil began to attract large crowds at which, Ted Chudyk recalls, he could "just crucify" E.C. Manning:

I don't think half of the stuff he said he could back up, but he was vague enough.

The NDP poured everything they had into the campaign. According to Bill Dryden it was an ugly campaign. NDP signs were continually torn down, and the business community tried everything to stop them. Social Credit nominated A.W. Leonard, the PC's J. Scott, and the Liberals nominated a man named William Switzer, a local resident, from a well known family in Hinton. The Liberals ran a good campaign. Late in the election, the Premier came into the riding, promising a new pulp mill for the area. As Neil observed, they were always promising a pulp mill somewhere.

On election night the results looked hopeful. The NDP got good votes in union towns like Jasper, Robb, and Edson. Neil led in the polls all through the night, until the last few votes were counted. When the final tally came in, he had lost by 90 votes to the Liberal, Switzer. The NDP had lost the town of Hinton because the town union leadership had gone for a "local boy." One of Neil's fears, being an outsider, had materialized. In retrospect Ted thinks that they could have won the campaign if they had worked harder. Parts of the riding were not covered adequately, and some organizational work was left undone.

But the defeat was not viewed as a defeat by the party. Such a narrow loss, in a riding where they had done poorly only two years before, electrified New Democrats. As Neil put it; "it was as good as a win," it was "quite a morale booster." For Social Credit it was bad news. They had run third, although a good third, but 70% of the people had voted against the government.

Unfortunately for the NDP two damaging lessons were learned from the campaign. The first, confirmed in their minds by the Switzer win, was that the Liberals were still the party to beat in opposition. The PCs had done very badly, ensuring that Peter Lougheed and his Conservatives would be ignored until 1967. The second lesson, that attacking Manning personally also paid dividends, would eventually damage the party in 1967. But at the time the near miss energized the party, taking it out of the doldrums of the previous year.

Throughout this period Grant continued to work at building the party, especially in rural areas. Most importantly, he activated and retained the loyalty of a number of key people. One of them was a farm woman named Irene Dyck, affectionately known to many in the NDP as "the Turnip lady.'' She was called this because she would cater banquets and use the money from her catering to pay the deposits of the Calgary NDP candidates. We first saw her when she emerged from behind a huge vat of turnips. She was born in Revelstoke, BC, but grew up in Innisfree, Alberta, where her father was postmaster. In 1930 she became a teacher and taught for 20 years. After marrying her husband Jack, they moved to a small farm near Calgary. Jack had been active with the CCF in the 1940s and 1950s, but Irene had remained on the sidelines. In 1962 the New Party discovered their names on an old CCF list, and Grant went to see them.

Irene was instantly taken by Grant. He was, she remembers, amiable, laughed a lot, and best of all, was a tireless worker. Irene was such a person, and greatly admired this in Grant. He persuaded Irene and Jack to come to the 1963 leadership convention, where Irene supported Ivor Dent. As she recalls, she was ''not much taken by Neil Reimer.'' She refused further elaboration, except to say that she was quite angry with Nancy Eng from Calgary (later President of the Alberta NDP) for voting for Neil.

Grant convinced Irene to run for the NDP in Drumheller in 1963, a riding held by Gordon Taylor, Minister of Highways. It was a thankless task, but Irene was philosophical about it. Grant came often to their home in the early years, between 1963 and 1968, when looking for donations, taking Jack Dyck with him. On one occasion they were directed to a farmer named MacDonald, whom they were told would give them a $5.00 donation. At the farm, Grant and Jack talked to the man, and eventually got $10.00 from him. Upon arriving home they discovered that they had gone to the wrong farm. They decided not to go to the right MacDonald, having already doubled their luck.

Irene's loyalty was typical of what Grant inspired in people. She worked tirelessly for him in Calgary over the years. Later, after she and Jack sold their farm for a sizeable sum of money, because Calgary had grown around it, Irene gave hundreds of thousands of dollars to the Alberta NDP. But at this time, she was just one of many rural people Grant counted on, and she responded enthusiastically.

Despite this kind of hard work, it was obvious that if the party was going to capitalize on the Edson euphoria, it would have to open the office and get Grant some organizational help into the field. In September of 1965 the Executive decided to hire an office manager on a full time basis. That person was Joyce Kurri who was born in Edmonton, went to school there, and eventually attended Concordia College. She did not get involved with the NDP until Neil Reimer became leader. She first saw him on television during the Edson by-election, and thought he was the answer to Social Credit. She was also very impressed with Ivor Dent, not as a person, but as a politician.

This interest in politics and her impression of Neil Reimer decided her on a course action. She called the provincial office and talked to Grant about volunteering for office work. Grant was still the only person there, and as she recalls, there was no money. He confided to her that they were looking for someone, and invited her to come down and meet Neil and himself. They met the next day.

I was never a member of the party. I think one of the comments I made was probably why Neil and Grant hired me. I said I would help anyone do anything to get rid of Social Credit.

She got a "real kick" out of Grant the first time she met him. She really liked him. (That impression changed for her over the years however.) To her he looked disheveled and unkempt, with a brush cut that needed cutting, not the world's sharpest dresser. But, in part, she decided this was because Grant did not want to be overdressed when he went out in the rural areas to ask people for a "few dollars." She contrasted him with Ted Chudyk, who was just the opposite. She concluded that in Grant's case, it was "just kinda him." She especially remembered that he had a terrific memory, but the office files were a mess. However, she thought that he was not totally responsible for this, because he had to rely on volunteers. Hours never meant anything to Grant. It was never too late to drive to the next farm. He was singleminded, and the party was number one with him at all times.

Neil, she thought, was the total opposite of Grant. Neil was dressed well and was very leaderly looking. She recalled that Grant and Neil worked well together, especially in the first years.

Joyce's first tasks involved the 1965 federal election, which the Liberals had called in hope of getting a majority. As usual, the NDP in Alberta fielded a full slate, and as usual they attempted to use the election for provincial purposes. Candidates were found, Grant assisted in arranging campaign managers and schools, and worked with Clarence Lyons, then prairie organizer for the federal party. The results were virtually identical to 1963. In Alberta the Liberals got exactly the same vote, 22%, but they lost the one seat that they had held. The Conservatives confirmed their newly acquired command of Alberta by taking 47% of the vote (up 2%) and gaining one seat, to 15. The Social Credit Party dropped from 26% to 22%, but held onto their two seats. The NDP, with its full slate, went up slightly from 8% to 9%, no great breakthrough. As it turned out, the national results left the Liberals in a minority government, and effectively ended the career of Lester Pearson.

This did not deter the provincial NDP, however. Still buoyed by the Edson result, the Executive made two significant decisions designed to bolster the party for the next election. The first, involved an agreement with the International Oil Chemical and Atomic workers which would allow Neil Reimer to become a full time leader up to the next provincial election. The second was a decision to hire three organizers and put them out into the field to raise money, candidates, and activity.

The question of Neil becoming a full-time leader had been discussed informally during the summer of 1965. It was in response to the good results in Edson, and a feeling that with some full time effort the party could become the official Opposition in the next election. With a full-time leader the party would be in a position to take maximum advantage of public and policy events, while the organizational side was left with Grant. But there was a rather large problem: money. It simply was not financially possible to replace Neil's salary for him. In order to overcome this problem Neil decided to try and get his international union to release him to a special project which would give him virtually full time for the NDP. But it was not easy. They were not terribly sympathetic to the idea of direct involvement in politics. The president of the union, A. Grospiron was, like most American union leaders, someone who leaned toward the Gompers style of political involvement, rather than toward the British and Canadian style of direct intervention in electoral contests. As well, Neil was still out of favour for his attempt at the presidency in 1963. The leadership balked at first, but eventually agreed to a compromise.

That compromise involved the Alberta NDP sharing the costs of Neil's relief. The amount involved was set at one half, or about $10,000. Such a sum was beyond the capacity of the party at the time, but the Executive agreed at its September 11, 1965 meeting to authorize up to $600 per month toward Neil's release. In a formal letter, which undoubtedly had been prescripted, Neil wrote to Grant on November 18, 1965 outlining the terms under which the OCAW would release him. In it Neil told Grant that the union was prepared to consider this option, but only if Neil would undertake a citizenship programme nation-wide, if the provincial party was willing to share the expenses involved, and if the NDP in Canada (read the federal party) was willing to consider this the entire donation of the OCAW for all of Canada. These conditions were accepted, but the Alberta party had no possibility of raising its share of the money. Accordingly, Neil arranged for local unions to lend the NDP $10,000, at no interest, to be paid back to them at a rate of $150 per month. The money was to be directed toward hiring organizers, but in reality there was little chance that the arrangement with Neil could have gone ahead without the loan. Grant included these views in a letter to Grospiron on December 13, 1966. The arrangement was finalized in an exchange of letters in March of 1966, allowing Neil to commence that year. It was a potent display of Neil's ability to organize the trade union movement behind him, a display which was recalled and resented a decade later when the trade union movement withheld substantial support from the NDP under Grant's leadership.

As the letters indicated, the question of hiring organizers was part of the local arrangement for the next election. It was discussed at the Executive meeting of November 28, 1965. The party had finally adopted the maxim that "you have to spend money to make money." The seeming possibility of electoral success, the re-opening of the office, and the proximity to the next election, all lured the Executive into a major expansion scheme.

The new organizational staff were not brought on until February of 1966. At the top of the list of prospects was Ted Chudyk. He had become quite close to Neil Reimer, and was eager to work for the party. He was approached by Grant in November of 1965, but nothing happened until three months later. Neil Reimer recalled that Grant delayed because he was still worried about Ted's communist connections, and was "checking him out further." This angered Neil, who relates that he did not care about this, and would not tolerate it. The delay by Grant was more likely related to Ted's closer relationship to Neil than to his ideological position. Grant was probably more worried about having control of his own office. It was obvious that Joyce Kurri was going to be a Reimer loyalist, and if Ted were also, Grant would have no one whose first loyalty was to him. Such feelings did not mean disloyalty to Neil, only that Grant wanted his "own people" working for him. The other possibilities for organizer were Ken Kerr from Edmonton, a friend of Grant's, and Allen

Early, later Provincial Secretary, from Calgary. Despite his misgivings, Grant realized that Ted was a very good organizer and fund raiser, making it difficult to refuse him. Ted was puzzled at the time as to the delay, but concluded that it related to funding. In the end, both Ted Chudyk and Ken Kerr were hired in February, 1966.

Activity in the party was galvanized by the addition of staff and a full-time leader. Ted Chudyk's appointment especially generated enthusiasm. Ted counts as his chief asset his ability to "fire up people," to get them to work for and donate to the cause. To do this he deliberately built an image as a flashy, self-confident playboy. He told tall tales about card playing, drinking and carousing, all of which, he now insists, were exaggerated. While modesty now overcomes Ted, he became a small legend in the Alberta NDP. He raised money, and expectations, and in substantial amounts. As he recalls, it became a contest between himself and Grant as to who could get the most money out of any given person or situation. Grant was very good, Ted says, but he was better. Eventually, when an important "pitch" was to be given, Grant would call on Ted to do it.

They travelled extensively, sometimes together, most often apart, building the NDP in Alberta. However the early results were not what the party had expected. At the May 15, 1966 Executive Meeting a major report on the first three months of the experiment was presented to the members of the Executive. It concluded that if nothing was done, at the current rate of expenditures the party would face a $5000.00 deficit by the end of the year. The problem was that the organizers, collectively, were not meeting the outlay for their salaries and expenses. This despite a philosophy which Ted Chudyk recalls as "payday was when you brought it [the money] in." Three proposals were put before the Executive. Keep going and hope that it got better, lay off the organizers, or try to increase sustaining donations (committed monthly contributions) to make up the deficit. Choices, one and two were unthinkable for the party at the time, and they decided to try and raise sustaining donations to keep the organizers in the field. By this time another organizer from the Peace River country, Allan Busch, had been added to the staff in an attempt to get more money from that area. The effort was only partially successful.

The financial implications, while important, were not as important as the overall mode which the party adopted as a result of these two decisions to put Neil on full time and to maximize organizational staff. That mode was a highly centralized, organizationally and electorally oriented party. The fight to cleanse itself of the old CCF element had been too successful in some respects. The party had been shorn of its policy people at the Executive level. If the old CCF had become too much of a debating club, the opposite was now true of the NDP in 1966. The President, Ivor Dent, as an elected Alderman, had an organizational bias. Neil Reimer was the same, with an almost savage dislike of Manning and Social Credit. None of the others on the Executive were what could be called left-wing, or policy people, with the possible exception of Ed Nelson, a farmer from central Alberta. This did not mean that Executive members were unaware of policy, or its importance. They simply viewed it as secondary to electoral activity. The result was that the NDP became an electoral machine, which led to some questionable decisions about electoral and organizational tactics during this period. Grant was part of that thrust, and agreed with it. Only later when he was in the legislature did he temper his views on this subject.

The Convention held in Edmonton in April of 1966 was an active one, but a disaster organizationally. It was held in the Edmonton Inn, which was newly opened, and not quite finished. Service was poor, and the facilities did not quite all work. As well, Joyce Kurri had never organized a convention and Verne Hardman had to be recalled to service to help organize. During the convention, there was much policy discussion, some of it undisciplined in the opinion of some members of the Executive. At a meeting of the Table Officers after the convention on April 6, the two matters were discussed. A decision was made to withhold final payment to the Edmonton Inn until they agreed to reduce their price as a result of poor service. In regard to policy Neil Reimer advocated tighter control of policy panels, which Ivor Dent agreed to implement.

In the late summer of 1966 the Table Officers met again to discuss a by-election. The incumbent in Pincher-Creek Crowsnest, William Kovach, had died earlier. The riding was a curious one, consisting of some ranching area west of Lethbridge, and a series of small coal mining towns including Blairmore, Coleman, and the little town of Frank, which had been levelled by the Frank Slide. The miners in the area had always been "Red," and the area had a history of communist activity. It was relatively good country for the NDP, an anomaly compared to the rest of southern Alberta. This by-election would provide a tremendous boost for the NDP, it was thought, although no one expected to win it.

Garth Turcott had come to Grant's attention several years earlier. Grant had observed at the time that Garth might be a potential candidate.

When Kovach died, the pressure to nominate Turcotte started immediately. However, Garth was not terribly inclined toward running for office. He and his wife Joan were quite happy with their life in Pincher Creek. Garth had a small law practice, and enjoyed his time at home. He had been a life long CCFer, soft spoken, and quite moral according to many who knew him. When asked to run, he was reluctant, to say the least. As Ted Chudyk remembered, "He would have been more inclined to run if we guaranteed him that he wouldn't win." Finally, as Ted recalled, he and Neil Reimer, went "on bended knee" to Pincher Creek and got Garth to agree to run.

Everyone who worked in Pincher Creek in 1966 has the same recollection. It was a great campaign. It was efficient, well financed, well staffed, and involved just about everyone. Early on it was decided to bring in Clarence Lyons, the federal organizer, to run the campaign. He had vast experience, and a good understanding of organization. However, Clarence was not as good a motivator as some others, so there was still a role for people like Ted Chudyk. All of the full time organizers, and Grant, were assigned a town of their own. Ted was in Blairmore, Grant was in Coleman, and so on.

It was also, according to Ted and others more of a "mechanical" election, an "organizers" election. He remembers in detail how much work was put in, going back to each door four times until people were convinced that the NDP was serious. He believes that the sheer determination of the workers was rewarded with votes. There were no great policy issues, no political issues. They were, however, able to "turn on the old juices" from thirty years before, when the miners were quite radical.

For his part Neil Reimer also got quite involved. He was in the riding often, and was instrumental in securing the Hutterite vote in the area. He recalls specifically that when he came to see the Hutterite elders he was able to talk to them in their own language and tell them about the discrimination they faced from the Social Credit.

Bill Dryden took a week off from the university and was assigned two polls in Coaldale. Together with a friend John Burke, they worked those two polls.

> I got to talk to miners. The Pincher Creek of that time is not the Pincher Creek, or Coaldale of today. The nights in their houses drinking beer and hearing all of the stories about British labour socialism. It really

crystalized all of the things I was doing at the university. I felt very heroic. I felt like I was really doing something.

Bill describes Garth Turcott as a good fellow, "a novice in politics who was in it for very strong moral reasons. It took a lot for Garth to leave his law office and run for the NDP."

Literally dozens of people came from all over the province to donate their time and effort. Among those people was Anne Dryden, Bill's wife. She remembers the campaign vividly. Bill had gone down but she was unable to go because of the children. Nevertheless, she and Lou Pocklington, went to sing at the rallies as they had in the Edson by-election. Anne immediately liked Garth Turcott and later got to know him quite well. At the time she had written a song about him, designed to help the campaign, which she and Lou, complete with her tambourine, sang at the meetings. Others involved were Gordon Wright, Bill Glass, and many new people.

On election night, the result was electric. Grant knew that they were going to do well, but nobody could predict the split. When the results were in Garth Turcott had beaten the Social Credit 1767 votes to 1631. The PC's ran third, and the Liberals fourth. It was quite simply overwhelming for everyone. Ted Chudyk described it as

. . . a night in a lifetime. To see the look on the faces. There was a guy sitting on a wooden bench in the Hall that we had rented and he was openly crying. Just sobbing. I said, "Joe why are you crying?" He said I didn't think I would live long enough to see this day. Just a genuine . . . moment. To see the eyes of these people. Beautiful.

The NDP had elected its first MLA in Alberta. The future, to most in the party, seemed very bright indeed.

Garth was not given much time to savour his victory, however. He was thrust into the legislature immediately in the Fall of 1966. Neil Reimer had become more convinced than ever that if the NDP was to continue its momentum, it would have to destroy E.C. Manning. As Ted Chudyk put it:

Neil was very much zeroing in on Manning himself, who by this time was a wealthy man.

But in Ted's judgement, this was an error, because the so-called "goods" that Neil had on Manning were shakier than he wanted to admit. Much of it was over-estimated, probably because, in Ted's opinion, Neil desperately wanted to find something.

For months before there had been reports in the media of corruption in the provincial government. Accusations had bubbled sufficiently that Neil decided to press these in the Legislature through Garth. With the benefit of hindsight, it is now clear that it was a monumental mistake. The evidence was not sufficient, Garth was the wrong person to carry the attack, and the party had come to have no other strategy other than attacking Social Credit.

At the time voices in opposition were raised against the decision. People like Tom Pocklington, Gordon Wright, and others tried to argue that the strategy was completely wrong. They advised that the party should hold Garth up as an example of how an NDP MLA, and therefore an NDP government, would operate: by being positive and stressing policy and integrity. They agreed that there was probably corruption, but they argued that it should come out naturally, not by NDP cloak and dagger.

Ted Chudyk had much the same impression, that the tactic was a mistake. But he is much more charitable to Neil, observing that there were large numbers of people in the party who supported the attack, many of whom were good Christians who resented Manning's use of the pulpit to forward the political position of Social Credit.

For his part, Neil now admits to ambivalence.

> I had never intended that it go as far as it did, because I felt that if you left a mark on the Premier, a question mark, and show that he had feet of clay . . . [that] was really all that we needed. We could allude to it and the suspicion in people's mind, and lingering doubts are likely in some respects more effective than proving a guy guilty at a certain point. Once a trial is over, it's over.

The strategy was to keep the pot boiling, to keep the issue of corruption, especially as it related to Manning, before the public. Neil felt that he had considerable ammunition, but no real smoking gun. Nevertheless, many who felt they had been wronged by the Manning government provided enough "smoke" to convince Neil and a majority of the Executive that there was "fire" involved. In any case, as Neil said suspicion alone was probably enough to hurt the Socreds.

Manning called a special two day session of the Legislature in November, 1966, soon after Garth was elected. It was decided that Garth should bring up these reports on Alf Hooke in direct questions to the Premier. According to Bill Dryden, Garth did not want to do so, but was persuaded by Neil and others that it was his duty as the party's only MLA.

As Neil recalls, Garth raised the matters not once, but eventually three times, which Neil felt was too much. He and Grant were watching in the public gallery. After Garth had raised the matter the second time, they left the gallery to talk to the press. Unknown to Neil, Garth raised the matter a third time. The first two questions had drawn "no comment" from the Premier, but on the third time he admonished Garth severely, and attacked Neil.

Alf Hooke, whose Ministerial conduct was at question specifically, recalls as well that the Premier spoke directly. In his book, *Thirty Plus Five: I Was There*, he says that Garth was repeating, "malicious and slanderous political propaganda that the Leader of his Party [Neil Reimer] has peddled in this province for months."[21] Hooke was prevented from replying by virtue of a motion to table the documents in the next regular session, but he recalls that later Manning questioned him about the wisdom of having an inquiry to clear the air. Hooke says that he was not opposed to an inquiry, but would have preferred to answer in the House on the spot.

The Liberal Leader in the House, Mike Maccaigno, managed to play both sides, by demanding that the government agree to an inquiry, while warning that if Turcotte was wrong, he would have to resign. To the Liberals it appeared that someone was going to lose from the affair, but they were going to gain.

When the regular session convened in February, Garth repeated his accusations. Bill Dryden remembers that it was a very hard time for Garth in the Legislature.

> It was awful to watch one person . . . take the abuse that Garth did from the Socreds. The noise, and the din, the hoots and the insults. It was abusive, absolutely abusive. And then when he would come out of the House, right beside him would be Neil, as the media talked to Garth . . . .

Bill says that Garth knew that the affair would eventually cost him his constituency, but that Neil and others did not think so. There were long sessions in which Neil and some members of the Executive pressured Garth on the matter.

> He wanted to represent his constituency. He never did get around to it. And he knew what they were like. Representation is the name of the game he wanted to get into.

The affair crystalized a deep split within the NDP which carried over into the 1967 election, a split between those, led by Neil, who wanted to continue the attack on Manning, and those who felt that it had gone too far, who felt that a social democratic party should not be playing this kind of politics.

For his part, Grant initially supported the Reimer strategy but, according to Bill Dryden, early on decided that it had become counterproductive. There is little to suggest that Grant was a major player in this affair. That he was deeply involved in all political strategy is true, but it is unlikely that he was a decisive voice. Nor is it likely that he was undecided on the general strategy of opposing Social Credit. This approach had been the norm for years, and Grant obviously agreed with it. What he seems to have been unsure about is the actual substance and tactics of the moment.

Although Reimer subsequently bore the brunt of criticism for the approach, Grant received criticism for his indecision. Bill Dryden was hardest on Grant when questioned about it.

> To me [his role] was disappointing . . . Grant played the "let's get together and solve this" role. He never did support Garth.
>
> I said to Grant that it was wrong, and Grant agreed with me. *Ex post facto* a lot of people said they made mistakes, but I'm saying that about half way through, a number of people communicated to Grant, and to Neil, that "is this what we did all of it [the Pincher Creek election] for? You go all of that time without a member and now you're going to sacrifice him?"
>
> Grant said that it had gone too far to stop, internally in the party, that Neil was committed to it, and that he didn't see how we could stop it.

Grant's ambivalence can probably be explained by two things. First he was still Provincial Secretary of the party and as such deferred to the leader and the Executive. The party was heading into a crucial election with what seemed like overwhelming momentum. It is inconceivable to think that he would have jeopardized his or the party's position at this juncture by taking a strong stand against Neil Reimer. Second, while he disagreed with this particular tactic, he still agreed with the long term strategy of running hard against Social Credit.

There are those who saw a more Machiavellian manoeuvre in Grant's action. They contend that Grant realized that both Neil and Garth were likely future competitors for the leadership, and he was not unaware that the Hooke affair was hurting both of his potential rivals. There is some plausibility to this, but little evidence. Many who knew Garth agreed that there was virtually no chance that he would have run for the leadership, even if he had been re-elected. As well, it was not so apparent to all in late 1966 and early 1967 that the anti-Manning strategy had failed. That conclusion was only realized completely after the 1967 election. More likely, Grant was undecided, ambivalent, and worried, but generally felt unable to argue effectively against Neil's leadership on the issue.

He was to draw a powerful lesson from the experience, however. When he entered the Legislature in 1971 Grant made it a strict policy not to engage in the kind of politics that typified 1966/67. He always took the "high road," and deliberately steered away from personal attacks on Lougheed, or his Ministers. It was a rule which he never violated.

At the first meeting of the Executive in 1967, there was little to suggest that anything was amiss. In every way the NDP was getting ready for what it thought would be a good election. Momentum was with the party, and there was even internal talk of forming the next government.

The NDP was not alone in this assessment. Few, if any, predicted the outcome of the 1967 election, and fewer still would predict the course of politics in the next four years. The long term indicators were there. The population of Alberta had become increasingly urbanized in the post war period, until in the mid-1950s more people lived in cities, than in the country. By the end of the decade of the 1960s this proportion had increased dramatically. The solid rural base of Social Credit had eroded considerably. With urbanization had come the oil boom, and the wealth that accompanied it. In Calgary this had created a new class of entrepreneurs associated with the oil industry. Although these "young Turks" got on well with the Social Credit government, they viewed it as old fashioned, religious, and moralistic. A relic of the Depression era, a "funny money" party out of the new mainstream of Alberta and Canada. They wanted someone more modern, which generated a growing perception of "time for change." Added to this was the age and longevity of the government. Although the "instant politics" of television was not yet a major factor, Social Credit had been in power for 31 years, an extraordinary length of time even by parliamentary standards. Manning had been Premier for most of that time, and was beginning to show his age. Finally, Social Credit had quite simply lost its momentum. Shorn of its radical wing, and now defeated federally, it was an anomaly in politics, clinging to power, much as the shell of a prairie grasshopper clings to a stalk of grain long after its death.

But in 1967, these signs were not as clearly or as easily assessed as they are now. The NDP seemed to have some momentum because of its attacks on Manning, and the two by-elections in 1965 and 1966. The party was much better organized and financed than in 1963, and it had the full backing of the labour movement locally and nationally.

However, the NDP was a socialist party in a province where the people had continually rejected the socialist alternative for 25 years. Although it was a new party after 1962, it was subject to the same attacks and misapprehensions as before. The labour base in the cities which Reimer counted on, had not yet fully developed. The cities were still conglomerations of immigrants, both domestic and foreign, who had little developed sense of class. Given this, the Liberal party seemed perfectly poised to take advantage of any "time-for-a-change" feeling. The Liberals had remained the Official Opposition in the legislature since 1963. They had added to their number in the Edson by-election, and had run respectably in Pincher Creek. Ideologically they were a "safe" alternative if the electorate was looking for change, and they had a long history as both government and opposition in the province. Finally, the Liberal party was doing quite well nationally, with the launch of a number of popular social programmes.

The party least likely to supplant the Social Credit seemed to be the Conservatives. At the time of the Edson by-election, March 1965, they had elected a new leader, Peter Lougheed, a lawyer from Calgary and grandson of Senator Lougheed. The provincial Conservatives had never been in office in Alberta, and had suffered from their association with R.B. Bennett and the Depression. But, although Diefenbaker was out of office in Ottawa, his victories had rewritten the federal political map in the province, reducing Social Credit to a minor rump. This meant that there was organizational help available, as well as successful MPs who could provide role models for the electorate. With hindsight, the Conservatives ought to have been taken more seriously in 1967 than they were. They had a young, hard-working leader, a stable federal base, a new more youthful electorate, and good financial backing. It was a potent combination when coupled with an ideological view that was hardly threatening to Albertans. Much of this was not evident to Grant or the leadership of the NDP. In Executive meetings prior to the election, the Conservatives were never mentioned.

Organizationally the NDP was very well prepared. It had decided to run a full slate of candidates, with concentration in several key ridings. Financially, however the situation was "critical" in early 1967. The office was $6,461.54 in debt,[22] a very large amount at that time. To ensure that funds were available for the election, a $20,000 loan was negotiated with the Credit Union, presumably guaranteed by the Executive members. It was agreed that this would be set aside exclusively for the election. Dunsky Advertising, a firm out of Winnipeg headed by Manny Dunsky was put in charge of advertising, and at least $13,000 was made available for this budget. It was also decided to advertise province-wide, in all three media, TV, radio, and print. As well, requests for outside organizational help were sent to other provincial sections, and the labour movement. By Alberta NDP standards, it would be a massive campaign.

The key candidates were all in place. Neil Reimer was running again in Edson. Garth Turcott was running for re-election in Pincher Creek. Grant Notley was running in Edmonton Norwood. Other prominent candidates were running in Edmonton Constituencies, people like Ivor Dent, Gordon Wright, and Tom Pocklington. In the Peace River country there was excitement, and even in Calgary and southern Alberta there was a full slate. At the April 4, 1967 Executive meeting, final plans were all in place. The convention had been successful, although there were ripples of problems with the "Novakowski crew" that would surface more vigorously in the future. The party was ready.

It had been decided to concentrate on a few ridings where chances of success were greatest. These were Pincher Creek, Edson, Pembina, Athabasca, Dunvegan and Edmonton East. Grant's riding, according to Neil, was not a priority, although Joyce Kurri remembered that it was. Neil had decided that it should be a tough campaign, what we would now call a negative campaign, criticizing Manning and the Socreds for not only their policy records, but corruption.

Ted Chudyk recalls that the polls, which the NDP had carried out showed that the NDP had caught the attention of the voters.

> When you asked people about the coming election they were considering Socred or NDP.

Issues played a small part in the 1967 campaign. It quickly became a referendum on Manning and the Social Credit government. Since Reimer and the NDP had been most vocal in attacking Social Credit, the media zeroed in on this aspect. Only the NDP and Social Credit were running full slates of 65 candidates. The Liberals ran 45 and the Conservatives 47, meaning that the NDP campaign got a disproportionate amount of time when measured against its previous electoral record. The continued attacks against Manning aided in securing that attention.

However, it also raised a major problem with the NDP. Many thought it was time to "shift gears," to move away from the negative and begin to outline positive policy alternatives. These included several candidates, as well as Ted Chudyk, Grant, and others. There was a worry that the continued attacks might leave too negative an image and eventually disgust the electorate. Neil listened to these arguments, but initially rejected them. He felt that candidates were just losing their nerve. He had warned them earlier about how tough the campaign would be. By mid-campaign this "loss of nerve" led to a mini-revolt amongst the candidates, with some threatening to resign. Neil, as he says, "made a mistake," bowed to that pressure, and changed his approach, making it more positive.

Ted Chudyk recalls that Neil was not very successful at this, even though he tried.

> Reimer spoke to me about this day after day. How do I change? The election is going well. How do I change my image. I've got to become a statesman. He couldn't grasp a handle. I [Ted Chudyk] said, you've got to stop hammering, and he stopped hammering.
>   Neil felt good . . . but couldn't get a handle on becoming Premier. He'd give a speech that would talk about medicare, housing, and all the rest of it, and the headline would read "The man who would have Manning in jail, said." He could not break the headline.

The NDP carried its image to the end of the campaign. As a result, Ted feels that it eventually cost the NDP the campaign.

That having been said, right towards the end they said yes, we want to get rid of Manning, but Reimer's too dangerous. And there was the smooth Lougheed just being nice up the middle. They wanted a change, but we over frightened them.

Others agree with Ted's assessment. Independent research conducted at the University of Alberta also confirms that voters gathered behind Lougheed because of an anti-Social Credit feeling.[23]

But there were other factors in the campaign as well. For one thing Social Credit concentrated on the NDP and underestimated the PCs. This was caused in part by the attempt Manning was making to get a coalition of conservative forces in Western Canada, but it was also fuelled by a feeling of animosity. Premier Manning wanted to defeat Neil Reimer and his party, as much as Neil wanted to defeat Manning. There was a mutual loathing, which led to an inevitable conflict. The PCs benefitted from this immensely.

In addition, the Liberals collapsed in Alberta. It is not clear what caused this. In part they failed to bring together the anti-Social Credit vote as effectively as the Tories. This seems to have been caused in part by their choice of concentration ridings but also by a lack of appreciation for the danger posed by the Tories. The Liberals felt strongly that the NDP was the party to beat for second place. As a result, they did very badly.

Organizationally the campaign went very well. The NDP had more advertising, the largest number of candidates ever, and an abundance of media attention. When the NDP released its platform on May 8, it got good publicity. It concentrated on "practical" programmes for people, avoiding matters which were not provincial priorities. The next day the Tories released their programme, and also got good coverage. One measure of NDP credibility in the campaign came from the Edmonton *Journal*, which on May 12 took the time to write a snide editorial entitled "The oh-so mild NDP."[24] In essence it accused the NDP of being socialist wolves in pragmatic sheep's clothing. Much was also made of some of the new candidates, with some scandalous generalizations about the character of New Democrats. In writing about Tom Pocklington, one newspaper columnist said:

He's a new style of NDP candidate. Neither a thick necked and inarticulate labour leader, nor an ineffective socialist dilettante of the CCF.[25]

A major debate between all four party leaders took place on May 16, 1967 at the McDougall United Church in Edmonton. Supporters of the NDP thought that Neil did well, but media reports described Lougheed as the winner. On May 19, in an editorial assessing the chances of the various parties, the Edmonton *Journal* said:

> And Neil Reimer being Neil Reimer, and the Socialists being the Socialist, no one in Alberta should take very seriously what they predict.[26]

Despite media opposition a successful Tommy Douglas rally was staged in Edmonton, complete with skits and characters playing the other party leaders. Everyone on election night had high expectations.

The results were a devastating blow. The NDP was shut out in all 65 ridings, losing Pincher Creek which they had won in the by-election only six months before. The NDP was close in several ridings, but not close enough for recounts. Neil had lost badly in Edson, to Social Credit. So had Ivor Dent in Edmonton East, and Grant in Norwood. As Ted Chudyk put it, throughout the party these was a "numbness." The hopes of the last few years, the bright promise of only six months before had been wiped out. Worse, the Conservatives had won six seats, including a seat for their leader Peter Lougheed.

Some of the media was gleeful. The day after the election the Edmonton *Journal* ran a cartoon showing Neil Reimer and Garth Turcotte in the Legislature dressed as terrorists, complete with barrels of gunpower, saying to each other "I thought you brought the Matches?" In an editorial the *Journal* gloated:

> Albertans have handed the Liberal and left-wing total welfare staters a resounding rejection . . . . The party [NDP] mouthed pieties about an "open society," but his campaign was an essentially negative, destructive campaign.[27]

The editorial congratulated Manning and Lougheed for their victories.

Grant Notley (first row, second from left) in Grade School at Westerdale School in 1944.

Grant Notley on his parents farm near Olds at age 14.

Grant with his mother Francis at the University of Alberta
in 1960.

Grant and his wife Sandy, shortly after their wedding in 1963.

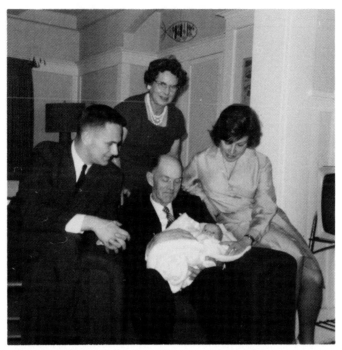

Grant and Sandy with Grant's mother and father and new daughter Rachel in 1964.

Grant's television debut in 1964 in Edmonton.

The famous Notley "brushcut" in 1966.

Grant and Sandy at Sandy's graduation in 1966.

Grant and Henry Thomaschuk in 1967.

Grant speaking at the First Nominating Convention,
November 10, 1970, in Rycroft Alberta. T.C. Douglas is seated
next to Grant.

Grant with Howard Leeson, Muriel Reiger, and other Council members at the NDP Council meeting in Fairview, Alberta, July 22, 1972.

"On the farm"—Grant with his children, Rachel, Paul, and Stephen, at their acreage near Fairview.

Grant in his first Legislative Office in 1972.

Nancy and Ralph Eng and their family during the Foothills
By-election in 1974.

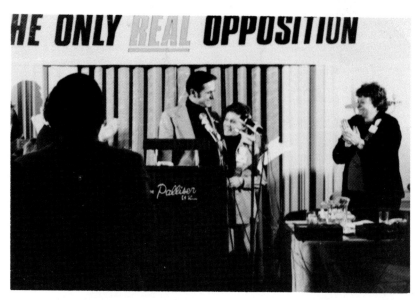

Grant with Sandy and Anne Dryden during the 1975 election campaign at the Palliser Hotel, Calgary.

Considering the problems.

At work in the office. Grant pondering constituency business.

Capturing the future vote.

Fighting for Canada. Grant with Ray Martin.

Grant (on right) with Ray Martin, Tom Sigurdson, Davis Swan, Ted Chudyk, and Henry Mendelbaum (from left to right).

"At home in Alberta."

Grant Notley in his office.

5 THE LEADER

FOR NEIL THE RESULTS were a bitter pill. The successes of the previous two years had heightened expectations, including his own. He had worked very hard, and given much of himself to the effort, even to the extent of virtually abandoning his own union during the two previous years. In retrospect it is clear that Neil's own personality and public image were part of the problem. His union background shaped his approach to issues and to politics. He was used to confrontation, to bargaining, to winning or losing. Compromise was something you did only as a last resort, when faced with far superior force. If you had an advantage, you pressed it hard for the good of your membership, and as a consequence, for your own career.

This approach dictated a tough, often abrasive style, a hard public image. This was Neil's approach to Manning and Social Credit, as well as politics in general. In private, with friends, he could be genial, even, as Joyce Kurri put it, "a teddy bear," but in public this did not come through. Thus, before the 1967 campaign, when Neil thought that scandals would bring Manning down, he pressed his advantage hard, as he would in negotiations. The result was to heighten a public image that was already hard-edged.

Such an image of toughness is acceptable in a political leader to some extent, but only if it is connected with activities that the public views as legitimate. Thus Manning as a Premier could be tough because being a Christian minister was an acceptable "calling." Later, Peter Lougheed could be tough because he was a lawyer, and was expected to be. But

Neil was a union leader, and in the 1960s being tough was still associated with the likes of Jimmy Hoffa. Unions were constantly portrayed as hot beds of communism or organized crime, and union leaders as slightly unsavory and illegitimate. Neil's toughness ultimately aided Peter Lougheed, not himself.

The decision to step down was a hard one for Neil, and not made immediately after the campaign. He obviously knew that a watershed had been reached, and that he would probably have to resign. He now remembers that several things prompted his decision. The first was that he needed to get a grip on his own personal life. He was almost fifty years old, had neglected his work for several years, and had suffered financially as a result of being NDP leader. A decision was needed soon, and that decision pointed toward resigning as NDP leader. The second reason was that Manning was stepping down, and there appeared to be a new opportunity that Social Credit would be displaced in the future. Neil concluded that there was a greater chance of those voters going to the NDP if he was not leader. The third factor was a strong desire on the part of his union that he return to work as its full-time head.

All of these were obviously important, but unspoken by Neil was another compelling argument. In 1967 it was crystal clear that the NDP was not going to become the alternative to the Socreds in the near future. The Conservatives had gained that position decisively by electing six people, and at best the NDP could only hope to gather a few seats as part of any Socred decline. The hopes of the NDP in the 1967 campaign that it would replace Social Credit were now delayed, if not destroyed. It would be a much longer road to power than any had anticipated in 1963.

Much of this was apparent in June of 1967, but the party faced some important business immediately after the campaign. First, it was bankrupt. The Executive had borrowed to finance the campaign. Money now had to be raised immediately. This work was left to Grant, who approached it in his usual methodical and diligent style. He launched a series of over a hundred fund raising meetings across the province, where he and Ted Chudyk raised a considerable amount of money. It was a long grinding process, one which Ted Chudyk looks back on with pride, but also with obvious relief. Grant gave the political speech at each of these meetings, and Ted gave the pitch for money.

The meetings served two purposes for Grant. The first was to try and raise money to keep the party afloat in the face of a deepening pessimism about its future. The second was personal. Grant knew that it was likely that Neil would step down soon, and that he had a good chance to succeed Neil if he did go. These meetings gave Grant immense exposure for any future leadership convention. The meetings were completed in three months and both objectives were met.

The second activity facing the party in the summer of 1967 was the Kirby Inquiry, called in answer to the allegations made in the legislature by Garth Turcotte before the election. This was coupled with a law suit against the party, all necessitating expensive legal help. That legal help was directed by Gordon Wright, who would contest the leadership next year.

Gordon had become quite active after 1966. He was born in Jamaica in 1927 to English parents, who subsequently moved back to Britain. There he completed his education, eventually becoming a lawyer. His family was quite active in the Conservative party, and he was a young Conservative. However, as he became more widely read he became more aware that the Conservatives were spreading, as he delicately put it, "half-truths," and after 1951 he supported the Labour party. In 1955 he came to Alberta, where he supported the CCF, although he did not take out a membership.

When the New Party Clubs were formed in 1962 he attended the founding convention of the New Party as a delegate from one of them. He attended functions, gave money (Grant used to come to him for post-dated cheques) but was not on the Executive. He was as he put it, "a curiosity" in the NDP. Not many lawyers supported the party in those years. Indeed, his law partners were not usually favourable to his activity.

In moving to Alberta Gordon fondly remembered that he continued an unbroken record of always voting for a losing candidate, until 1986, when he voted for himself and was elected to the legislature. Before his death in October of 1990, he was able to vote for himself one more time. He is remembered by all party members as thoughtful and principled, a man who always provided sound advice to the party. He is also remembered as someone who could fall asleep at any time, especially in court, which he did during the Kirby Inquiry. However, this seemed not to bother his understanding of events, or his ability to perform, since he would always resume his critiques or comments exactly as if he had not fallen asleep.

In 1966 he was recruited into formal activity. As he recalled:

Reimer and Notley took me out to lunch . . . or I went to lunch with them . . . in the first part of 1966, and they asked me to be a candidate in the forthcoming election.

(Gordon was no more successful in extracting a lunch from Grant than anyone else). He was asked to run in Edmonton North. He did not know what to think at first, but after some pressure from Neil and Grant, and after talking to his law partner, who was "appalled," he decided to run.

Gordon did quite well in the campaign, running third, but raising the vote of the NDP. When it became apparent that the NDP would have standing at the Hooke-Hinman Inquiry (Kirby Inquiry), Grant asked Gordon to take on the legal case for a "reduced fee," as Gordon recalls. He agreed, and concentrated on the first portion, which began in September and went for two months.

The other person involved in the Kirby Inquiry was Anne Dryden (now Ann Hopp). Anne was not a lawyer, but at this time the Editor of the Alberta *Democrat*, the New Democratic Party paper. Anne was born in Tyler, Texas in 1933. She lived in Texas and California until 1954, when together with her parents, who worked in the oil industry, she moved to Alberta. Her education was completed in the United States, high school in Texas, and an Associate Arts degree at Yuba College, in Marysville-Yuba City in California. She studied journalism and communication, because as she says she was, "a bit of a ham," and eventually produced a radio request show in the early fifties, called "Lonesome Anne." She also produced a children's show, a TV cooking show, although she admits that she "really couldn't cook a lick," and a TV interview show. In the U.S. she was not involved in politics at all, although her mother was quite active in the Democratic Party.

In 1955 she met Bill Dryden. They were married and quickly had three children. They kept her very occupied, together with working at first with the Edmonton *Sun* as a rewrite editor for rural news. Her work for the *Sun* gave her a feeling for rural Alberta that she wouldn't have had otherwise. In 1961 Anne went back to work at the School for the Deaf. Her keen interest in current affairs, and Bill's involvement in the New Party brought her into some contact with the NDP. Her own inclination was to the left of the political spectrum because of her antipathy toward McCarthyism and segregation. That involvement took the form of entertainment as she perfected her technique with a baritone ukelele, and in 1963 she wrote some political songs. She does not recall meeting Grant directly, but she began to do volunteer work at the office, just as her husband Bill had done.

Bill was involved with Tom Pocklington at the university, and so Anne became good friends with Lou Pocklington, his wife. Together, they put together a little set of songs to perform. The lyrics were novel, but the tunes were taken from "old favourites." Over the years these songs became standards in the party, which Grant dearly loved to hear. In 1965 she and Lou went to several meetings during the Edson by-election.

> We had these pretty hokey costumes, sort of long dresses that were vaguely reminiscent of a Nun's Habit. Dark and flowing down to the ground. I had my ukulele, and she had a tambourine, and we sang songs.
>
> Once we went up with Tommy Douglas, and two or three times with Neil. We loved it. The crowds responded well. The crowds have always responded to the singing . . . because the words are blatantly partisan. And because they're hokey rhymes to familiar tunes. Plus the fact that neither one of us could sing. So weren't up there showing off our wonderful talent. We were just the person next door.

She and Lou continued to perform for various functions during the Reimer era, especially for the Pincher Creek by-election, and during the 1967 campaign, in Tom Pocklington's riding. As she said, the words were universal, and could be applied to any candidate.

Gradually she came to be more involved with Grant, and more impressed with him. In particular she remembers helping him with his speaking voice, something she could do as a result of her speech therapy training. His voice was too high and too nasal. She decided to show him how to moderate it. This was accomplished by having Grant lie on the floor in the office, with two large books on his diaphragm. No one is quite sure if this accomplished the purpose. Grant never mentioned it as a key turning point in his later ability as an accomplished speaker.

Just before the 1967 campaign the Executive had decided to put out a party newspaper. Again, Sandy Notley, with her media background, had worked on newsletters and other papers in the period up until then, and wanted "madly" to be the Editor. However, Grant would not hear of it and Anne was hired. Sandy was quite hurt, and naturally blamed Anne at first. (Later they became good friends.) Anne's first job at the paper was to report on the Hooke-Hinman affair. As it turned out this really became the only function of the paper.

Anne remembers that the only reason that the paper was able to go out was because they had a justifying typewriter. It required hours and hours of typing, all of which Anne did voluntarily. The results of each session in the Kirby Inquiry were published in the paper by Anne. Actually, these long, cogent, and very explanatory articles were written by Gordon Wright. However, Gordon was reluctant to publish under his own name, for obvious reasons. Consequently, the articles, though written by Gordon, were attributed to Anne.

As it turned out the inquiry went badly for the NDP. The evidence was more ambiguous than the NDP thought, and the Chief Counsel for the inquiry more "inert" than Gordon expected. Despite the best efforts of Gordon Wright, the inquiry found in favour of Hooke and Hinman. It was a long, expensive, and ultimately useless effort, part of a broader strategy which backfired completely. For Gordon Wright, it was personally a defeat, but it gave him positive exposure within the Alberta NDP, enough to make him a contender for the leadership.

The culmination of the election, the Kirby Inquiry, and other events, put a tremendous strain on the NDP internally. As 1967 came to an end, it became obvious that the unity of the previous five years was beginning to crack. By 1968 there were three factions in the party. The first was the traditional group surrounding Neil Reimer, including Roy Jahma, Ivor Dent, Joyce Kurri, and other union members. A second group consisted mostly of young New Democrats from the Calgary and Edmonton university campuses, headed by Ken Novakowski. This was a pro Waffle group, intent on moving the party to the left. It was supported by the Woodsworth-Irvine Fellowship and other CCFers originally opposed to the Reimer leadership. Finally, in embryo, there was a group of mostly rural people which was prepared to support Neil as long as he was leader, but ready to coalesce around Grant Notley if a leadership race was declared.

It was a delicate time for Grant. In later interviews he was generally silent about this period, and seemed to take less pride in his election as leader than one would expect. After the election of 1967 he was organizational head of a rapidly sinking ship. The party had outstanding debts of nearly $50,000 (this amount has been reported as high as $100,000, but party documents refer to a lower level. It really is difficult to pinpoint what it was exactly). At the June 2, 1967 meeting of the Executive the organizers were laid off. Ted Chudyk was put on OCAW staff for a number of months. Only Joyce Kurri and Grant remained. It was imperative that the party recover financially, but it was a very difficult if not impossible job. The 120 day marathon raised some money, but not enough. It was supplemented by the sale of the now infamous debentures, or promissory notes. These were quite simply loans from party members at what were then good interest rates. No due date was attached, and interest was seldom if ever paid. Indeed, these were only found again in 1973 when the holder of a large note died and his estate demanded repayment. These debentures were an indication of how desperate things had become, especially when one considers the fact that the party owed over $20,000 for the Kirby Inquiry.

Grant's position then, was delicate because of the financial state of the party. But more importantly, it was delicate because when it became clear that Neil would step down as a leader, Grant was forced to remain loyal until the official date of the convention. He could not dissociate himself from the Reimer leadership without alienating the Reimer loyalists. On the other hand, if he remained absolutely loyal and unquestioning he would alienate those in the rural areas and on the left who viewed the Reimer strategies and leadership as part of the problem in the 1967 election. It was the classic "Crown Prince" dilemma.

In order to deal with this Grant made two key decisions. First, he decided to abandon the hope of securing the support of Novakowski and the Waffle group. They were a loud, but very small group. To placate them would have cost him support in other areas. Second, he decided not to overtly distance himself from Neil Reimer. The consequence of this was that when open warfare broke out between the Novakowski and Reimer factions in December of 1967 Grant supported Neil. It was a delicate balancing act. It left Grant very much in the position of the "organizational" right wing candidate.

Several months prior to the announcement Neil discussed his decision to step down with several people. One of these was Grant. Grant urged him to stay on for at least two years. Neil recalls that Grant urged this because he did not feel that he was ready yet to run for the leadership. Sandy Notley agrees that Grant urged Neil to stay on, thinking that it was too soon. She also recalls that Grant talked to Ivor Dent and tried to get Ivor to run. Ivor would have been a logical choice, but by this time had his sights set squarely on being Mayor of Edmonton. After the 1967 results it was not a auspicious time to take over the NDP in Alberta.

Ted Chudyk remembers that Neil knew that the 1967 results were the end of the line.

> Neil had tired out. He also looked at his family, and said, I better pay attention to my union. They're my bread and butter. Neil made [sic] a very good conclusion at this point. He gave it his best shot. Maybe some errors [were] made, but then we all make errors.

When it became apparent that Neil would be going, Grant talked to Ted about running for the leadership. Ted was surprised. He still thought of Grant as a "green kid." As Ted said, "He still had a brushcut. I sort of looked at him as a kid." Grant wanted to know from Ted what his chances were. Ted thought that Grant had a good chance, and that ultimately he would be the best choice. It is not clear that Ted's recollections on this are as precise as possible. There were many at the time who did not think that Grant was the best choice, but the years between have blurred a good bit of vision.

Whatever the estimations involved, Grant was forced to campaign for almost a year for a leadership position which publicly was not open. According to most accounts he did this very discreetly. However, Joyce Kurri, who remained as Office Manager and was a self-admitted Reimer loyalist, disputes this view. She contends that from her vantage point, it was obvious that Grant was seriously undermining Neil's leadership after the 1967 election. It is a view which she supported in two separate interviews, thirteen years apart.

> After the '67 campaign the wolves were after him [Neil Reimer]. You wouldn't believe it. Our own people inside. I mean our organizers, I'm not going to name them, did as good a hatchet job on him as anyone else . . . . Nothing ever surprised me, because I know the way people are in politics, and what ends they'll go to. And Grant was behind most of it.
>
> As I say I typed up the news release which nearly broke my heart when Neil resigned. I was nearly in tears. Because Grant was so excited about it and he didn't hold it back. I can see them all today coming out of that little conference room.
>
> From that day on, I couldn't stand the sight of him [Grant].

Before he announced his retirement Neil made a point of ensuring that there would be a contest. He was determined that it would not be simply a crowning of any one candidate. Neil did not think that Grant was the best person to succeed him. He believed that Grant needed experience outside of the party, and was too young. It was an assessment shared by a number of people. Anne Hemmingway, a supporter in the Rycroft area of the Peace River country, who later became provincial President, supported Neil on this point.

> I used to hear of this Grant Notley, and that he was Secretary, and . . . I would say what kind of man is he? Well they would say "he is a kid," and of course when he ran that is exactly what he looked like. To see him stand up and speak with Gordon Wright and Allen Busch speaking at the same time I thought, well that kid looks like he's good, but he needs four or five years, he's got to grow up. Therefore, I did not support Grant for the leadership in 1968.

Gordon Wright recalled this matter when Neil approached him to run for the leadership.

> There were many supporters of Grant who didn't think that he was old enough to do the job. Some of these asked me to throw my hat in the ring. Reimer encouraged me, and Roy Jahma.
> But only one person came forward to be my campaign manager, and that was Ken Novakowski, who had a reputation as being a radical and a nuisance . . . I think it distressed Neil Reimer.

It was apparent to everyone that Grant had an overwhelming advantage over other candidates. He was well known throughout the party, and had maintained those contacts regularly. For people like Irene Dyck and hundreds of others, the contest was a foregone conclusion. Graham Thomlinson, later President of the Spirit River-Fairview constituency when Grant was the MLA, had one regret about supporting Grant.

> I remember I was backing Grant. I think probably our only regret would be to lose him as Provincial Secretary because he was very good at the job . . . . But he definitely had a lot of things going for him as leader . . . . He was a better speaker . . . and a more practical type of person. He always got along well with the media . . . .

Throughout the province, Grant had accumulated considerable support. Joyce Kurri, although she did not support Grant, also thought at the time that the race was a foregone conclusion.

At first there were four candidates, an optometrist, a teacher, Grant and Gordon Wright. But the first two dropped out almost immediately. This left only Grant and Gordon to go on the leadership tour sponsored by the party. The stops included the Peace River country, Lethbridge, Pincher Creek, Medicine Hat, Red Deer and Edmonton. By the time that the tour was underway Gordon was very enthusiastic, and wanted to win. He hoped to overcome his own lack of exposure by going on the tour.

It was a very friendly affair. They travelled together, and in the southern tour they even went in the same car. Allan Early, as Acting Provincial Secretary, accompanied them. Gordon was annoyed that Allan although supposed neutral, was supporting Grant and had not taken a leave of absence. Gordon's campaign manager, Ken Novakowksi, was quite angry, but they did not publicly criticize Allan because they did not want to be perceived as "whiners." Gordon, in his usual courteous manner did not think that Grant was directing Allan:

> I don't think so. Allan was bending the rules a little, but within the bounds of decency. It really wasn't important.

Many of the labour people were prepared to support Gordon, but were put off by his association with Novakowski. As Reg Basken put it, Gordon showed "bad judgement" in this. It was a strange coalition, made especially difficult because the convention was being held in Calgary.

Gordon's impression of Grant was instructive. He remembers that Grant was "not much of a speaker." On the tour he was "not outstanding" and had no sense of humour.

> He always did appreciate a joke, but at first had almost no capability in telling one. His skill as an orator was small. He wrote out all of his speeches beforehand. It was wonderful over the years to see him develop into a first-class speaker.
>
> But even then he knew his facts, and he was dedicated. He had the time to devote to it.

By the time that the candidates made it reached the convention, it appeared that the race might be somewhat tighter than expected. A further complicating factor arose as well. A third candidate, Alan Busch from the Peace River country, an Anglican Minister and a former organizer for the party, had decided to run. Alan had thought about running against Neil in 1967 but had been dissuaded by some blunt talk from Joyce Kurri. In 1968 he was encouraged by Bill Dryden and Anne Dryden.

The speeches at the convention did not change much. Grant gave a good, clipped, and careful speech. As predicted, he did not rock any boats. At the time Bill Dryden did not like Gordon, and assessed his speech as too pompous, and British labour oriented. Others thought that Gordon's speech was excellent. Allan Busch performed well, but had no organization, and little backing.

The result was as predicted, Grant won on the first ballot, getting slightly over 50%. It was far closer than any, had expected. Gordon Wright believed that if the convention had been held in Edmonton, he would have won. Others, like the Drydens, agreed.

Looking back now it is easier to see why it was such a narrow victory for Grant. Despite his familiarity to a large number of New Democrats, Anne Hemmingway's assessment that he was too young is probably correct. Neil's assessment that Grant was too socially restricted and did not have enough "real life" experience is also valid. Bill Dryden's criticism that he was not sufficiently policy oriented or ideological enough can also be accepted. He carried with him a variety of defects that cost him support, and made people uneasy about him.

If anyone of more stature in the NDP, such as Ivor Dent, had run for the position, Grant would not have won. But no one was interested. They had all done their "political sums," and come up with the conclusion that 1968 was not a good time to become leader of the Alberta NDP. Social Credit was slipping but the Conservatives were coming on strong. The NDP was in terrible shape, electorally, financially, and ideologically. It was a party riven with internal splits, ripe for discord, and probably about to become politically irrelevant.

Only a gangly, hard-working, boyish, and socially immature young man like Grant would even consider taking over, a person who realized that this was probably his only chance to become leader. All of the smart operators sat back, waiting for the next time. All of the calculators agreed that there was little chance that Grant would succeed, and that a new leadership convention would be held in a few short years. All of the pundits agreed privately that this leader had little chance to succeed.

They were all wrong.

What should have been the best and most exciting years of Grant's leadership were in fact the hardest. The party was broke. It was as Grant put it, "almost in continual war" between the factions, Reimer on one side, Novakowski and the Waffle on the other. The coalition that Grant had led to a leadership victory was spread across the province, but with little base in Edmonton. Worse yet, the labour movement in the NDP, still controlled by Neil Reimer, pulled back from support of Grant. This withdrawal was caused by actions on both sides. For his part Neil did not think that Grant was the best person for the job, and felt that he would be a short-lived occupant of the leadership chair. As well, Joyce Kurri had passed on stories about alleged disloyalty by Grant and the organizers, causing hard feelings. From Grant's point of view, the shoe was on the other foot. He believed that he had been both loyal and helpful to Neil throughout Neil's leadership. He had worked long and hard for Neil, giving up much to ensure that Neil and the NDP were given the chance of success. He was personally stung and hurt by Neil's support of Gordon Wright, a relative newcomer. As a consequence, he and Alan Early acted petulantly taking down all of the pictures of Neil in the office the day after the campaign, an action that only served to widen the gap between the two men.

However, in later 1968 Grant was faced with more than an internal party split. The political scene in Alberta altered swiftly after the 1967 election. The Conservatives under Peter Lougheed were the Official Opposition. The Liberals, as a result of their poor showing in 1967, were in disarray. In 1968 Mike Maccagno resigned both as leader and as Member of Legislature for Lac La Biche. In the subsequent by-election on August 20, 1968, Social Credit won the seat handily for the first time in several years. Ominously, the Liberals ran a poor third to the Conservatives and Social Credit. More ominously, the NDP candidate, R. Stuart, got only 4%. It was clear that a polarization between the Conservatives and Social Credit was growing.

But the big news of 1968 was the resignation of E.C. Manning as Premier of Alberta. After 33 years in the Legislature of Alberta, 25 of them as Premier, the dynamic and charismatic leader of Alberta Social Credit was leaving the political landscape. Elected in his place was a quiet and soft-spoken southern Alberta rancher, Harry Strom. Just as importantly, the provincial Social Credit party abandoned its federal wing, endorsing a policy which allowed Social Crediters to support whatever federal party or candidate best served the interests of the right wing in Canada. In retrospect this policy, dubbed Social Conservatism by Alf Hooke and others, was a disaster. It isolated the provincial Social Credit, making it a minor provincial party in a small prairie province. If it was logical to vote Progressive Conservative federally, why not provincially? It was a calculation not lost on voters in 1971.

The most immediate result, however, was a by-election, held on February 10, 1969 in Manning's seat of Strathcona East, an Edmonton area riding. Grant had just been elected leader, and there was pressure from Neil and others for him to run in the riding. In his own mind he had not sorted out where he wanted to run, but as Ted Chudyk recalls the main consideration was whether or not the seat was winnable.

> Grant at that point became the strategist, really for his own good. Grant very much wanted to distance himself from the gutter fighting. He wanted to be . . . seen as Premier material. But more importantly he didn't want to establish in his new position a track record as a loser. He wanted to have a pretty good shot at winning before he got in the race. That I know for certain. He wasn't going to run just to represent the party.

Ted agreed with Grant's strategy. In his mind the NDP had won the battle with the Manning government but lost the war to Peter Lougheed. There should be a deliberate effort to distance Grant from the Reimer approach to politics and to establish a winning record.

Neil Reimer disagreed. He wanted Grant to run in the by-election. He now argues that by deciding not to run in the Manning Seat Grant actually delayed the development of the NDP in Alberta.

> In my view Grant was motivated in that decision not to contest in Edmonton out of his imagined fear of Ivor Dent and Neil Reimer. No question in my mind. Let me take a look immediately at the first decision that he made which proved so successful for the Conservatives and, I think, fatal for us.

> Manning resigned the seat where I live. Ray Field . . . had run there before, and had a credible showing, in terms of the showings of that day. I know the people of that riding.

The by-election was immediately after Grant got elected. He put in some absolute non-entity to run. He didn't come to me. He didn't go to Ivor, or to any name. Didn't even ask us. He didn't make an attempt. He didn't want to win that one. He never would have admitted to that, but I was shocked . . . .

We could have won that one. Just as much as Yurko [the PC candidate] could have won it, because in 1968 there was no Conservative ascendency.

Neil's charge that Grant avoided the by-election because of a fear of Neil and Ivor is debatable. Ivor had only two months before declined to run for the leadership. Neil had just stepped down as leader. It was a reasonable assumption on Grant's part that neither would be interested. It was also predictable that he would not ask Neil or Ivor to run. As a new leader, it would have been difficult to have the previous leader elected to the House. Finally the seat had been a Socred stronghold. Everyone expected that it would be retained by Social Credit. In the election which followed the NDP candidate Gary Allen, a graduate student at the University of Alberta, got only 4.7% of the vote, but more importantly, Bill Yurko won the seat for the PCs.

The results for the Conservative Party in Alberta were electric. Observers of Alberta politics have agreed with Neil Reimer that it was one of the Conservative Party's "biggest successes."[1] Social Credit was in shock, and some disarray.

That disarray was to be continued by yet another by-election loss. The death of Bill Switzer, MLA for Edson, who had defeated Neil Reimer twice, opened the door to a second by-election and a real challenge for all of the parties.

For the Liberal Party it was a straightforward matter. They had lost the Lac La Biche seat in 1968. If they lost this one, it would likely mean the end of the Liberal party as a significant force. For Social Credit it could provide the momentum needed to get the Strom government back on track. They needed badly to win. For the Lougheed Conservatives it was a dream. Since they did not hold the seat, and had run fourth, any increase would be viewed as positive. If they won, it would give them overwhelming momentum. For the NDP, it was a big, big problem.

Sandy Notley recalls that Bill Switzer died on the July 1, 1969 long weekend, when she and Grant were in Olds.

We were at Olds at the farm for the long weekend and Grant had been out for a walk . . . . I heard the news and when he came in I said, "Grant, Switzer has died. There is your by-election." For the first few weeks he would say, "well, I don't necessarily have to run."

However, Grant soon came to the conclusion that he would have to run. Ted Chudyk remembers that decision.

He didn't want to go. I think it was because he felt that he had no choice, in his credibility as Leader. It was a very uncomfortable by-election, trying to rekindle the old people.

In many ways it was a bad situation. He was following in Neil's footsteps, trying to win in Edson, where it was apparent that the chances were not good. Grant was not a union leader, and could not command the organized resources in Edson that Neil had. Worse, there was real strain between Neil and Grant, meaning that the trade union movement would not fully support him. However, it was impossible to duck the election. To do so would allow the Conservatives and Socreds to strengthen their grip on the next general election, making the NDP irrelevant. Grant could not allow this, and made the decision to go ahead.

Once into the by-election, Grant determined that they must do everything possible to win. The best organizational talent from around the country was solicited, and many came. Stephen Lewis, later NDP Leader in Ontario and Canada's Ambassador to the United Nations, ran the campaign. It was a lesson for Stephen according to Sandy.

Stephen Lewis was the organizer and I remember poor old Stephen talking about urban people. He didn't know how to read a range and township map. He assigned from the voter's list off this road and up that road sort of thing, and didn't understand.

Grant remembered that the party decided to spend $20,000 dollars, a large sum considering that the cupboard was bare. There was a big nominating convention, filling the Legion Hall, standing room only. But Ted remembers that it was very difficult to get people to work. Many people from outside, including Sandy, were brought in to canvas, put up signs, and telephone supporters. Technically it was a good campaign. But there were few overriding issues.

The Conservatives ran a young candidate called Bob Dowling. He remembered Grant as "nervous, unschooled, and wet behind the ears."[2] The Socreds ran a man named Jorgenson, and the Liberals a Mr. R. Woods. Sandy remembers that on the night before the election Grant told her that they would lose. He estimated that they would be 1100-1200 votes behind. The result, stunningly, was a PC win with 2445 votes. Social Credit ran second with 1743 votes, and Grant third with 1524 votes. The Liberals ran fourth, effectively ending their immediate provincial chances.

For Grant it was a dismaying result.

> It just didn't click. I ran third. I think at that time I probably felt more personally defeated and shattered than at any time in my twenty years or so.

But when asked if he considered stepping down as leader he said no.

> No not really. I don't think there was any other alternative, in my judgement. There were people who certainly would have come in, but I don't think that there were any serious alternatives.

The most immediate result of the by-election loss was the obvious financial difficulty. All of the staff were again laid off, and the party office was closed. For Grant, it was the lowest point of his political career, a low point from which it was going to be very difficult to recover.

However, he attacked the job with his usual energy. He tried to do two things. First, he went on the road continuously, trying to raise money to keep the party and his family together. It was an incredibly hard job. Second, he tried to keep his name and the party before the media, commenting on every issue. From this he earned the nickname "Fastest Press Release in the West."

In the early part of 1970 Grant continued his attempt to keep the party afloat. He was aided in that task by Sandy, and by his long time friend Mark Johnston, who became the voluntary, unpaid Provincial Secretary, in part because some of Mark's stock portfolio could be used for an ongoing loan. As Sandy recalls, "There was always the loan." Joyce Kurri continued to keep the accounts for the party, but did not come into the party office. She accomplished this task from the OCAW office of Reg Basken, who was then Treasurer of the party. The split between Grant and the trade union movement became even deeper at this time.

During this period Grant's two sons, Paul and Stephen, were born, Paul before the by-election, and Stephen after. Sandy, having completed her Bachelor's degree, went to work at the University of Alberta as a research assistant in Medical-Sociology because they needed the money. As Sandy recalls, her working at the time did not bother Grant. Nothing in their marriage had changed since his election as leader. Grant was totally devoted to the party and to the leadership. His every waking hour was taken up with party activity, especially during this period.

In the early spring of 1970 Grant went to a meeting in the town of Athabasca. It was a regular meeting, designed to raise funds, and keep interest in the party alive. Prior to the meeting a young man by the name of Hart Horn had been asked to do some organizing. Hart was born in Cologne, Germany in 1935. In Europe he had been streamed into a training programme involving business management. In 1956 he emigrated to Canada, and went to work with the CPR in Calgary. Although he had not been political in Europe, he leaned toward the left wing parties because of the American policy of splitting the two Germanies. He became a citizen of Canada in 1961, and decided to go to university at the University of Alberta campus in Calgary. His English was sufficiently proficient that he was able to secure a teaching degree in 1967, and stayed on to do Master's work. After that he taught part-time, and eventually wound up in Edmonton at the University of Alberta in 1969, doing post-graduate work. By 1970 he had moved to Athabasca, commuting to the University, finishing his work with the aid of a Canada Council grant.

Hart was a blunt-spoken, hard-working person. He had not been politically active, but had been impressed by Neil Reimer in 1967, and voted NDP in Calgary. He does not recall why he was asked to organize the Athabasca meeting, but he set about it diligently. The result was a larger than expected turnout, something which impressed Grant. That night Grant stayed at Hart's home, and they talked politics late into the night.

Hart was immediately captivated by Grant, and by his work in politics. When Grant asked him to do some further work in the constituency Hart agreed, selling 60 new memberships and setting up an interesting race for the nomination. The nomination meeting was a big success, and a candidate, Peter Oprysko, was nominated in the early spring. For Grant it was a small ray of sunshine in a bleak landscape.

Grant and Hart became quite good friends, and after an Edmonton meeting which Hart had organized, Grant asked him to consider becoming Provincial Secretary. It was symptomatic of the state of the NDP that

Grant would even suggest this to the Executive. The post of Provincial
Secretary had, since 1962, been a paid position, a position of influence
and power within the Alberta NDP. To be considered for this position
usually meant that someone had long experience within the party. None
of this was true in 1970. The party could barely afford to pay Grant, and
the Secretary's job had become a voluntary unpaid one. Hart Horn knew
nothing of the party, its structure, its membership, its policy, or its
history. In normal times, he would not have been considered for an
organizational position, much less Provincial Secretary. But these
were not normal times, and Grant desperately needed someone who was
a hard worker and willing to do so without pay. To Grant, Hart seemed
to be that person. He proposed Hart's name to the Executive, and it
was accepted.

Hart's first days as Secretary were a shock. The office had been closed
for months. Everything was, as he recalled, musty and dusty. There was
no list of current or past members. Indeed, there was no list at all, only
some old addressograph plates piled in a corner. It was a mystery to Hart
that the organization functioned at all. He spent the next several months
trying to straighten out the mess.

That he did not know what he was doing was an understatement. He
quickly enlisted the help of a retired pensioner named Stan Gee. Stan
was reluctant at first, indicating that he really was more of a Communist
than a Social Democrat, but eventually agreed to lend a hand, strictly
unpaid, of course. (Eventually Stan stayed on for many years, keeping
track of his membership lists. He was a kindly, cheerful, and dedicated
person, whom everyone liked.) Other people, like Lou Pocklington, also
helped out when possible.

Hart did not consider himself to be used by Grant or the NDP during
this period. He was very impressed with Grant. He considered him a
thoughtful, hard driving person, concerned about human dignity and the
oppressed. He realized that Grant was also personally ambitious, but he
felt this to be necessary if anything was to be accomplished. The two were
of similar temperaments, both being very hard workers. They got along
well and eventually Hart became something of a confidante of Grant's as
they travelled around Alberta. Hart was also impressed with Sandy.

Sandy was an enormous boost to Grant. A big, big crutch. Even bigger
than I was . . . . She was the mainstay at home. If ever there was a wife,
who did the duty of supporting her husband, it was Sandy Notley.

The one thing that distressed Hart about Grant was the way that he treated Sandy. He felt that Grant was oblivious to her contribution and took her too much for granted. But, along with everyone else, he excused Grant's attitude on the basis that Grant simply did not have the time to be the perfect husband. He also felt that Sandy accepted her role. He compared her to someone who had taken a vow and was continuing to accept the consequences of that vow. As with everyone else, Grant was able to command a great personal loyalty from Hart, something which continued throughout the rest of their relationship.

By 1970 there was only one thing which could save Grant's career. He had to get elected. Grant knew this.

I was certainly aware that if I had lost [in 1971] I would have had enormous problems within the party and probably would have not been able to remain leader. I'm sure that that would have been true.

The decision about where to run was absolutely crucial.

The choice provoked a bitter internal debate which took place on several levels. The first debate was the most explicit. Which riding held the best chance for Grant to get elected? There were really only two or three choices. The first was Norwood, where Grant lived. It was an inner city Edmonton riding, with mostly working class people. From a class perspective it would be good territory for the NDP. But Grant rejected Norwood for two reasons. The primary reason was that city ridings tended to swing widely with electoral changes. They were more vulnerable to media concentration, and tended to be affected by it. Grant's analysis was that a leader in a single city riding, without a strong provincial campaign, could easily lose. As well, Grant was worried that the informal party strife between the factions in Edmonton would not enable the party to unite behind him. There was little local organizational help in Norwood to offset such losses from the rest of the city.

The second riding was Edmonton Beverly, another east Edmonton working class riding, but with a much stronger unionized segment. It was probably the best riding in the city. But Grant had not run there before, and many of the arguments against Norwood applied to Beverly. But most importantly, the split between Grant and Neil Reimer had widened into a total break. It was not likely that the trade union movement would rally behind Grant unless the breach with Neil was repaired.

This really meant that Grant would need to go to Neil cap in hand, something he was not prepared to do.

This left the Peace River country, and in particular, Spirit River-Fairview.

> It wasn't a good internal situation in Edmonton. I had come to the conclusion that the cities weren't good grounds for us because of the media. That the Socreds, would try to hang on, the Tories were coming on strong, that in a media backlash people would say, well they're [the NDP] nice people, but we've got to vote for whomever [Socreds or Tories].
>
> So the question really arose, where could I run where I would be on an equal footing with the other parties? So we chose the Peace.

Grant's analysis included some persuasive arguments. In the Peace River region there was only one TV station, the CBC. Grant felt that he would at least get fair coverage on CBC, not equal to the others, but more than on the private media. On radio, the costs were small enough in the Peace River area that the NDP could be able to match the Socred and Conservative advertising, dollar for dollar. In addition to these tactical considerations the North was in a desperate economic situation. There was considerable unrest and that restlessness meant that the NDP got good crowds. In his own mind then, Grant decided that the constituency of Spirit River-Fairview was his best chance.

Spirit River-Fairview also fit well with Grant's personal background. He was more at home in a rural riding and more familiar with the issues. He had worked hard in rural constituencies, including the Peace River country, and gotten to know the people. The splits of the city did not matter in the area, although there was the problem of being an outsider. Finally, Grant was determined to broaden the base of the party, to make it more representative, and less a union dominated organization. His own CCF background led him to the conclusion, perhaps erroneously, that rural Alberta in the north was still an area that could be counted on for a progressive politician.

Once decided, it remained to sell the idea to the rest of the party. He started with Hart Horn. According to Hart it was not a difficult job, but he thought that they ought to have some evidence of the state of support in the riding. They decided to ask Cliff Scotton, then Federal Secretary, to come to Alberta and accompany Hart Horn up to the Peace River country to "assess" the situation. In October the two of them toured the ridings of Spirit River and Smoky River.

Both ridings are far from the centre of Alberta, in a small area of the northwest where the glacial residue has produced a pocket of very fertile land. But farming there was a chancy business because of unpredictable weather and frost. The area has tended to grow feed grains and fescue in an attempt to minimize the chance of crop loss. The towns of Spirit River and Fairview are north of Grande Prairie, separated by the spectacular Peace River valley, an area where Grant and Sandy eventually built a home. The people are used to disappointment, are rugged and tough, but also band together for collective purposes. For example, the National Farmers Union found this area to be fertile ground for membership. Even in 1970 the farm community had been marginalized, and the area around Spirit River, Rycroft, and Fairview were in deeper crisis than the region further south near Grande Prairie. But it is beautiful country, and the people there were dedicated to remaining and succeeding.

For Hart and Cliff Scotton this was very much a business trip. Their purpose was really two-fold. The first was to assess support. The second was, if support was high enough, to convince local people that Grant should be accepted as the candidate. Neither was assured before they got there.

Hart remembers asking people how they felt about somebody coming in from the outside, and in particular, someone who had just lost the by-election in Edson. He remembers that the response was quite positive. Graham Tomlinson, a long-time supporter of the CCF and NFU in the area, and later president of the riding association, remembers that they thought that their riding would be a good one for Grant.

> We were fairly good, we were fairly strong then. We had a pretty good membership. We had one of the best memberships in the province, I guess that is why we felt that if he was going to run some place he better try it here.

Anne Hemmingway, also a local farmer, and later President of the Alberta NDP, has a more explicit recollection of the meeting. She remembers that Hart and Cliff met with about eight local people, including herself, Sam Simpson, Bill Sidorko, Nick Schmeer, and Graham Tomlinson. Initially the discussion centred on finding a candidate, not on Grant.

When the question was popped as to what we had done about a candidate everybody looked uncomfortable. I didn't, that's how naive I was. I didn't know what the hell they were talking about. And the first thing I knew was that Bill Sidorko said, "Well, I think Mrs. Hemmingway should be our candidate."

I remember Nick Schmere said "Well, I think either she or Earl Burton . . . " I said, "Just a minute I want some questions answered."

Her questions had to do with the level of support in the constituency. From the answers Anne concluded that if support was so high in their riding, Grant should be asked to run there. In retrospect she realized that both Hart and Cliff Scotton were angling for an invitation for Grant to become the candidate, and Anne provided the opening.

After meeting with the local officials in the Smoky River constituency as well, the two men returned to Edmonton. Their conclusion was that Grant ought to run in Spirit River-Fairview, and that the local people would be willing to accept him, despite all of the problems of running an outsider. It now remained to sell it to the Executive. Cliff Scotton's role was critical, since it provided an air of legitimacy to the assessment. At the Executive meeting held at the party office, the discussion was predictable. Hart Horn remembers the opposition:

> There was lots of disagreement about that [the recommendation for Grant to run in Spirit River] Reg Basken didn't want him to run out there. I don't know what the motivation was. I think sometimes, I wasn't sure whether Reg really wanted Grant to succeed. I could be totally mistaken in that, but I certainly wondered about that sometimes. It could be that Reg simply felt that if Grant would wipe out in the Peace River, that the party would be so discredited that it would be all but dead . . . . But Reg was not in favour of Grant running out there.

Hart remembers that Gordon Wright was more supportive. Gordon was willing to trust Grant's judgement, especially the assessment that there was more political unrest in the Peace River Country and a dissatisfaction with Calgary Power and the electrification program. Other members of the Executive, Ethel Taylor from Red Deer and Everett Baldwin from Calgary, also supported Grant. Finally, the decision was made. Grant would go to the north to run.

Of all of the turning points in the life of Grant and the Alberta NDP, this was the most crucial. Several important ramifications flowed from his decision. The most important was that Grant would run in a riding where he was finally elected. Had he failed, his political career would have been considerably shorter. Just as important, however, was the fact that the party itself took on a distinctly more rural flavour. Not since the days of the old CCF had this been the case. With the leader in a rural riding it meant increased credibility for the NDP on rural issues. Grant believed at this time that the CCF rural/urban coalition was not dead, at least not in the North, and that it could be revived to provide a strong coalition of progressive forces. Finally, for Grant personally, running in the North provided a power base within the party that was undeniably his. The rural areas had always supported him, but he was viewed as an urban person, an adjunct to Neil Reimer. As a candidate in a rural riding he could shed himself of the problems of an urban identity and especially of the problems of Edmonton.

While all of this was of great importance to the NDP, it was of small consequence to Albertans. In early 1971 they were in the process of making up their minds about Harry Strom and the Social Credit Party. Not since 1935 had such an undercurrent been present. By 1970 several long-term social trends were maturing. Much of Alberta had become urbanized and increasingly involved in the petroleum industry. The population was younger, with almost 15% as first time voters. Religion and its importance had declined in Alberta, with fewer people attending churches. The attitudes of Albertans was more buoyant, less pessimistic. An entire generation of voters did not remember the Depression.

More immediately, the feeling that it was "time for a change" had begun to set in. Social Credit had been in office for 35 years. Harry Strom seemed mild and tentative by comparison to E.C. Manning, while Peter Lougheed seemed fresh and competent. The Conservatives were cautiously pushing the time-for-a-change theme. They were careful to emphasize that they were young and different, but not radical. They were supported by the oil companies and their owners, and wanted to assure voters that a new hand at the helm meant more competence, new attitudes, but not radical ideas. It was also an age when television was becoming increasingly important to political campaigns, with its emphasis on style rather than substance. By 1971, Social Credit seemed old fashioned, while the Conservatives seemed in tune with a changed Alberta.

All of this meant a more marginalized NDP. Only two things worked in favour of the party. The first was the wave of progressive politics and protest which had swept western democracies. Although many of the ideas of the Waffle in Canada were deemed too radical by party establishments, they nevertheless provided energy and enthusiasm to the whole party. The second point in favour of the NDP was its reputation for honesty, integrity, and sound government. The Schreyer government in Manitoba had been in for almost two years with good results. In Saskatchewan, in June of 1971, the NDP under its new leader Allen Blakeney, swept to power with a huge majority, giving all New Democrats a big boost. Grant and the Alberta Executive hoped that some of this would spill over into Alberta.

Before anything could happen however, it was necessary for the party to do two things. It had to raise money, and it had to nominate candidates. In the latter case the Council of the party had decided not to over-extend itself as it was argued had been done in 1967. The Council had ruled against a full slate and in favour of concentration. This was not a new debate. It had been fought and refought within the party since its inception. But usually Grant and Neil had been able to convince people of the wisdom of running a full slate of candidates and of concentrating in certain ridings. This time was different, however. The Council knew that the party was broke. Worse, it was still in debt, and that there was little chance of raising anything in the way of substantial cash for the campaign. The party desperately wanted to elect someone, and they felt that concentrating their efforts was the way to do it.

For Grant and Hart, the decision meant abiding by the letter of the Council decision, if not the spirit. They decided to kick off Grant's campaign with a big nominating convention, and then to nominate as many as possible without nominating in all ridings. They convinced Tommy Douglas to come and speak at the Spirit River-Fairview meeting on November 14, 1970 in Rycroft, Alberta. It was a huge success.

Anne Hemmingway remembers being part of the organizing committee.

I had volunteered to organize a pot-luck supper because I wanted to ensure that women came to that nominating meeting as well as men. I felt that I could make them come by making them feel that the banquet would fail without them being there.

We ended up feeding 450 people, in a hall that's only supposed to hold 250.

As the meeting time approached, Grant was very nervous. He had heard from several sources that Anne Hemmingway planned to run for the nomination against him. If she did, it would fracture the riding and highlight the fact that he was from outside. Sandy recalls Grant telling her this, and concluding that Anne was still hostile to him from the leadership convention. Such was not the case however, since Anne had been active in the organization of the meeting, and insisted that she wanted Grant to run.

> I made no bones about supporting Gordon [Wright] at the [leadership] convention in 1968.
> That didn't mean I disliked Grant, just because I supported Gordon. He seemed very nervous. But the meeting went beautifully.

Grant, in his modest way, claims that so many people came out because they wanted to hear Tommy Douglas. But the people of the area were pleased to have the leader of the party running in their riding. It was a typical rural Alberta meeting, with two tables drawn up as a head table, a white table cloth across both, with a pitcher of water and several glasses. Seated at the table were Sandy, Grant, Graham Thomlinson, Tommy Douglas, Earle Geurtin, and three others. There was a single microphone, and no podium. In those days politicians were expected to be able to speak extemporaneously, or from a very few notes. Pictures of the meeting show Grant in a classic Notley pose: head cocked to the left, left hand lightly holding the mike stand, and right hand extended downward. Another shows him peering owlishly out at the meeting, undoubtedly counting how many people were there and how much money could be raised. Tommy also sits in a classic pose, arms folded across his chest, looking up at Grant as he spoke. Grant gave an excellent speech. So did Tommy. It was, as Anne Hemmingway said, a beautiful night.

The rest of the preparations in early 1971 went well. Hart and Grant were eventually able to nominate 70 candidates, five short of a full slate. The mandate from the Executive was to run Grant's campaign in Spirit River-Fairview, and then to pull together as much of a provincial campaign as possible. To do this they decided to set a $20,000 campaign budget, of which $5,000 would be spent in Spirit River, $5000 in the rest of the Peace River area (mostly on advertising) and $10,000 in the rest of the province. It was, by comparison to 1967, an absurdly low budget. But the party had no money, and no choice.

Of the other ridings only a few were more than paper candidacies. In Edmonton Beverly, after a fight between the trade union movement and the Waffle, Barry Chivers, a local lawyer associated with Gordon Wright, won the nomination. Barry was a good candidate, and ran a strong campaign with some support from the Steelworkers union. In Calgary two relative newcomers to the party, Ray Martin (later to become leader after Grant's death) and Jim Staples flipped coins to see who would be candidate. Jim lost, and had to run while Ray became campaign manager. Throughout the province the party geared up, and with the Saskatchewan result, gained some momentum. It was a shoe string party on a shoe string budget, led by a last chance leader, that headed into the summer campaign. It faced two awesomely financed opponents, set to do battle to the death for the government. In this campaign the NDP was indeed a minor player.

Eventually the campaign went much better provincially than anyone expected. Grant split his time between Spirit River and the rest of the province. But things did not start off very well. On the day the writ was issued Reg Basken, the Treasurer, was in Florida, and stayed there for ten more days. Without Reg, the party could not get any money. Hart Horn frantically called Reg, leaving messages, but got no response. At the time Hart did not know if Reg's lack of response was deliberate or not.

> I don't mind saying that I was deeply disturbed by the whole thing. Reg and I from that moment on had a total and complete falling out. Because I was not impressed by that event. It was very difficult for me to muster the start of a provincial campaign. We did well considering that kind of handicap.

Reg Basken recalled the incident of the "ten days" quite well. He deliberately did not release any funds because he had no faith in Hart's ability to spend it wisely. As it turned out, despite the lack of money, the party did very well, mainly because of a set of crucial accidents that came together.

> We managed to get hold of, and I'll be damned if I remember how we paid for it, some kind of a plane that was rented, with a pilot that came out [from] Manitoba, who was on summer holidays. Somebody came up with him, probably Cliff Scotton, who piloted Grant all over the countryside and that gave us an instant mobility.

A large number of people from outside also Alberta came into help, including Dave Barrett, later Premier of B.C., Lorne Nystrom, an MP from Saskatchewan, and Joe Borowski, a Manitoba Cabinet Minister. Another Manitoban, Wiley Simmons, coordinated all of the TV and radio. Hart Horn managed to develop a silk screen sign operation and to keep the signs uniform throughout Alberta. All of this was done with volunteer labour, including Hart, who was paid only a stipend of $500, which went into the Edmonton Park Allen constituency where he was a candidate.

There were some problems with a few of the candidates. In one case a candidate had a complete breakdown. In another there were problems with welfare payments. Perhaps the most bizarre incident happened in Edmonton Whitemud, a suburban, upper middle class riding in southwest Edmonton. Don Hamilton, an Executive Assistant to Premier Strom, was running for Social Credit. Don Getty, a former quarterback for the Edmonton Eskimos, was making his second venture into politics for the Progressive Conservative Party. It was a hotly contested campaign, with both candidates spending a considerable amount of money. Into this contest the half dozen NDP members of the riding attempted to field a candidate. No one in the riding would run. The name of a young man originally from northern Manitoba was suggested to them, a man named Joe Mercredi. They met with him one evening and he agreed to run. The campaign went fairly well, although Joe was no match for Getty and Hamilton at the public meetings, until the police arrived at Joe's house one day and collected him, ostensibly for evading outstanding warrants. The NDP campaign in Whitemud was quietly folded up, and Joe got an appropriate vote. Don Getty won, and eventually became Premier of Alberta after Peter Lougheed retired.

In its campaign, the NDP concentrated on the Social Credit government. According to Hart Horn, there was no reason to believe that they should not. It just did not seem credible that the Conservatives could beat the Socreds. In Spirit River-Fairview the campaign was very much against Social Credit, who made it a nasty contest. Grant's main opponent was the Minister of Northern Development, Al Fimrite. Grant thought that he was a highly decent man, but a little disorganized. For example, during the campaign Premier Strom made a visit to Fairview to boost the Fimrite campaign.

Strom was a highly decent guy as premier, but not imperial . . . . So anyway, Strom comes into the Fairview airport, because they were going to have a meeting.

They let him off at the airport, and there is no one there to meet him. The local Social Credit organization had forgotten that there should be someone there to meet him. The airport's three miles out of town. There's no phone, and the meetings at 2:00 p.m. So Strom has to start hotfooting it down the road, . . . walking. A farmer, coming along in his truck . . . picked up the Premier and delivered him to the meeting.

It was one of the few comical things that Grant remembered about the campaign. Throughout the riding NDP signs were defaced with stickers which said "outsider." Toward the end of the campaign, pictures of swastikas and the hammer and sickle were drawn on signs. It was a bitter and ugly campaign.

Grant singled out two old timers as crucial to his campaign, Bill Sidorko and Sam Simpson. They both loved to campaign with Grant. He also mentioned Anne Hemmingway in the Rycroft area. There were two offices, one in Rycroft, and one in Fairview. Grant sensed that they were doing well until the last ten days, when he felt that things turned down. During that period former Premier Manning taped some commercials that attacked Grant and the NDP specifically.

The campaign was ugly. On the last few days of the campaign Manning came in, not in the riding personally but with little pre-recorded commercials saying that these outsiders are attempting to destroy your way of life. A really hard sell. Really attacking me personally, and attacking everything that the NDP stood for.

But Manning's attack was not enough, and on election night Grant got 39% of the vote, just enough to push him ahead of Al Fimrite in a three-way campaign. The Socreds were stunned of course, but the defeat in Spirit River was overshadowed by the incredible victory of the Conservatives province wide. In his victory speech Grant facetiously thanked Senator Manning for his part, saying that it was Manning's mudslinging that had turned the tide. As someone who had fought them all of those years, Grant could not resist the impulse for one more shot at the mighty Social Credit.

Of course, as a result of winning 49 seats, the Conservatives formed the government. Social Credit, for the first time in its history, formed the opposition with 25 seats. Grant was the sole New Democrat elected, and he won with a margin considerably less than a majority. The reaction in the NDP was ecstatic, however. The leader of the party had been elected for the first time, and in a general election. Despite all of the problems, the years of frustration, the absolutely dismal state of the party after 1968, and even the active resistance of some people within the party, Grant Notley was in the legislature. One would have thought, from the internal reaction within the NDP, that they, and not the Conservatives, had won the election.

6 THE MLA FOR SPIRIT RIVER-FAIRVIEW

THE ELECTION ENDED WITH some internal wounds which needed healing. Hart Horn had provoked considerable hostility by some of his actions. About ten days before the end of the campaign Reg Basken and Hart Horn had had one final fight. When the smoke cleared, Reg had fired Hart (although he agrees that he really had no authority to do so), had taken away Hart's keys, and taken over the remainder of the central campaign himself. Coincidentally, or perhaps because of the continual pressure, Hart became ill with a kidney infection, and remained in hospital until after election day.

For his part Reg Basken, who was then Treasurer, disputes Hart's contention that the campaign left the party with no debt. He recalls that the financial situation was as grave as ever, and that this led to a decision once again close to the provincial office. It was to be the last time that this happened. Grant's election to the legislature changed the role of the NDP in Alberta decisively in the future.

Grant recalled that he had little time to savour his victory. Within a week of the election, several things happened. First, he was called by Stephen Lewis and asked to participate in the Ontario election. Being the good soldier that he was, and perhaps not yet fully aware of his new role, he spent the month of September in Ontario in the Nickel Belt riding. During the Alberta campaign he had promised to move to Spirit River-Fairview if he was elected and upon his return from Ontario he and Sandy went house hunting in Fairview. They found what Grant described as a "terrible old house, drafty and cold," for the princely sum of $10,000. They moved to Fairview in November of 1971.

> The house was really quite a place. It was a ramshackle old place. Right in the middle of a weed patch. We spent hours and hours and hours scraping down the plaster, and repainting. It had the most hideous kind of siding on, imitation stone. It was falling off. That year we stuccoed it. We brought in all kinds of loads of dirt and built up the lot, and smoothed it all out, seeded it down to grass, but of course grass takes a time to take hold so for a year it was a very big mudhole . . . . It was an awful looking place.

In October Grant lost no time in beginning what was to become the trademark of his tenure, the constituency tour. Twice a year Grant would hold office hours in every town in the constituency, making himself available for service to everyone. He knew that a potent way to win people over was to ensure that he used every effort to satisfy complaints, look into problems, and be a helpful ''fixer'' whenever possible. It was what Garth Turcotte wanted to do, but was not able to undertake.

However, Grant also had larger considerations to deal with. He correctly understood that he was now in a changed position within the party as a result of his election. Whereas before the election he had had to plead and wheedle for support for his decisions, or money for party activity, he was now the indisputable head of the organization. His power base was secure and he set out immediately to ensure that the Alberta NDP became his party. To do this he had to make several changes. First, and most important, he needed a Provincial Secretary who was his person, someone loyal to him and willing to work with him in building the party. To hire a Secretary he needed to get Executive approval to re-open the office and appoint someone acceptable to him. Second, he needed to ensure that he did well in the Legislature. If he was to get re-elected in four years, and if he was to add colleagues from other ridings, it would require organizational help in the form of a research or executive assistant. Both moves would cost money, something that the NDP did not have. But Grant correctly concluded that given an adequate performance by himself, and a reasonably aggressive office staff, money that was not available in the dark days between 1968 and 1971 could now be raised. He set about getting Executive approval for both actions.

It was as a result of his search for legislative assistance that I first met Grant in 1971. Although a native Albertan, I had spent the years 1961-1970 in the United States, where I had completed an Arts degree in European history before returning to Edmonton. I had applied for and been accepted into the Master's programme in Political Science at the University of Alberta, and as a consequence had come into contact with people like Bill Dryden, Tom and Lou Pocklington, and other New Democrats. My experience in the US during the 1960s had driven my political views to the left, and upon my return I joined the Alberta NDP. I had just completed my first year, and was writing my Master's Thesis, when Grant began his search for a legislative assistant. One of my fellow students in the programme was Myron Johnson, who had been a journalist and whom Grant already knew. Myron was also from Alberta, and was also attempting to finish a Master's Degree. We became good friends, sharing an office for the first year.

In typical fashion the Council of the party approved hiring research assistance for Grant, but agreed to pay only $400 per month during the legislative session. Grant, being Grant, decided to maximize this money by hiring two people, part time. He asked Lou Pocklington, who was a Vice-President of the party, to see if Myron Johnson was available, and perhaps someone else. I turned out to be the someone else. After meeting with Grant and Gordon Wright, Myron and I proposed that we share the duties when they materialized, with one of us coming in during the morning and the other in the afternoon. As it turned out we were to share the salary, which we did, but usually found ourselves at the Legislature for a full day instead of just half. In this way Grant got two of us for the price of one.

My first impression of Grant was that he was quite "ordinary." I was quite prepared to be impressed, since I was fascinated by politics and politicians. But Grant in person simply was not that impressive. He dressed rather cheaply, he had conservative tastes and a conservative demeanor, and was at that time hardly older than I was. Aside from being elected there was little difference between us. However, as I worked with him we quickly developed a camaraderie and affection which persisted throughout our relationship. In short, I quickly became one of Grant's loyalists, like so many before me.

The first days at the Legislature were not very promising for Grant. Although he was Leader of the NDP, he was only one MLA and therefore did not head a recognized "group" in the House. He quickly found out that he was going to be given as little help as possible. Although the Leader of the Official Opposition had a position, an office, and generous funds attached to his position, Grant was to get only what an ordinary opposition MLA would get, which was virtually nothing.

At first, there had been no office at all. That was provided only after a meeting with the new Premier, Peter Lougheed. The meeting was arranged on an afternoon in November of 1971. Grant and I both went up to his office. We were kept waiting for sometime, chatting with the Premier's new Executive Assistant. When we were admitted things went very well. Lougheed was gracious and friendly, turning on the famous smile and charm for us. At that time no ill will, no sense of combativeness had yet developed. Both men were new at their roles and both were still focussed on Social Credit. Only later, after Grant had been in a legislative session, did the combativeness assert itself. Indeed, this meeting was to be the first and last in the Premier's office.

Grant produced, as he put it, a little list for the Premier. The primary items were office space, a secretary, and a seconder for Grant's motions. The rules required a seconder to all motions, meaning that unless someone agreed with Grant, or a courtesy seconder was arranged, Grant would never be able to introduce a motion in the House. Lougheed was positive on the office space, sympathetic but noncommittal on providing a secretary, and not optimistic on a courtesy seconder. Actually, Grant had not expected to achieve the latter goal, since few of his motions would meet with approval by the other MLAs. The meeting ended on the same cordial note on which it began. In retrospect Lougheed probably thought that Grant would be a momentary blip on the political landscape, a 39% member unlikely to be around after the next election. It was an under estimation made by many people in 1971. As it turned out, a one room office was provided and Grant was allowed to share a secretary with the Speaker, Gerald Amerongen, a man whom Grant grew to dislike intensely. This meant a fair bit of crowding as everyone was jammed into one room.

With the provision of Myron and myself, an office, a phone, and some secretarial help, Grant's career in the legislature was launched.

During December and January we concentrated on developing questions for the session, researching specific issues, and arranging a team of people outside of the legislature to provide volunteer research help. Ultimately this included a wide range of people from all parts of the province, all dedicated to helping Grant provide an effective opposition. They proved to be very helpful, and contributed significantly to his performance.

On the party side Grant pressed ahead with his intention to appoint a new Provincial Secretary and re-open the provincial party office. As with the two legislative assistants, Grant wanted someone who would be personally loyal to him, someone whom he could count on in a fight with the various factions of the party. As well, he wanted someone who knew the party, was acceptable to the membership, and was hard working. That person, he concluded, was Bill Dryden. Although Bill had supported Allan Busch for Leader, he had remained active with the NDP and was not associated with either the Reimer or Waffle factions. Grant asked Lou Pocklington to approach Bill about the position. At the time Bill was eager to leave his job as Administrative Assistant in the Department of Political Science at the University of Alberta. Things there had not worked out as he had hoped, and he had never really gotten politics out of his blood. He also had acquired a good deal more respect for Grant, whom he perceived as having matured and developed considerably. This allowed Bill to consider working closely with him. In November of 1971, he agreed to allow his name to be put forward to the Executive and Council.

The Executive of the party agreed with Grant that Bill would be the best candidate. Fourteen people applied, some with good credentials. Grant made it clear, however, that Bill was his choice, just as Neil had done with Grant in 1963. At the Council meeting in January Bill was opposed by two candidates. In an attempt to derail Bill's selection, a motion for a mail ballot was made, but defeated. The Council agreed with Grant that the candidate ought to be selected immediately. Three names were put forward, Bill Steemson from Calgary, who was nominated by Nancy Eng, who would become President the next year and Richard McLellan, who had the support of outgoing Secretary Hart Horn. Both were defeated in the ensuing ballot and Bill became Secretary. It was a measure of Grant's new position in the party, and his control of it, that he could force Bill's appointment through in the face of stiff opposition.

The internal arrangements were now set. Grant had successfully re-organized the staff side of the party. His own riding association was now catapulted to a new prominence in the party. According to Bill Dryden, Grant's election, his re-organization, and his position now contrasted sharply with the Reimer period of leadership.

I think that Grant has always been best when he has had someone to contrast himself with. He did set up where the party should go in contrast to Reimer when he was Leader. He really did turn those people on up in the Peace River country. Now finally his rightful chance [was] going to come.

All that remained was for Grant to perform well in the Legislature. He had always wanted to be an MLA, but when faced with the actual job he realized how daunting it would be. However, he had an instinct for what was important about House work and he had the willingness to work hard at the job. He knew that the Question Period was most important. This was the part of the day that all of the media covered, the part of the proceedings most likely to get attention. In plotting strategy for the session, he keyed in on this activity. He also knew that his first speech, and subsequent speeches on major issues would be important, but just as important was the coverage of them. This meant that each time Grant spoke someone had to ensure that a press release was distributed and Grant was available for comment. The speeches themselves did not attract much attention since few reporters stayed in the House for them. A media strategy was needed if he was to get good coverage. Since he was unlikely to get a courtesy seconder, the matter of motions in the House was of little consequence, but he did not need a seconder to introduce bills. It became necessary to have a strategy on what bills would be drafted and introduced. All of this had to be couched in a general approach, in an ideological framework of action which would serve as a guideline for all issues. Finally, and most importantly, his work and effort as Leader had to be related in large part to the needs and interests of his own riding, of Spirit River-Fairview. All of his effort would be of little consequence if he was not re-elected in four years time.

Before the session then, Grant sat down with Myron and me to work out duties and responsibilities. Given Myron's media background it seemed useful for him to deal with press releases, media strategy, and general public relations. I was to concentrate on questions for question period, research on certain areas like energy, and the drafting of bills. On some things we coordinated, like constituency work. In addition we contacted and secured agreement from people like Adolph Busse in Economics at the University of Alberta, Neil Reimer, Reg Basken, Barry Chivers, John Worton, Jean McBean, Ed Daniels, Jim Anderson, and many

others to act as research contacts for us in each of the areas of government. When a question in that area arose, or more specific research was
needed, we would contact each person for help, all on a voluntary basis.
The legislative team was larger than it seemed, but not as coherent as
it should have been.

With the legislative team now organized, the larger question of "to
what end" was raised. More succinctly, what would the policy goals of
Grant's legislative career be? While Grant had been forced in the past
to deal with specific questions on policy during his term as leader, he
had never been confronted with questions arising from the broader
sweep of ideology. That is, he had never been forced to consider a
coherent and long term approach to government and governing.

As with most of us his views had been shaped by a variety of often
disconnected and *ad hoc* events and decisions. Seldom are we allowed
the luxury of single minded pursuit of specific goals in life. Too often
we become hostage to streams of events which carry us far from our
original destination. Grant was no exception. He had pursued largely
organizational and electoral goals throughout his adult life, with little
opportunity to express coherent public policy, and even less apparent
inclination to do so. He was not a rigid ideologue. His electoral goals
dictated a flexible and even pragmatic approach to questions of public
affairs. As far as he was concerned there were few boundaries. Notwithstanding this pragmatism, he had a well developed sense of social
conscience. He knew and accepted what was socially moral and proper.
This in turn dictated that certain questions ought to be pursued in his
political universe, despite the fact that they might not be optimally advan-
tageous politically. Quite often this required a fine distinction, but one
which he managed with remarkable success. Finally, he was a convinced
regionalist and Albertan. That is to say, his views of Alberta and Canada
were fixed with a regional bias tempered by the CCF centralist approach
to national issues. He was the perfect hybrid of CCF and NDP, of Albertan
and Canadian.

Most of this is discernable only by careful examination of his legislative career, or through past personal contact with him. There are few
comprehensive statements that substantiate these conclusions, save
perhaps his maiden speech in the legislature. Whatever the personal goals
of Grant Notley, or the general approach to public questions he adopted,
most of what he did and said was dictated by events which surfaced during his career in the legislature. That is to say, outside forces most often

shaped the agenda. This meant that to a large extent he was reacting to, instead of acting on, issues and problems. Fortunately, this suited Grant well. He was not a careful long-term planner. He was not someone who committed elaborate thoughts or plans to paper. He was, however, bright, attentive, verbally agile, and possessed an excellent memory and a well developed sense of politics about issues. All of this was superbly suited to his position as a single member from the left in a Legislature with 74 other conservative members.

Grant brought all of this to bear during his first session in the House, which began on March 2, 1972. His long career was so successful, and his mastery of the necessary skills of the House, so complete, that it is difficult to evaluate which if any of the several sessions were his "finest hour." Each of us who worked with him can look back and point to a number of instances which would seem to qualify. However, his first session was unique, if only because it was the first time that he stepped onto the stage of the Legislature. He was able to fix in the mind of the media and the public a favourable "first impression," a thing of great value for any politician. In that sense, his first session was both his most important, and his most successful.

With this in mind, careful planning went into every aspect of the impending session. The most important event was going to be a review of royalty arrangements with the oil industry. This review happened every ten years, but in 1972, with a new government, it was particularly important. For Grant, and the NDP, it was central to key aspects of NDP policy in the province. Oil was the single largest industry. It was responsible for provincial prosperity in the post World War era, provided jobs, tax revenues, and a large part of the fiscal base of Alberta. It was also foreign owned and was dominated by an ethos of buccaneer capitalism which jangled the nerves of most socialists. Setting the new royalties would be crucial to the future of Alberta, and Grant wanted the public to know both the importance of the issue and the position of the New Democratic Party. Thus, in January and February of 1972, he and Bill Dryden mounted a series of meetings throughout the province on the royalties question, gatherings designed to get some media attention for the NDP position. These rallies were not entirely success- ful, but they did establish the importance of the issue, and set the stage for Grant's role in the House. Not surprisingly then, much of the planning and research for the first session was directed toward this topic.

The subjects of the first question period were discussed at length between the three of us. We selected four subjects for their topicality and for their relevance to the NDP. Since the Leader of the Opposition always got the first set of questions, it was important that Grant have questions that would not be asked by Social Credit with their 25 members. We thought that we were well prepared. Grant remembered the first question period day this way:

> That [day] was the biggest test because that was the first time I spoke in the Legislature. I remember being so upset because we had gone over the areas of questions, and at that time you just got up, and dog-gone it the Socreds got up first, and they stole all of the questions that we were going to ask. We'd spent so much time on it. I remember Howard in the Gallery, he was absolutely appalled that one by one all of the questions [were asked]. So I got up on supplementaries, but I certainly got my share. I probably asked more questions than anyone that day, but they were all supplementaries.

They were indeed supplementary in every way. One was on National Parks, another on an inquiry, and several on hog marketing, a subject of much attention later on in the session. At the end of Question Period, Grant asked for House approval to send best wishes to the Alberta entry in the National Brier, since the rink came from his riding. It was unanimously approved. Interestingly, Grant thought this was necessary to establish that he would be a positive figure in the House as well as a critic. Grant probably did it for two other reasons. First, he wanted to dissociate himself immediately from the bad memories of the Turcotte days in the House. Second, he wanted to be accepted by the "club," by his peers in the Legislature, as a legitimate member. While he succeeded on the first, he was never completely successful on the second.

Grant's first question period was judged a success by all. Not because of the quality of the questions, or the astuteness of the research involved, but because he was quick enough, bright enough, and not too intimidated to think on his feet and take advantage of opportunities. As one member he would not be accorded any special privileges, despite the fact that he was Leader of the NDP. His performance would depend almost completely on his ability to exploit advantages and to think on his feet. He had quick young haunches, an asset in the Question Period of the Alberta legislature in 1972 and they were coupled with a quick mind. His first day was a success, almost entirely because of his own ability.

If his performance in Question Period was good, his ability to draft and deliver a good set speech in the House was equally as good. He knew that his first speech would be a matter of record for the rest of his political career. He took considerable care in its preparation. One of the small points involved was how to get the Speaker's attention. Grant wanted to speak early, in order to establish his role as a party leader. As it turned out he was able to speak on Monday, March 6, just the second full sitting day. We went over the speech with considerable care, with suggestions from both Myron and myself. But essentially it was Grant's speech, and in many ways it encompassed his entire approach to politics.

It was his speech in reply to the Speech From the Throne, and as such was limited in some respects by the conventions of the House and by the need to address the government programme. Nevertheless Grant took the opportunity to explain his own political philosophy. Two things stand out about the speech. First, it attacked issues, not personalities. Grant was careful to avoid any confrontation on a personal basis. Second, the issues he attacked were securely woven into his own social democratic approach. On the latter point some excerpts are instructive:

Now the [Socred] white paper of 1967 outlines the conservative perspective of government: that government should leave the major initiative to the private sector, . . . that it should be passive, not active . . . in short, that government should be a repairman for the private sector rather than the primary instrument in forging economic and social justice. It is the difference between a passive philosophy of government and an activist view of government . . . . It is a more subtle . . . a profoundly more important difference than the classic debate over ownership itself, for today's socialist knows the need of a private sector based on the small business and family farms . . . .
But it is a critical issue of where and when public intervention, whether government should plan ahead and anticipate problems, or simply react when disaster strikes . . . . In my view, passive government is bound to fail despite the sincerity of its advocates. It is bound to fail because of its limited philosophical perspective . . . . [1]

It is a classic statement of social democratic philosophy. On the one hand he squarely rejects the Marxist approach that unless the means of production are socially owned no real change can take place, while on the other hand he rejects the concept of a society dominated by the market place. In today's post-Thatcher/Reagan age, the speech's commitment to an activist role for government rings clear and decisive. Grant believed that by using government one could change society. By using the power of the state one could redress the injustices and maldistributions that result from unbridled capitalism. Implicit in his approach is an acceptance of democratic theory, of the assumption that governments can be removed, unlike private capital, and can therefore be trusted to act for all citizens. Finally, Grant made it perfectly clear that public ownership is not an end in itself, but an end to social justice.

It was a remarkable statement, made more remarkable because it came from a man who had never previously put such thoughts to paper during his political career. There were many who doubted his ability to do so, many who were pleasantly surprised.

The remainder of his speech is instructive as well. The issues were carefully selected. The first issue Grant raised was agriculture, a clear signal to his constituency and the party that rural affairs were going to have a high place on the NDP agenda. Unfortunately, as he began to address this issue, by chastizing the government for not supporting an emergency debate on grain transportation the previous Friday, he was interrupted by Hugh Horner, then Deputy Premier, on a point of order. It was not a point of order at all, but an attempt to debate Grant's assertion about whether or not the government wanted an emergency debate on this issue. It was one of the few times that Grant was completely surprised. He had not expected such an interruption. Indeed, it was very unparliamentary, especially during a maiden speech, and Grant sat down immediately with a look of bewilderment on his face. However, as soon as he realized that he was the object of a deliberate ploy, he stood up again, brushed aside Horner's point, and continued on as if nothing had happened.

He would make his points on agriculture again and again in his career. He emphasized the need to preserve the family farm, ease the cost-price squeeze through federal government programs, lower costs of power and other inputs, provide a mechanism for land transfer from one generation to another, and develop, adequate rural services, especially in education. He went on, however, to attack corporate farming and integrated agriculture as the ultimate threat to farmers, a theme which he continued to hammer on throughout the session. A week later he again addressed this issue when a motion guaranteeing a fair share of production for small producers was placed before the House by Social Credit.

The second major issue addressed in the speech was poverty, and the plight of poor Albertans. In this instance he marshalled facts and figures in defense of his primary thesis, that many Albertans were not sharing in the general prosperity. He concluded by calling for a declaration of economic rights in the proposed Alberta Bill of Rights.

The third major issue involved the energy and the upcoming royalty review. He argued that it should go far beyond a simple review of royalties, and ought to look at all aspects of the oil and gas industry, especially foreign ownership and export policies.

Agriculture, poverty, oil and gas were the cornerstone of his policy approach. By speaking to agriculture he hoped to address rural Alberta and rebuild at least in the part, the broader base of the left in Alberta. By addressing poverty he addressed questions of the distribution of wealth, and the role of government in redistribution, an approach to urban Albertans in areas that were depressed, or to families that were excluded from the benefits of the province's prosperity. By addressing the oil and gas questions he hoped to convince all Albertans that the NDP had a distinct, viable, and workable alternative to the market place development of the province's primary resource.

He closed his speech with a quote from a famous Tory.

So, I conclude my remarks. I began by quoting from a famous Alberta socialist, the late William Irvine. Let me draw my remarks to a close by quoting from a famous British Conservative, Benjamin Disraeli, who said, "though I sit down now, the time will soon come when you hear from me again."[2]

It was an excellent speech, and Grant received very favourable reaction.

I'd worked very hard on that speech. I wished I did as much work these days on a speech. We had a lot of good reaction afterwards. Almost every columnist wrote about it.

There were a lot of little notes [from other members] afterwards, quite a surprising number.

The media did indeed respond positively to Grant's speech. The editorial comment in the Edmonton *Journal* was typical:

> [It was] an eloquent and well researched speech. If they [the NDP] have to make do with one, they are fortunate that the one is Notley.[3]

The Session was off to an excellent start, but it was to get better. Social Credit was largely dispirited and disorganized after the election. They had never been in opposition, and although some members, like Gordon Taylor, were more feisty than others, a large number were still in shock, and simply waiting to retire. This included Harry Strom, former Premier, who everyone knew would step down as leader before the next election. It was perfectly tailored for Grant, who was consistently able to grab more than his share of publicity. Much of this involved good planning and research, and more because of Grant's personal ability, but some was simply the result of good luck. Two incidents Grant recalled illustrate this point:

> One of the key, I guess, exposés if you like, that I uncovered in 1972 was the fact that there were ceilings on all the royalties, on all the leases. They couldn't go beyond 16 1/2%. It was written in. In other words, to change the royalty structure we would have to remove the ceilings.

The fact that legislation would be required was a major problem, and Grant was rightly credited with raising this issue. It was the result of good research by all of us. A second incident, by contrast, was just dumb luck.

> The other incident that shows a bit of the luck of the draw if you like. Howard Leeson had been at a party with a judge with fairly close connections with the Conservative party, who was talking about the change of auto insurance for the government fleet from a Social Credit firm to a Tory firm. Howard immediately went into the bathroom and wrote down as much as he could remember on some toilet paper and brought it out. On the basis of this less than researched information we posed a series of questions in the legislature and brought down the first patronage storm.

As the Session progressed, the Conservatives became increasingly irritated with Grant, whom they had tended to ignore initially. They began to concentrate on him, heckling and attempting to discredit him. This occurred with some ferocity in the debate over a proposed multi-million dollar development in the Banff National Park called Village Lake Louise. However those attempts backfired, as noted by Harry Midgley, a political columnist covering the legislature.

> First, it should be said that one reason for Mr. Notley's success last Tuesday is that he is an attractive and expert speaker in the House . . . . He had a sense of timing . . . . He does his homework. He had them hopping mad and dancing to his tune. They kept jumping up with ill-conceived points of order. [Like Errol Flynn] Mr. Notley kept brushing them off with contempt, or metaphorically running them through with shafts of scornful wit. [At one point he advised Don Getty] to toughen up. Because of their numerical superiority in the House their ill humour, ill becomes them.[4]

This rivalry soon carried over to relations between Peter Lougheed and Grant. Lougheed was justifiably proud of his new mandate and new government, and was unwilling to share much of the spotlight in the first session with the NDP leader. It was evident that their positions would soon increase the competition between them. It was also evident that Social Credit was dying, and the Tories did not want a new opposition party to succeed them too quickly.

In the final analysis two main issues emerged during the 1972 session. The first was the new Alberta Bill of Rights, and the second was the week long hearings on new royalties. Grant participated in the debate on both with vigour and ability. The Bill of Rights and the Human Rights Commission Act, were the jewels of the Lougheed government's legislative programme in 1972. They were debated in mid-May as the Session drew to a close. There was general support for the legislation from all members, including Grant. But he placed on record some key differences between himself and Lougheed on the question of rights and how they ought to be interpreted.

> I really believe that there is a case to be made, Mr. Speaker, for going beyond the specified rights in this Bill, and taking a close look at economic and social rights.

Now, Mr. Speaker, the argument that we cannot include economic and social rights in our provincial legislation is not really valid when we recognize the importance, the overwhelming importance of the Universal Declaration of Human Rights.[5]

Grant went on to talk about the importance of political rights, the rights of civil servants, and finally the right to organize and strike. It was a classic statement of NDP politics in this area, one which clearly differentiated him from Conservatives.

On the question of royalties, Grant was extremely well prepared. The oil industry was an enterprise which he had studied and understood completely. The royalty regime of the industry had to be reviewed and reorganized. The government was intent on getting more money, but did not want to be threatening. Ironically, this was just prior to the OPEC crisis which would fundamentally alter energy relationships around the world.

The government decided to hold a week long series of public hearings in May, and in a dramatic move closed down the Legislature in order to hold them in the Chamber as a Committee of the Whole. This meant that all witnesses submitted briefs and were questioned by all members of the House. It was an extraordinary procedure, and one which Grant used to his advantage. He recalls the episode with some pride.

I continued to press for royalty revision through the Spring session. Over and over again I demanded that. In May of 1972 we had open hearings. For an entire week I was, I guess, the chief arguer for higher royalties. We had scores of people there. Somebody had to go over the briefs. I remember my long weekend, May 24 was spent reading over all of these briefs.

In a sense, I was almost an ally [with the government] on this issue.

In fact, Grant was the perfect foil. His more radical views made the government look reasonable by comparison, and allowed Lougheed to change the royalty arrangements, unilaterally, by legislation.

When the session ended in June of 1972, it was a weary but pleased Grant Notley who went briefly back to Fairview. He had done well. Fred Kennedy, the right-wing columnist for the Calgary *Albertan* grudgingly admitted that Grant was the "number one star." He wrote, "Here is a chap who went from a junior league right into the majors." Harry Midgley of the *Journal* had a more profound insight.

People have tended to sigh for him. In my view this sympathy is mis-placed. If you can't be the leader of a great party exercising power, probably the next best thing by far is to be one man parliamentary party. Besides, with political antagonists like those Mr. Notley faced, who needs a lot of boring old party colleagues.[6]

Ironically, from the standpoint of some within the party, he had done too well. They contend that he was so successful that he became the party in the public mind. As a result, they argue, he was unwilling to share that spotlight with anyone else. This meant that in subtle ways he worked to ensure that he remained the sole member, never allowing other strong people to emerge. While these arguments seem plausible, they are largely *ex post facto*, arguments which seem more plausible now than they did in 1972. At that time Grant firmly believed that his performance was the key to a larger caucus in the next election, and maybe, just maybe, the government in the future.

Anxious to capitalize on his legislative performance, Grant immedi-ately began a series of post-legislative meetings throughout the province. Bill Dryden arranged the tour, which was to become a fixture in the com-ing years. At every stop he was greeted with great enthusiasm. He gave his "legislative report" (now including some humour) on what had actually happened in the House. This was followed by a short pitch for money from Bill Dryden. Unlike the past the crowds were larger and more donations began to come in. As Grant had predicted, his presence in the House boosted the party immensely.

As usual, Grant spent considerable time in Calgary and the South, an area which most northern New Democrats considered a wasteland. For Grant however, it was a welcome relief from the splits of the Edmonton region. It also coincided with his strategy to build the party in areas out-side of Edmonton. In particular, as he said to the press after the Session, he was setting out to make the NDP the "voice of rural Alberta." In order to facilitate that end he and Bill Dryden decided to hire a southern Alberta organizer on a temporary, part-time basis. The organizer's name was Pat Waters, an instructor at the Southern Alberta Institute of Technology. It was Pat's job to sell memberships and gather donations in Calgary and the South. This job was made considerably easier by the fact that a revival of the party had taken place in Lethbridge where a former farmer and then University of Lethbridge student Tom McLeod and his wife Anne had set to work diligently to ensure an NDP presence in that city. Tom came from a family of left wing farmers in the Carmangay area. He had worked for the Alberta Wheat Pool, and at the local level for the NDP. After 1972 he took on a larger role, and built a solid party organization in Lethbridge. This sort of activity began to occur elsewhere as well, ensuring that the South, which had looked very bleak only two years before, was now moving in the opposite direction.

In Calgary in particular, a hard working nucleus of people emerged after 1971. Irene Dyck and Everett Baldwin continued to keep a small office open in the Calgary Labour Temple, called the Metro office. They donated their time, organizing events and raising money. Everett, a retired teacher, was also on the Provincial Executive, elected as a Federal Councillor. It was not easy to get people elected to that post in those days, since it entailed spending your own money to fly to Ottawa for meetings. Ralph and Nancy Eng were the key Calgary people in the organization. They had moved to Calgary from Rimbey several years before. Ralph was a research chemist, and Nancy was a teacher. Both had supported Gordon Wright for the leadership in 1968, but after 1969 they had become good friends with Grant. When in Calgary Grant usually stayed at their house instead of a motel. Nancy was a bright, articulate, and personable woman. Since the next provincial convention was slated for Calgary, Grant asked Nancy to organize and chair the event. Later he asked her to run for President of the party. Along with the Engs a group of younger people, headed up by Ray Martin and his wife Ede, also got enthusiastic in the election. From 1971 to 1975 they were key workers in the area.

At the provincial office Bill Dryden attempted the revival of a largely dead party apparatus. He had changed his mind about Grant completely.

> When he was elected, and into the Legislature, I think he took on such a different stature, and my respect for him came together at that time in a way that I've just never changed to this day.
>
> That was a new Grant Notley. He opened a lot of eyes, including mine. I then wanted to see the party shine. We had to match up to him. He was a real role model.

But the office was moribund. Bill had to go to the owner of the building in which the NDP office was located on 97 St. to even get back in. He had to beg the landlord to give the party back its typewriter and desks, which the owner had repossessed for nonpayment of rent. The place was dirty, dusty, and in the wrong end of town. Stan Gee, the volunteer who had been pressed into service by Hart Horn in 1970, had taken most of the records to his home, and carried most of the membership list in his memory. Stan was convinced yet again to come back to work, on a volunteer basis. His only reward was the occasional doughnut or raison bun purchased from the Bohm Bakery located below the office and run by a Hungarian couple, who, although quite anti-leftist, took pity on successive employees by extending credit for various baked goods.

Bill also recruited Verne Hardman to return once again to help set up the office and reorganize membership lists and material. In turn Verne recommended a young woman named Dianne Lorieau for the position of Office Secretary. Dianne was eager and bright, but with little experience. Unlike Verne she did not have a long history in the party. But she was a hard worker, with a good sense of humour, and proved to be a valuable asset for the party through the 1975 election. Together with Bill, Pat Waters, Stan Gee, and a number of volunteers, they formed the nucleus of a new administrative staff.

Needless to say, the people of Spirit River-Fairview were ecstatic with their new MLA. He quickly became the hero of the Peace region. He was constantly in the news, raising local issues, dealing with local problems, and generally representing the people, especially the farmers, in a way that they had never experienced before. Grant settled in very comfortably in the riding. Farmers accepted him immediately because he could converse with them knowledgeably about agricultural problems. But he was equally at home with the town people, who perceived him as urban. As Sandy recalls, the only problem for many people was that he was a New Democrat, not that he was urban. Within the party he was quite conscious of the fact that most members of the NDP in his riding were more radical than he was, particularly on economic issues. It required considerable skill on his part to maintain both his provincial image, and his local one, something Graham Thomlinson, the constituency President, thought he did well.

The hectic pace begun by the legislative session did not lessen throughout the summer. When the BC election was called in July Grant went to manage a campaign for Graham Lea, later a Cabinet Minister in the Barrett government. While he was there the federal election was called, the first with David Lewis as leader. The party in Alberta responded well. There was good enthusiasm, new candidates, and solid campaigns. The election itself, dubbed the Corporate Welfare Bum election because of

Lewis's attack on corporations that were not paying taxes, went very well for the NDP. The result in Parliament was a virtual tie between the Liberals and Conservatives, with the NDP holding the balance of power. It was a minority government which continued for a year and a half. In Alberta the NDP did better federally than it had since the depression. Vote totals jumped in every riding, especially in Edmonton where constituencies like Edmonton Strathcona increased by a full 10%. There was little doubt that a new and confident mood pervaded the party.

Right after the election the Fall Session of the Legislature was convened. This was an innovation by the Lougheed government, part of its pledge to democratize politics in Alberta. It was a short session which dealt with only a limited number of items. In Committee of the Whole on the Alberta Bill of Rights, Grant again strongly urged the inclusion of political rights. He also raised the question of the emergence of the Ku Klux Klan, which had attempted to register in the province earlier in the spring, urging that such organizations not be protected by the Bill. He also pressed for more public housing, and supported the City of Edmonton in its bid to gain a fair share of revenue from Alberta Government Telephone. In the latter case it is likely that his old friend Ivor Dent, then Mayor of Edmonton, had something to do with this posture. After the Spring Session, the Fall sitting was a bit anti-climatic.

With the session over, Grant was able to turn his attention again to the party. He had accomplished two of three of his objectives. He had regenerated the staff and the office of the party, and installed people loyal to him. He had also solidified his position as Leader through a brilliant performance in the Legislature. What remained was to reshape the Executive of the party in order to bring in new people and make it more representative. At least this was the public reason for advocating new faces. Privately, Grant wanted to rid himself of the factions loyal to the Reimer and Waffle contingents, and bring in new people from the country and from Calgary. Bill Dryden, as Secretary, was intimately involved in what became a purge of labour representation from positions of influence on the Executive.

Bill had already clashed with Reg Basken in 1972. As Provincial Party Treasurer Reg continued to keep close watch on expenses and played the role of watchdog for the party. Bill chafed under this close direction, believing that the Secretary should have much more autonomy. He got support from Gordon Wright, who was still President, when Reg was being "particularly obnoxious." In November of 1972, Bill asked the Executive for more leeway, but was largely unsuccessful. It was natural, therefore, that he would support Grant's efforts to remake the Executive at the upcoming convention in Calgary, in February of 1973. Fortunately, Reg Basken had just been elected President of the Alberta Federation of Labour, and was unable to continue as Treasurer, making the whole effort much easier.

Two other considerations motivated Bill and Grant to undertake this action. The first, according to Bill Dryden, was some pressure from ordinary members for more influence in the party.

> Constituency people were asking me for a bigger say on the provincial bodies, more members on the Executive. At that time we had ten or twelve members on the Executive, of which six, seven, and sometimes even eight, were considered to be the private domain of labour. We didn't even get to say which member of labour it might be.
>
> It certainly wasn't my idea, it came from the constituents, it was my plan, and Grant agreed.

A second reason for purging labour was Bill's perception that the Alberta labour leadership had tacitly supported Peter Lougheed in 1971, despite their public support for the NDP.

> I can remember—and I tried to pass it on to Grant—I can remember going to nomination meetings or political affairs in the city in which I saw more labour people around Tory things than I saw in the NDP. I saw their contributions fall incredibly to our candidates and yet as I understood from talking in the political education side of Alberta labour, that they were operating at a higher level than ever before. And it was plainly understood that they supported Lougheed unofficially in 1971, plainly understood. And yet, [they were] still wanting to hold on to their role within the NDP. But I think they had become part of the coalition to elect Peter Lougheed.

Neil Reimer and Reg Basken dismiss this as nonsense and a misimpression. Reg points to the role of labour in the party before and after 1971 as evidence for their support. Still, Grant believed that organized labour had not been as loyal as it should be. In his mind it fit well with the single minded determination of many in labour like Neil Reimer to get rid of Social Credit at any cost. Indeed, as a short-term tactical measure, labour support of Peter Lougheed in 1971 could be rationalized as necessary to remove Social Credit and eventually allow the NDP to become the real opposition to the right wing Tories. Whatever the truth involved, or motivation, both Grant and Bill perceived this to have happened, and it added to their determination in the matter.

For them to succeed in a purge it was necessary for Bill to do several things. He had to have good people to compete for each position, and he had to ensure that there were sufficient delegates from outside of Edmonton. The first problem was solved by asking Gordon Wright to step down from the Presidency and run for Treasurer. This opened up the President's position for someone outside of Edmonton for the first time since the party was founded in 1962. The person chosen to run was Nancy Eng, the organizer of the Convention.

Nancy was an excellent choice. She was personable and articulate, in her early forties, well known in the party and tough when needed. She was by now a strong supporter of Grant, and would also be the first female President of the party. In the contest for the vice-presidencies Bill worked hard to ensure that there was strong support for regional representation, resulting in more candidacies from each part of the province, including the Peace River, thus reducing the role of Edmonton labour candidates. The stage was set for a confrontation.

During the convention Bill told Reg Basken and Neil Reimer that their choices would not be ratified. Indeed, it was likely that Neil would not get elected unless he talked to Grant. At first there were threats and counter-threats. Neil accused Bill of becoming a "Notley shill." Ivor Dent also entered the fray for Neil. Bill says that Ivor threatened him about Neil's position. Bill was not surprised by this, since Ivor had a long relationship with Neil. In the final analysis Bill and Grant decided that Neil should stay on, but only after Neil confided to Bill that he thought that the party owed it to him.

It was a stinging repudiation of the labour movement's role and history in the Alberta NDP. At the convention itself, Harry Kostiuk, a labour representative who was later to become President of the Alberta Federation of Labour, was defeated twice for the post of Vice-President by hand-picked candidates from Peace River and Lethbridge. The rout of Neil Reimer's labour influence was complete. With the 1973 convention Grant put his final stamp on the Alberta NDP. For almost a decade there was virtually no challenge to him or his leadership. While there were those who opposed him, they were effectively silenced during this time, overwhelmed by the magnitude of his success and stature. Only a personal election defeat could bring him down, and Grant knew it.

His carefully scripted plans suffered a small setback in early spring, however. Bill Dryden and his wife Anne separated, and Bill decided to leave Edmonton, accepting a position as Assistant Federal Secretary of the national party. This left Grant with no one as head of the staff organization. As a result he asked me to postpone my Ph.D. dissertation for two years, and take the job as Provincial Secretary. I agreed, and was appointed Acting Secretary in April, and permanent Secretary in the summer. We worked very well together, although I did not have Bill's administrative or party background.

The 1973 Spring Session was another good one for Grant. Since Myron Johnson had gone to Saskatchewan, he hired another graduate student, Jim Anderson, as his assistant. Jim continued the tradition of excellent service for very low pay. Grant hired a new secretary, Helen Strickland, a hard working amiable woman who stayed on for several years despite enormous demands on her. Grant was as active as ever in the Question Period, raising issues and pursuing them with determination. Social Credit, which had now elected a new leader, was still rudderless, waiting for Werner Schmidt to get into the House. In retrospect the choice of Schmidt was a costly, even fatal, choice for Social Credit.

Grant continued to highlight agriculture and rural issues in every session. In particular he supported small family farms and farming. In 1972 he had introduced a Corporate Farming Act, which would have regulated corporate farming. Needless to say, it was not passed. He continued to press for protection in 1973, and ridiculed the government half-hearted efforts against foreign ownership in general.

> Mr. Speaker, first of all it seems to me that the Bill we have before us is really pretty much "Mickey Mouse" type of legislation, one which is not going to achieve the proposed result . . . . The Bill is rather pallid compared to the Ontario government Report on Foreign Ownership. I find that rather surprising. It would appear that Alberta Tories here are much more meek and mild . . . than are their brethren in the Province of Ontario.[7]

He also pressed on the issue of rural gas co-ops, elevators, and rail line abandonment.

In the area of energy he opposed private development of the large gas reserves under the Suffield military base in southern Alberta, calling for a crown corporation to develop these reserves. He also spoke out strongly on labour issues, for the Metis on housing problems, and re-introduced a Bill which I had drafted designed to regulate the release of credit information on individuals. In all, it was a rerun of the success of the previous year, with everyone becoming comfortable with the idea that Grant was the star of the Opposition.

When he completed the session, Grant again launched into a round of party meetings throughout the province, designed to raise money and sell memberships. It was my first set of trips with Grant in my new role. We were accompanied by Annie Dryden who had become an admitted "legislature freak." Anne brought her ukelele, singing her reworked party songs at each stop. The crowds loved them since they skewered the Tories and lauded Grant's role as the only effective opposition voice. Grant, although embarrassed by this kind of personal tribute, neverthe-less was anxious to have Anne along, a throwback to his university days when he enjoyed singing with the other youth members. Anne became a close confidenté of Grant's during this period, and was involved in every subsequent important party event and election campaign.

The trip was an eye-opener for me. Grant gave his speech, the legis-lature report, and I gave the "pitch" for money. By now Grant's whole approach to speaking had matured. At a meeting in Andrew, Alberta he gave a "report" but it was actually a well crafted and well delivered speech. He had only a few notes in front of him to recall the subject areas. The remainder of his speech was entirely extemporaneous. He began with humour, a joke about his solitary position in the Legislature, shifted to the importance of politics at the time, outlined the enormous problems involved in the regulation of the oil industry, and finished by remind-ing his audience that only the NDP stood between Lougheed and the waste of a golden opportunity to use the resources of Alberta in an humane, socialist way. Throughout his voice was well modulated, his gestures precise and well timed, and his delivery flawless. He had come a long way from those early years as Secretary.

By contast, I was no Ted Chudyk. At my first meeting, after Grant had spoken, I gave a long, dry academic dissertation on why it was socially desirable for the membership to support the party with donations. The people at the meeting sat with bewildered looks on their faces, plainly per-plexed as to what they should do. After a minute Grant intervened to say:

Well, those forms won't do any good at home on the mantle. Take out your pens now and fill them out, together with a cheque.

And they did. I learned a valuable lesson in directness. The tour was a big success.

The party financial position had improved tremendously by then. Members were excited, and willing to give. At the 1973 Convention Bill Dryden had launched an election fund which he called "74 in 74," asking everyone, in February 1973, to sign a post-dated cheque for $74 to be cashed in July of 1974. He correctly understood that people were willing to sign a post-dated cheque where they would be unwilling to sign one on the spot. It had raised nearly $30,000. In 1973, as a result of federal NDP pressure, Parliament had passed a new electoral law which allowed tax rebates for contributions to political parties. By providing substantial rebates for smaller donations, up to 75% on the first $100, the new law made the task of fundraising much easier.

In the spring of 1973 the Conservative member for Calgary Foothills, Len Werry, died in an accident. A by-election was needed. The new Leader of the Social Credit, Werner Schmidt, announced that he would seek the seat. Grant and I knew that the NDP needed a good candidate and a good effort in the election. It was a suburban Calgary riding, which the NDP did not expect to win, but it was important that the party establish itself as a force.

On the way back from Ottawa we decided that Nancy Eng was the logical candidate. She was President of the party, lived in the riding, and could get time off for the campaign. When we talked to her, Nancy was reluctant, but finally accepted. The by-election was announced for June 26, 1973. It was an excellent effort. Nancy was a superb candidate, and those of us on staff went down to organize, including Pat Waters who was already there. The local Calgary people turned out in force to help, Ede Martin (later Ede Leeson) ran the office, and Pat Waters managed the campaign. The Liberal leader, Bob Russell, also ran in the riding. New Democrats even fertilized the hillside near the riding hoping to grow a giant NDP in the grass, but no rains came; and it did not show up until later.

Again the result was dramatic. The Tories won with 5430 votes, and the Socred leader was second with 4219, but Nancy got 2,133 votes, a very respectable showing in a riding where the NDP had not done well in 1971. Everyone was pleased. The party was definitely on a roll toward the next election.

The rest of 1973 was to be occupied with the growing federal provincial dispute over oil and gas pricing, generated by the actions of OPEC in the Middle East. As a response to the poor showing of the Liberal party in Western Canada in the 1972 election, Pierre Trudeau called a Western Economic Opportunity Conference in July of 1973. It was attended by the four Western Premiers and the Prime Minister. While some dismissed it as a cynical attempt to bolster the Liberals for the next federal election, the Western Premiers decided to take it seriously, and worked out a series of papers which they presented to the federal government. It was a remarkable effort considering that three of the governments were NDP, and Lougheed was the lone Conservative. However, he managed to get the other governments to take a strong Western approach, no mean feat with Ed Schreyer and Dave Barrett, Premiers of Manitoba and BC respectively, who had more centralist inclinations. By contrast, Allan Blakeney, who had been elected Premier of Saskatchewan in 1971, was closer to Lougheed on many issues than the other two, despite party affiliation. For his part Grant tended to support Blakeney, with his stronger regional views, but this still made him much more of a "national" Canadian than Lougheed. Because there was a consensus with the NDP Premiers, Grant's voice on the Alberta position at the conference was muted.

However, as a result of the OPEC oil embargo, prices for oil began to rise sharply during the summer. The federal government announced a freeze on domestic prices and an export tax on oil exported to the US designed to recover the difference between the international and domestic prices. Both Alberta and Saskatchewan reacted sharply, again catching Grant in the middle. He tried to bridge the federal provincial dimensions of the issue, that is the jurisdictional issue of control over resources, by attacking Lougheed for allowing foreign companies to reap millions through low royalties, but also condemning the federal government for its export tax. A Notley press release stated the NDP case:

NDP Leader Grant Notley charged Premier Lougheed with grandstanding and theatrics in his dispute with Ottawa over the oil export tax. By focussing his attack on whether the federal government had the right to impose the tax, the Premier has failed to protect the provinces' legitimate interest in the more important question of who gets the money from the tax, Mr. Notley said.

"If we are to take the Premier's remarks seriously," the NDP leader argued, "his position is an extreme provincial rights stand which if successful would balkanize the country, erode the powers of the national government, and leave a divided Canada to the tender mercies of giant multi-national corporations."

If the government of Alberta is using the royalty review as an excuse to sabotage federal price restraints and profit taking, it must be opposed by all Albertans who realize that a pseudo-separatist oil policy is not only bad for Canada, but bad for Alberta too.[8]

Privately, Grant was furious with the federal NDP over the issue. It had taken a hard stand against any price increases, supporting and even forcing the Trudeau regime to oppose Alberta and Saskatchewan. Grant and the Alberta NDP were caught in the middle. With a single provincial member, and no federal members, the party had little influence over the federal New Democratic party which, because of the Liberal minority government in Ottawa, was able to dictate Liberal policy on the issue. For New Democrats in Ottawa the issue was clear. World prices were artificially high, and Canadians in central Canada ought not to pay them. For Lougheed the question was just as clear. Oil and gas were a provincial resource and if circumstances were such that the price of those resources had increased that money ought to go to the provincial government and the producers. In fighting the federal government Peter Lougheed had discovered the equivalent of the political Midas touch, something which he exploited mercilessly over the next decade. Only Grant Notley was caught in the middle.

The division within the NDP resulted in some bad feeling. In October of 1973 David Lewis proposed to visit Alberta to explain his views on the matter. He asked the provincial party to arrange some meetings. At the October 26 meeting of the Alberta NDP Executive a unanimous motion was passed instructing me to write a letter to Lewis telling him that a visit "would be inappropriate at this time." Lewis was angry and called Grant directly, referring to me privately as "that parochial beast from Alberta," not understanding that this was a general feeling with the Alberta party. Eventually, Grant retreated, and he agreed to facilitate the visit. At the end of the visit to Edmonton, David took some revenge on Grant.

On David Lewis's last night in the Alberta capital, it was decided that he, Grant, myself, and David's assistant would go out for Chinese food.

At the restaurant, the owner recognized David and Grant. Since he was impressed with David Lewis, we allowed David to take charge of the ordering. He instructed the owner to "just bring us a good Chinese dinner." In turn the owner provided us with a very expensive meal. When the cheque came it was put between David and Grant. It sat there for two and a half hours before Grant's gnarled hand reluctantly moved over and took the check. David carried on talking as if nothing had happened. Not only had Grant not gotten Lewis to change his mind on oil, but in one of a very few instances, Grant was also forced to pick up the check.

At the Federal Council meeting in early 1974 the oil pricing issue was addressed in detail. The Saskatchewan and Alberta parties argued strongly that all money from the export tax should come back to the province. David Lewis and Tommy Douglas disagreed. The matter stayed unresolved until an agreement was reached on the issue between the federal government and producing provinces in the Spring of 1974. That agreement froze domestic prices and fixed the price of oil for the next 12-15 months. It was to be only a truce, however, in a longer war. This became clear when the new federal budget proposal in May made provincial royalties nondeductible for federal tax purposes, effectively catching the industry between the two orders of government. As well, part of the agreement in effect traded off the proceeds from the federal export tax for a higher domestic price, leaving Lougheed open to the charge that he had lost both the battle over jurisdiction and the money. Speaking in the House, Grant said:

> On Thursday the Premier reported on the conference in Ottawa. He came back and made it very clear that he felt the right decision had been made to surrender any proceeds from the export tax in return for a higher price for crude oil . . . .
>
> I submit, Mr. Speaker, that the Premier may have misjudged the situation rather badly and far from being a stalwart defender of provincial rights, he may, in fact, have allowed the federal government to latch on to a whole new area of taxation by getting 100% of the revenues of the export tax . . . . [9]

Grant went on to talk about the need for a *quid pro quo* for sheltered energy prices, and the need to ensure that the oil companies did not get the windfall profit from the new higher prices. He closed by emphasizing that the money from the windfall profits should be expended in Alberta for economic diversification and to alleviate poverty. It was the core of a political theme which Grant would carry into the election less than a year later.

Throughout the latter part of 1973 and the early part of 1974 the NDP had been gaining political and organizational momentum. At a successful convention in Edmonton the party had raised considerable sums of money for the coming election. It was decided to spend some of this money on organizing prior to the next election. Three organizers were hired, Tom McLeod, David Elliot, and Larry Schowalter. Tom came from Lethbridge, and had been very successful in regenerating the constituency organization there. With his rural background it was decided that the party would move him to the Peace River Country, to take charge of organizing the four provincial constituencies up there. Everyone understood that it was imperative that Grant be re-elected, and that the NDP try to win at least one other seat up there, probably Smoky River.

David Elliot had been a long time supporter of the NDP, starting to work for the party in the 1965 election at a very young age. He first met Grant in 1970, but remained unimpressed with him, growing eventually to really dislike him. The feeling was probably mutual. Nevertheless, Dave was available and was an extremely hard worker. He was assigned to the central Alberta region, where he drove endless hours organizing, collecting money, selling memberships and setting up nominations, at which he was very successful. Larry Schowalter was assigned to the Edmonton area. A young man with little experience, he found the job quite daunting, especially since the residue of the Reimer-Notley fight remained. The expectation from all of the organizers was that they would ensure that the party had candidates, campaign managers, and real campaigns in all of the key ridings. As well, they were as usual expected to raise enough money to pay for themselves. As in 1966/67, they were only partially successful.

As soon as the organizers were hired, the federal election of 1974 was called. Most effort was concentrated on that task in the spring. Tom McLeod was first pressed into service in the Lethbridge area but was then transferred to Grant's riding to begin the process of re-electing Grant. In his personal diary he recorded the experience:

Today was a busy day as I drove 12 hours to get from Lethbridge to Peace River, picked up Leeson to drive to Grande Prairie, which was another 150 miles. Once there, we went to the [federal] constituency organization meeting. People were very friendly but after introductions they passed a resolution which in effect stated that they welcomed me as an organizer, but that I would have no authority at all in the coming election campaign. Before I had a chance to get either Leeson or Notley, who were also in attendance, alone, to ask them what this meant, both of them left by car to go back to Edmonton. I felt like getting back into the car and following them back to Edmonton and then back home after telling them what to do with their job.[10]

It was not an easy job. The longer he worked the more Tom realized that despite all of Grant's efforts, and the size of the membership in the area, it was going to be a large task. Other excerpts give an idea of the area Tom organized.

May 31, There is something that makes it [the Peace River Country] so unique compared to any other place I've been, People here . . . keep no regular hours. It's not uncommon for them to get into a car at 10:00 p.m. and drive to a friend's 50 or 60 miles away for coffee.

June 1, I'm surprised by the size of the donations. People here don't look prosperous enough to give the amounts they do.

June 2, Muriel Reiger, the Official Agent, is a very efficient woman. She should be Provincial Treasurer, for she is very tight with money.

June 5, I asked the owner of the building [campaign headquarters] if it was possible to put campaign posters on the outside of the building. He flatly refused.[11]

In other areas of Alberta it was even more difficult. Candidates were very hard to find. In the Yellowhead riding, held by Joe Clark, no one was willing to run. Finally, the candidate from the previous election agreed to stand again. However, at the nominating meeting, when the motion to run a candidate was debated, an elderly gentleman rose and said that although he was in favour of running someone, he certainly hoped that it would not be the candidate from the last time, since he had been terrible. Needless to say, the previous candidate was miffed, and decided not to run. Luckily, someone else came forward. In Medicine Hat the nomination meeting produced no one, and to the sounds of the *M.A.S.H.* theme, "Suicide Is Painless," the meeting had to be rescheduled. When it was finally held the young woman who had agreed to run froze completely. When she was just starting her nomination speech she simply said, "thank you very much" and sat down. She was nominated anyway. It became apparent that the 1974 election would be quite different from the one in 1972. When the campaign was over David Lewis had lost his seat, the Liberals had a majority government, and the NDP was reduced to a rump of 16 seats. It was a disaster. Alberta fared much the same. In the Peace River constituency, the incumbent Ged Baldwin won handily, but most importantly, the NDP ran third for the first time ever. It was not a good sign for Grant.

The formal results caused Grant and the provincial NDP to refine some of its strategy. The goal was still to become the Official Opposition, but it was now clear that the provincial party would not be helped by any national trend. It was decided that that upcoming provincial campaign would focus more heavily on Grant maximizing the party's provincial possibilities and the chance for Grant to be re-elected in his own riding.

Locally, Grant redoubled his efforts to provide service and fulfill the expectations of his constituents. As Tom McLeod soon found out, Notley was a prodigious worker.

> I don't know how Notley can survive at the pace he sets for himself. He draws up a list of communities he wants to visit, and the dates. This routine is followed until every community is covered. The usual period is about a week, which includes several hundred miles of driving and about a hundred phone calls. During these trips the pace is fantastic with no thought of stopping for lunch on his part.[12]

He continued to try and solve every local problem, however small. In one instance in 1972 we got a call at the Legislature from a local farmer. The man began by saying, "I've lost my pig." I sat on the line, completely baffled, and said "Oh." He went on to say that he wanted Grant to find his pig for him. I then ventured to ask him where he thought that it had been lost, did he think that it was near his place? "No, no," he said. "I sent it to market, and I've never been paid. I want Grant to find out why." Relieved that it was somewhat more official than I had thought, I advised Grant, who then dutifully tracked down the hog in question and made sure the farmer was paid. In another instance, an irate constituent called Grant and demanded that he come to his farm to discuss a problem. When Grant asked what the nature of the complaint was, the man refused to disclose it, demanding that Grant come to his farm first. Grant finally agreed. When he arrived the nature of the problem became apparent immediately. Grant had to be rowed to the farm house in a boat, since it was surrounded by water. The Department of Highways had forgotten to put a culvert in a new section of road, backing the water up until it surrounded the house. We joked later that perhaps we should have asked the government for a new outboard motor for the man rather than a culvert.

Despite the humour of these instances, most issues were serious, and Grant pursued them tenaciously, usually providing a successful resolution. In each instance he built respect, albeit grudging in some cases.

By the fall of 1974 the run-up to the election was well underway. Grant was convinced that it would be in the Spring of 1975. Despite the federal setback the provincial party was again buoyant and nominations were moving smoothly toward a full slate. The issues had really boiled themselves down to two groups. The first was oil and gas, and what to do with the huge revenues that were going to accrue to the public treasury. OPEC had provided Alberta with an incredible bonanza, so much so that people were beginning to call Lougheed a "blue-eyed Sheik." The NDP strategy centred around how these revenues would be used. In an attempt to pre-empt the government on this issue the NDP issued a mini-budget, drafted by Grant, his assistant in the Legislature Jim Anderson, and myself. We were aided by some experts in the industry like Joe Yanchula from Calgary, who would run for the NDP in the upcoming election.

The document stressed three goals for the mini-budget—tax reduction and reform, human resource programmes, and diversification of the Alberta economy. The first use was blatantly electoral, but it was weighted toward low and middle income earners, and was complete with a commitment to reform the tax structure. The second grouping brought in traditional NDP programmes like medical care, dental care, pensions and allowances, but it also committed money to rural education, and free tuition at post-secondary institutions. Finally, in the area of economic diversification the document committed the party to acquiring equity in all public utilities, the creation of an Alberta Development Corporation which would acquire the then proposed Syncrude development, and finally made a major commitment to diversification in local and agricultural industries.

The attempt was successful in two respects. First, it reinforced the perception of Grant and the NDP as thoughtful and constructive critics of the government, people with a different but practical approach that encompassed both urban and rural Alberta. Second, it also reinforced the perception that the NDP was the only real alternative to the Lougheed Tories.

This led smoothly into the second major approach of the upcoming campaign, that the NDP was the "Only Real Opposition." It was an approach calculated to appeal to those voters who were not going to vote Conservative, to entice them to amalgamate behind the NDP as the party of the future, the only real home to provide effective opposition to the Tories. Tacitly, it conceded the election to the government, while deliberately concentrating on supplanting Social Credit. In retrospect, it was also tailored perfectly to maximizing Grant's re-election chances in his own riding, since it highlighted his legislative performance. In all ways Grant became the embodiment of the party in 1975, and no one disagreed with that strategy.

Although the party had raised almost $100,000 for the election, an amount unequalled in any campaign in the past, it had no money for professional polling. However, none was needed. It was clear that there were going to be only 4-6 ridings where there was a reasonable chance of electing anyone. Two of those ridings were in the Peace River Country; Grant's riding and the riding of Smoky River, where Victor Tardif had come within 190 votes of winning in 1971. Two others were in Edmonton: Beverly and Norwood, both working class areas with heavy union involvement. Other ridings were nominally designated concentration ridings, but no one had any illusions about winning in them.

Throughout the province the process of nominating candidates went well. Good candidates were running in key constituencies, Victor Tardif again in Smoky River, Ray Martin in Calgary McKnight, and a labour candidate in Edmonton Beverly. Incongruously, some constituencies like Grande Prairie and Pincher-Creek Crowsnest, which had been good ridings for the NDP, were experiencing difficulty in finding a candidate. At one time it looked as if Tom McLeod or I would have to run in Grande Prairie, but on the very day of the nomination meeting a candidate came forward.

Grant's nominating meeting was a key event. We decided to hold it back-to-back with the nomination meeting of the adjacent riding of

Smoky River where Victor Tardif was running. They had to be big events if we were to regain the momentum lost in the region by our poor showing in the federal riding. Tom McLeod organized both events. The meeting in Smoky River was small, but Grant's nomination was a huge success, with 600 people attending.

> [At] Notley's meeting in Spirit River on Saturday we had a great crowd of almost 600 people, a meeting I think they will talk about for years to come. I think this will really shock the Tories and should give Notley a good start toward re-election.
> More important than the money is the NDP supporters have now saved face after last summers election. This night has been a great moral victory for our side.[13]

But the victory was temporary at best. The other two opposition parties were having difficulty attracting candidates. This was especially a problem for Social Credit, who under their new leader Werner Schmidt were the Official Opposition and held 25 seats in the House. The last thing that they wanted was to see Grant Notley re-elected. One of the places where they did not try very hard to find a candidate was in Grant's Spirit River riding, and ultimately they did not field a candidate.

By contrast, the Conservatives were in an incredibly strong position. The opposition parties were weak and disorganized, especially Social Credit. The provincial economy was buoyant. The Conservatives first term in office had been a public success. And most importantly they were now closely identified as the defenders of Alberta's interests. They had tapped into the well-springs of western alienation in a significant way. They were, in short, unstoppable. They also wanted to rid themselves of Notley, and were quite prepared to do what was necessary to accomplish that. On the surface it did not look too difficult. Grant had won only because of a three way split. Without Social Credit, and with overwhelming provincial momentum, there was every expectation that they could win in Spirit River in a two way fight. But taking no chances, they nominated a strong candidate. Grant himself says that he did not know if there was a secret deal between Social Credit and the Conservatives, but he did remember that the Tories felt "they had it in the bag."

For the NDP it was imperative that they launch themselves into 1975 with a good annual convention in Calgary. All efforts were bent toward making it a success. One of the key elements of that convention was the attempt to get Premier Dave Barrett as the keynote speaker. Barrett was considered the premiere NDP speaker and was much sought after. I had written to him earlier in 1974 and was turned down by an Executive Assistant. Grant then wrote him and was turned down by Barrett. We were both in despair about the matter when our convention chairperson, Ede Martin, offered to write and try to get him, "since the party heavies had failed." In her letter she reminded the Premier of all of the help he had received from Alberta people, including herself in 1972, when she had worked in an NDP campaign office, lived in a candidate's house that was flooded and required constant attention to a sump pump to keep it open. It was a "vigorous" letter, and much to everyone's surprise Barrett wrote back saying that he would come. When he arrived he asked to meet the woman who had written him the "shit hammer letter." He was a huge success, and so was the convention. It now remained only for the Conservatives to call the election.

True to Grant's prediction, the Premier opened the House in February, presented the budget, and then had the Lt. Governor dissolve the legislature for a general election on March 26, 1975. The NDP was ready. It had literature, signs, a leader's tour, and almost all of its candidates in place. As well, it had commitments from the other sections of the party in Canada to supply organizers. A large number of people came in from elsewhere. Although this was an NDP tradition, the sheer number was greater than ever before. Even people like Tony Penikett, later Premier of the Yukon, was in Grant's riding to help out.

Social Credit continued to have difficulty and was able to field only 70 candidates, several of whom were nominated at the last minute and were not serious candidates. The NDP had a full slate of 75, the only opposition party to do so, but several of its candidates were also "slim." The last candidate nominated was in Pincher Creek-Crowsnest on March 3, 1975. This was the riding which Garth Turcott had won only nine years before. However, the local members now wanted to support the Social Credit candidate, Charlie Drain, to keep the Tories out. Charlie had been quite "Red" earlier in his life, and was still considered to be progressive. However, the Council of the NDP had ordered every riding to nominate, and I was dispatched to the riding to see that it happened. The local people set up a meeting and a time, but deliberately sent me to the wrong town. I was able to find them, however, and met them just as they were leaving the hall. I insisted that they reconvene the meeting. They agreed but insisted they would not nominate. Once the meeting was reconvened I told them that they had no choice but to nominate. They then changed tactics, pointing out that no one would run. I declared that Dave Elliot, one of our organizers, was prepared to run. I asked the Chairwoman to open the floor for nominations, and I nominated Elliot, all of which was completely unconstitutional. I then had the meeting adjourn. Everyone at the meeting told me that they would be supporting Charlie Drain instead of Dave. I acquiesced and announced proudly to the media later in the day that the NDP had a "full slate." Poor Dave got just 3% of the vote.

As the campaign progressed it became apparent that the election was a foregone conclusion. However, not taking any chances, Lougheed made a series of costly announcements during the campaign. He was criticized by some in the media for overkill. The NDP campaign provincially went well, with considerable advertising (by NDP standards) and exposure. Grant was superb on the leader's tour, consistently getting good coverage. In particular his ability to speak to a large crowd had become very impressive. At the rally in Edmonton he preceeded Tommy Douglas as a speaker. It was not an enviable position. Tommy was still at the peak of his oratorical abilities. And yet, Grant delivered an excellent campaign speech which brought the crowd to their feet several times. He was not yet a Tommy Douglas, but he was now clearly an Alberta understudy. Throughout, he concentrated on northern rural issues, where NDP strength was concentrated. In the final analysis, however, issues were unimportant. The real fight was for a handful of individual opposition ridings, one of them being Grant's.

As he recalled the election Grant used to dwell on the two-way fight in Spirit River-Fairview, and the Tory arguments.

[They used to say] if you want anything done, you have to have a government member. That was the sort of high road: [or] Notley's basically a communist. He doesn't care about the riding, he spends all of his time running around. They tried to use that. That sort of thing. It was not an edifying campaign.

But these arguments were not very potent in 1975. They flew in the face of facts. Grant has been a good MLA, had worked hard, and won the admiration of non-New Democrats. By 1975 he had a strong personal following. People were proud to have one of the party leaders in their riding, and were even more pleased that he was so accessible. As the local President Graham Thomlinson said:

> They were impressed by the fact that he was Leader of the party. He was a good spokesman for the agricultural community. He voiced their concerns. And he was so good with his constituency people, that was really what put him in good stead there as much as anything else. He always had time to meet and talk with anybody who had a concern. He developed a tremendous model for any politician.

In all, he had made a good impression. The organization in the riding was also much better than in 1971. There was more money, more media, and more organizational help. Tom McLeod had been in the riding for nearly a year at that time, together with his wife Anne and family who had moved up as well. Ted Chudyk was brought back to run the campaign, together with Joyce Nash, wife of the Federal Secretary. Everything was organizationally sound.

But as Tom McLeod also recalls, Grant was not at all sure about the outcome.

> The closer you got to the election, the more hyper he got. He was like some sort of an alien being. The longer the hours you worked, the more energy he seemed to have, and the less you had.

Graham Thomlinson also recalled that Grant thought that it would be close.

> Oh I think that he thought that the chances were good but it was close, there was no way anybody could foretell the results accurately.

It was much closer than anyone expected when the polls closed at 8:00 p.m. on March 26, 1975. Four years of brilliant performance in the legislature, four years of hard constituency work, four years of making the NDP deal with rural issues, four years of organization, and four years of combined effort all came down to the decision of a few voters.

As soon as the polls closed the size of the Tory victory became apparent. At 62% of the vote, they simply annihilated the opposition. Statistically, no one but government members should have been elected, but four Socreds hung on, including Bob Clark, Grant's old competitor from

4H days in Olds. In the Peace River country, all the NDP hopes of a break-through were dashed. In Smoky River Victor Tardif lost by a large amount. In Peace River and Grande Prairie, the Tories were victorious. Only in Spirit River was it a fight. Grant trailed the PC candidate all night as the count trickled in. With only two polls to come he was still behind. However, when those last two polls were received, Grant surged ahead and won by 99 votes. As he said later, "I hung on by my fingernails." In a huge Tory landslide Grant had survived as one of those statistical oddities of the election, an opposition member.

7 THE SOCIAL CONSCIENCE OF ALBERTA

THE 1975 ELECTION BROUGHT many changes to politics in Alberta. The Conservatives, like their predecessors the Social Credit, were now the undisputed masters of the province. Money was pouring in from oil revenue undreamed of even five years before. The economy was booming, the cities growing, the farm economy healthy, and in general Albertans were feeling good about themselves and their future. The result of this was that opposition politicians were marginalized, forced quite literally into a tiny corner of the Legislature and the politics of Alberta. For Social Credit it was a most unpromising time. There was little that could raise their party from its abysmal state. They were a party with a powerful past, now reduced to four members. As it turned out, within ten years the Social Credit party would be dead.

For Grant and the NDP the situation was somewhat different. Tom McLeod put it best when he said that expectations within the CCF and NDP had been so low for so long that the election of Grant in 1971 had been perceived as a major breakthrough. His performance in the House had been a bonus. His re-election, in the face of a huge Tory landslide, had been considered another major victory. People were not inclined to view the failure to elect other New Democrats as a reason to criticize Grant. The campaign of 1975 had been well run, and in the estimation of most New Democrats it had accomplished all that it could in the face of the Tory tide. At 62% of the vote the government ought to have won every seat and the fact that Grant hung on was enough for most New

177

Democrats to cheer about. In particular, the members of Grant's own constituency were ecstatic.

There were those who criticized the result, however. There was still a group within the labour movement who felt that the strategy of the previous four years, reaching out to the rural areas, concentrating on Notley's seat, and not concentrating enough on other seats, had netted the expected result, the re-election of only Grant Notley. At the bottom of this criticism was bitterness over the purge of 1973 and the continuing sullen analysis that Notley was more interested in ensuring his own re-election than in forwarding the interests of the NDP. Supporters of Grant Notley disputed this assessment, calling it sour grapes, arguing that Grant had made precisely the right decision in 1971 and 1975, and by so doing kept an NDP presence in the Legislature. Even more importantly, Grant was a superb MLA, and if the public perceived him and the NDP as synonymous, that was all right with the membership. Grant himself recalls there was no real challenge to him after 1975.

> I was much, much, stronger in the party than ever before, because I'd survived . . . . We gained votes, we went from 11% to 13%, so that we ran second in most of northern Alberta. It looked good. We even had second place in Calgary McKnight, where Ray Martin ran. It was a good time in terms of the party. No challenge at all.

If the leadership did not change, almost every other position did. Nancy Eng, who had been a superb President and a very close confidante of Grant, discovered prior to the election that her cancer had re-occurred. This caused her to step down as a candidate in the 1975 election and to resign the Presidency in 1976. Nancy was one of those rare women who was a convinced fighter for women's rights, but did not appear threatening to men. As the first woman President she worked hard to make sure that women took their rightful place at all levels of the party. She used to joke that she would only make coffee when she could make policy as well.

In the summer of 1975 I left my position as Provincial Secretary to return to the University of Alberta. I was succeeded by the candidate for McKnight, Ray Martin. Ray was born at Delia, Alberta, and took his education there. Later he went to university and secured a degree in Education. He worked as a teacher and a guidance counsellor in the Calgary school system in the 1960s. In 1970 he became interested in the New

Democratic Party through a friend of his, Jim Staples, who had asked Ralph Eng to approach Ray and try to interest him. As he says, one thing led to another, and soon he was an active member. He campaigned for Jim Staples in the 1971 election and became one of the small group of active members after the election. The first time that he met Grant he was very impressed. He thought he was a very polished person. He also met David Lewis that year, and it galvanized him into action. Grant often stayed at Ray's place when in Calgary. In 1973 he decided to seek the nomination in Calgary McKnight and did quite well in the 1975 election. After the election both Nancy Eng and Grant urged Ray to take the job as Secretary.

> What I did do at the time was . . . to get a year leave of absence from the Calgary School Board, which was my employer. To show you what a shrewd businessman I was, I recall taking a $7,000 cut in pay for the thrill of being Provincial Secretary. I remember coming up, and Gordon Wright was on the Executive, he was the Treasurer, saying, "God if he's stupid enough to take a $7,000 cut in pay, we'd better hire him."

At the time he intended to go back to Calgary after one year, but decided to remain in Edmonton. He became very good friends with Grant.

At the Legislature, Jim Anderson left, and Myron Johnson, together with another young man, John McInnis from Lethbridge Alberta, took over the duties as legislative assistants. There were other changes as well at the 1976 convention when Gordon Wright stepped down as Treasurer and I succeeded Nancy Eng as President. Interestingly, despite Grant's protestations about his own security, he was still nervous about Neil Reimer and the labour movement. I found out much later that Grant wanted me to run for President because a rumour was around that Neil Reimer would attempt to run for the office. Grant was still unwilling to have Neil as a major figure in the party. He was convinced that if I ran, Neil would not. Whatever the truth of this, it was something that Grant failed to mention at the time.

The result of all of these changes was to shake up the party in its central apparatus from top to bottom. With the exception of Grant it was a completely new look. Even Grant took on a new style, and a new attitude.

I became a much better listener in the four years . . . . I couldn't appeal just to the people who were there as a base. I had to deliberately move beyond that. It was a case of how you move beyond that without alienating your base. You do that on the basis of being honest and straightforward. You do things you say you're going to do.

In Alberta between 1975 and 1979, this meant appealing to all of the small groups and individuals who were not sharing in the new found wealth of the province, who were marginalized or deprived in a society which still had few mechanisms for ensuring equal opportunity, much less equal condition. This meant appealing to special interest groups, rather than attempting to build a mass party on the basis of appealing to all working people. Grant was convinced that class analysis was irrelevant to the Alberta of the 1970s, a province still alienated but now wealthy enough to be a force in Canadian federalism. Implicitly he was still aiming to be Leader of the Opposition, expecting that it would be at least two elections before the NDP would become a significant force. However, he also kept up his deliberate strategy of strong support for rural issues, both to keep his own seat intact, but also to be perceived as having broad enough appeal to be a Premier in waiting. Thus his work in the Legislature during this time centred on questions of social policy to a greater extent than in the first term, bringing him a reputation as an ombudsman, as Alberta's social conscience.

The list is impressive. Throughout Grant's career there is a consistency, a devotion to the rights of the underprivileged, the disadvantaged, the "little guy" in society, that cannot be completely explained by electoral opportunism.

In the Legislature Grant was a strong defender of aboriginal rights and in particular he championed the cause of the Metis people in Alberta. This was not always popular in his own riding or in rural Alberta in general. In 1973 he raised the plight of Metis people in Grouard who had to truck water 30 miles to their community. The government had proposed a programme which would take 10 years to provide adequate water supplies to them. As Grant said in the House:

It seems to me that there are certain basic things that Albertans should be entitled to . . . surely an adequate water supply. What we are talking about is a community well . . . . That's not an excessive proposition at all.[1]

In 1977 he attacked the government for bringing in a new Land Titles Amendment Act, which he argued was an attempt to stop the filing of native claims on crown land, and short-circuit negotiations.

> Mr. Speaker, . . . to take away an important legal instrument on a retroactive basis . . . says [something] more . . . about their [the government's] understanding and concern for the powerless, the small people, the defenceless people in this province of ours . . . . In Bill 29 we are trampling justice rather than pursuing justice.[2]

Later the next year the provincial government cut funds to community advisory boards of natives in the north, in what Grant called "an outrageous attack" on the boards, and "a blatant attempt to divide and conquer," because they had opposed changes to the Land Titles Act. In June of 1979, when officials of the Metis Development Branch of the Department of Social Services seized files from eight Metis communities Grant defended the Metis in the Legislature, calling the raids "commando style." He was vindicated by the Ombudsman's report on this matter. Most importantly, he consistently defended the Metis right to land as well as the right of all aboriginal peoples to land settlements, and in 1981/82 he strongly defended inclusion of native rights in the constitution. His record in this area was consistent, and from all indications, appreciated.

Although Grant was, to put it delicately, traditional in his home life, he spoke out often in the legislature on behalf of women and women's rights. In 1974 he sought to correct inequalities in the level of pensions between male and female teachers. In 1976 he raised the matter of affirmative action, pushing the government to accept the principle. In 1978 he gave a major speech on the Matrimonial Property Act, taking a strong position in favour of equal sharing. Speaking against judicial discretion, or other considerations he said:

> But I think that we need to keep another point in mind . . . the thing that has always worried me about the argument that we're going to have to sell the business, or the farm, . . . the suggestion that the preservation of the property is more important than the right of the spouse to receive her fair share. Mr. Speaker, however sympathetic I am to maintaining the small businesses, or family farm operation, we cannot place property rights before the individual rights of the citizenry . . . .[3]

He also brought out the plight of women in poverty in Alberta at a time of great oil prosperity. Although Grant was not a convinced feminist, his own socialism brought him to progressive conclusions about the role of women in the party and the society.

There were many instances when Grant took up the cause of the "little guy" in Alberta society. Those who were powerless always found his office to be open. Service station operators came to him in 1973 when they had problems with leases with the major oil companies. Hutterites asked Grant to speak out against the Communal Properties Act, and he did. He spoke out for physically challenged people and their right to employment, for children as wards of the province, and even for trappers in northern Alberta. Specifically, in the latter case, Grant was asked to try and secure better compensation and notice from seismic crews and large oil companies searching for oil. He was successful in getting the government to admit that they were leaving the process to private negotiations, something which graphically illustrated the relative imbalance of power between the two groups. Later the government looked at a levy on the industry to compensate trappers. Often Grant would introduce Bills in the House to highlight his concern for a particular group. In 1972 and 1973 he introduced legislation to regulate private credit information agencies in an attempt to protect the privacy rights of Albertans. In an attempt to protect small farmers from takeover, and preserve the role of small agriculture in the province, he introduced the Corporate Farming Bill in the 1973. It was modelled after similar legislation in North Dakota designed to restrict the entry of corporations into farming. In 1978 he introduced the Small Business Act. It was designed to ensure more government contracts for small Alberta businesses to encourage the breakup of large contracts, to provide appropriate grants to small business, and to establish a Select Committee of the Legislature to review government approaches to small business. Speaking to the Act he said:

> I submit to the government . . . that it really isn't good enough to put all of our eggs in the basket of large projects. I know they capture the headlines . . . . But the long term future of this province is going to be written more in the way we deal with the less striking project, the project that will involve smaller operations; . . . countless hundreds and thousands of small business enterprises, particularly related to the renewable resource sector.[4]

Consistent with his philosophy on small farms, Grant never viewed supporting small business as a problem, although he took considerable criticism within the party for this stand, and vicious attacks from the government for being a socialist wolf in sheep's clothing.

Grant was especially concerned and eloquent when it came to young people. He viewed his own youth as an awakening, an opportunity to try and change a small part of the world. He admired those who tried to change the status quo, especially young people.

> I am not saying that the young people are necessarily any better than the adults of today, but I think that there is at least some evidence to indicate that there is greater idealism and that in my judgement Mr. Speaker, is certainly very desirable.
>
> Another thing I find refreshing when talking to high school students is their healthy scepticism of politicians, scepticism of institutions, scepticism of ideology . . . what I find rather different to the part of young people is . . . a willingness to set on the table the shibboleths and say alright now, you say such and such is a good thing . . . you have to show them. I find that extremely encouraging.[5]

Adequate shelter and housing was also an area of concern for Grant. Immediately after the election in March of 1975, the House was called into session to pass the budget and other unfinished legislation. The huge influx into Alberta of money and people generated by rising oil prices had put enormous strain on the availability of affordable housing in the major cities. By mid-1975 it had reached critical proportions. Rising interest rates, low vacancies, conversion of apartments into condominiums, and a lack of public housing units all contributed to the situation. With less than a 1% vacancy rate in Edmonton, rents began to rise sharply.

In the Legislature in June Grant proposed that the House adjourn the regular business for an emergency debate on this matter. The Tories resisted, but the Speaker ruled that the motion was in order. Caught between the Speaker's ruling, and obvious bad press on the issues, Premier Lougheed rose in support of the debate. It was the first time in the life of the government that this had happened. Grant followed this action with motions, bills, and petitions on the issue. He staunchly supported some form of rent review and control over the next several years. In 1978 he introduced a Tenants Bill of Rights in the House. The legislation was designed to protect tenants from unfair eviction, and protected tenants on matters like damage deposits. Grant made affordable housing one of his major priorities, supporting all efforts to get government to move on the issue.

While the energy issue was never far from the public agenda, in the period 1975 to 1979 the major issue was what to do with the money. The government's response to the inflows of vast amounts of spare cash was to create the Heritage Trust Fund in 1976. This was a fund dedicated to putting away excess revenues for a "rainy day." Thirty percent of all resource revenues were earmarked for the Fund, and it had an initial capitalization of $1.5 billion. Lougheed justified the Fund on several grounds, but the most important was diversification.

> Mr. Speaker, the investments of the fund must meet both of two important challenges, and that is what's going to make the fund so difficult. It must offset the probability of declining revenue in the future . . . . At the same time, it must be a vehicle for diversification and for strengthening our economy.[6]

In his speech Grant supported the concept of a trust fund. Ironically, he seemed not to anticipate that a fund like this could eventually be more of a curse than a blessing. Instead, he concentrated on two other aspects. The most important was the lack of legislative control over the fund. As it was designed only 20% of the fund was to be invested in a manner which would need legislative approval. The other 80% would not. He emphasized the importance of legislative approval.

> The fact of the matter is there should be debate in the Legislature, where there can be open accountability. Mr. Speaker, the fact of the matter is that this government is asking us to pass a bill which will give it the opportunity to pick up companies . . . without debate in the Legislative Assembly.

> Let's look at why parliament attempted to gain control of the purse strings in the first place. By using the power of the purse, parliament could control the king or the king's representatives . . . to suggest somehow that we shouldn't be debating the issue in the House is just completely wrong.[7]

This debate, and others on this issue, exemplified Grant's commitment to British parliamentary democracy and the power of the legislature. Undoubtedly, he was committed in part because he was an opposition politician. Had he been Premier, running a government might have tempered some of his zeal. But more importantly, Grant revered the legislature, its traditions, and its power. Membership in it had been his single-minded goal, and he was unwilling to see its role minimized by the government. He was a strong and consistent fighter for parliament and the rights of parliament. In that sense, he was more of a CCFer than a New Democrat. His own quest for social justice seemed to him to be best fulfilled within the orderly chambers of parliamentary democracy and any who attacked it certainly found little favour with Grant.

While Grant had internal differences with some members of the Alberta labour movement, he never let that interfere with his overall relationship with organized labour. He consistently supported their causes and their attempts to maintain the right to organize and the right to strike. He demonstrated this many times in the House. More importantly, although under him the Alberta NDP emphasized rural issues, he never abandoned the CCF idea that a natural electoral coalition could be maintained between working people, and working farmers. He fully accepted organized labour's integral role in the New Democratic Party.

> We've had some very good people on our Executive. Some senior people like Harry Kostiuk have always been close to us. We have several people who were active in the fed [Federation of Labour] who were on our Executive. George Olexiuk, who was with AUPE.
>
> But to be honest, people don't like strikes, and that's one thing that they don't like about the NDP. It goes with the turf.

Perhaps the toughest time for Grant was his support of organized labour in their fight against the Trudeau wage controls. Less than a year after its re-election in 1974 the Trudeau government announced a set of wage and price controls for the country. Provincial governments were asked to adhere to them, and the Alberta government agreed. But the labour movement fought them vigorously, denouncing them as simply wage controls. In retrospect they were right. The NDP governments in Manitoba and Saskatchewan were caught between appearing not to support Canada, and their affiliation with the trade union movement. For Grant, the choice was tough, but he did not shy away. On the national day of protest, October 14, 1976, he marched with over a thousand people, leading a solid contingent of New Democrats. In the Legislature he alone had voted against the Anti-Inflation Program. Speaking to the rally from the steps of the Legislature, he said:

> As I stand here today, and see this huge crowd, I know that I no longer stand alone [in my fight] to get the province of Alberta out of the wage control programme.[8]

It is perhaps no great surprise that Grant was a keen supporter of quality education. His mother's influence, his own early experiences, and his good memories of university, all propelled Grant to become a cogent critic of provincial government policy on education. One of his major preoccupations was with the financing of rural schools. In particular he criticized funding formula that weighed against quality education in the rural areas.

> Mr. Speaker, the new grant system, as I understand it appears very fair at first glance . . . . But . . . I am quite concerned that as a result of the new grant structure [we] will have no choice but to close down rural high schools.
> Now how are we going to preserve those rural high schools? The only way we can possibly do it is if the government makes provision in the grant structure.[9]

In post-secondary education he was concerned with the quality of education, and our Canadian identity. Speaking to non-Canadian influence in the province's institutions he not only supported the role of Canadians in their own institutions, but he insisted that it had to be coupled with institutional autonomy and a cosmopolitan atmosphere.

> Many of the speakers this afternoon have made reference to the value which arises from having many people at a university from different cultural backgrounds . . . . I think generally that is true . . . but, . . . you must have some vantage point, and that vantage point must be an identity which is rented [rooted] [sic] within the community and the country.[10]

It was a pan-Canadian view which he expressed often, and one which placed him firmly on the side of Canadian nationalists. It was a view which was not always welcome in the Alberta Legislature of the 1970s and early 1980s.

Grant was also a strong supporter of public education, that is, publicly funded education. While he supported the right of people to choose a private school, he vigorously opposed giving them *carte blanche* in terms of content. In his opinion the world was not something that you "believed" in, it was something that "was," and this required that each individual be given facts about the universe around them. This required standards and quality educators, and some provincial control over the curriculum of each school. In short, he was opposed to allowing private schools to control their curriculum, except as it came to religious instruction. Even more importantly, he opposed the kind of "freedom of choice" which would lead to a two tier education system, one for the rich and one for the poor. But in spite of this, he also strongly supported the autonomy of local school boards within general guidelines.

In the field of university education, Grant adopted the concept of an open university, with full accessibility for all who had the ability to go. Indeed, when he was leader of the party, it maintained a policy of opposition to tuition fees, which he perceived as detrimental to the prospects of poorer students. On March 15, 1978, when approximately 5000 angry students marched on the Legislature to protest cutbacks, Grant supported them. The students booed both Peter Lougheed and Bert Hohol, then Minister of Advanced Education.

Perhaps Grant's own philosophy of education was summed up most eloquently in a speech to the Legislature on May 11, 1978.

> Finally, Mr. Speaker, the . . . [goal] of education [is to] develop a sense of purpose in life and ethical or spiritual values which respect the worth of the individual, justice, fair play, and fundamental rights, responsibilities and freedoms.
>
> Really, one of the things we should strive to achieve in our education system is to liberate and to develop to the fullest extent the creative potential of all individuals, while cherishing and showing respect for diversities. I think that has to be the goal of the education system, to release the tremendous potential that exists in every single person.[11]

Grant was also in the forefront on the health issues in the province. Belief in a universal medicare system was deeply rooted in his early CCF years and in his admiration for the Blakeney government in Saskatchewan.

Consequently, he tended to concentrate on improvements to the system rather than substantial change. This included a call in 1973 for the abolition of premiums for medicare, a step already taken by the Schreyer and Blakeney governments. In 1974 he proposed universal denticare and pharmacare programmes, again pointing to other provinces as examples. In this case he was able to point out the wide differences between the urban and rural areas in the availability and quality of dental care.

In 1980, at the height of the dispute over "balance billing," or extra-billing by doctors, Grant introduced a bill in the Legislature to outlaw the practice. He was scathing in his criticism of the government for their reluctance to deal with this issue, and of the 15% increase that had been given to doctors, despite the government's willingness to hold the line with nurses. Needless to say, the bill was not passed.

He also took up the cause of smaller groups, and addressed local health issues. This was especially true in his own riding. His position on health issues was very traditional. In particular he avoided questions like abortion, where he perceived little political gain and considerable heart-ache for the party. Nor, as already stated, did he advocate wholesale changes to the system. Quite rightly Grant estimated that the NDP had a good record with the public on health issues and he fought to maintain that perception.

But, despite his close attention to major issues like health, Grant was always mindful of his own perception that the NDP had to be relevant in rural Alberta. This meant appealing to people on rural issues like health and education, but it also meant speaking out often on agriculture. In this area Grant's ideas were almost entirely shaped by his CCF background. He strongly supported orderly marketing, the Wheat Board, and the Crow Rate. He believed in rural co-ops, and most importantly, the small family farm. His support of the latter was conditioned by his own rural background, and his romanticization of the place of the small farmer in the history of Alberta. But he also believed that family farms were the most efficient, productive, and environmentally sound way to grow food. He strongly opposed corporate farming, and found his support in the National Farmer's Union rather than the Palliser group. All of this meant that he and his staff spent considerable time on this issue. Grant thought that he had an impressive record in this area:

> Our track record, hog stabilization plan, $40 for cow-calf operators, Crow Rate, commitments long before government moved in some areas

of infrastructure, more money for railways, terminals, hopper cars, orderly marketing, forced them to back off. They were going to try and get out of the Wheat Board last year, they backed off on that. It's a good track record on farm issues.

He was especially supportive of the Wheat Board:

I've always been a strong supporter of orderly marketing. I have defended that to consumers even though it might mean higher prices in the short run, in the long run it will mean a constant flow of production, so it's better for everybody.

I think that the Wheat Board has done basically a good job. It's perceived, because you've got the right wing propaganda here, as being a federal agency . . . too bureaucratic, a little more private enterprise. I don't subscribe to any of that.

One of Grant's fondest memories was of the tractor demonstrations in late 1975. These demonstrations resulted from a disastrous drop in beef prices which was threatening to bankrupt small producers, particularly in the North. Small groups of farmers began driving their tractors on roads, sometimes as many as 40 of them. They were angry. Grant spoke to many of them, and introduced a motion for emergency debate on the issue on November 18, 1975. The government ministers minimized the problem, and eventually speaker Amerongen ruled against an emergency debate. However, the government did come through with a $40 million programme some months later, which Grant probably correctly took credit for.

The issues Grant developed in the Legislature tell us some things about him. The first, and perhaps most important, is that he was profoundly influenced in his selection and strategy by his own social background. In particular his rural roots and belief in the family farm ensured that rural issues were near the top of his agenda. It also partially explains why he saw himself as a link to the old CCF, rejecting Neil Reimer's claim in that regard. A corollary of this approach was Grant's deliberate strategy to try and break through in the rural areas. He was most comfortable with rural people, but more importantly, he saw them as the most uncomfortable in Lougheed's Alberta. Considerable discontent was to be found in these rural pockets, and borrowing from his own analysis and experience in Spirit River, the most vulnerable for the Tories. If the NDP could gain access to these "niches" of discontent, it could elect enough people to become the Official Opposition, and then the Government.

The second thing that is apparent from Grant's treatment of issues was his own driving sense of equality. Throughout he was consistent in his support for the powerless and the underprivileged. He always took time to listen to groups or individuals, to arbitrate their complaints and criticism of government. It was this "Ombudsman" function which so wove him into the political fabric of Alberta. He quite literally touched thousands of individual people. But his ideology was always the ideology of opportunity. He wanted to ensure that people had equality of opportunity, not necessarily equality of condition. Again, he was "in tune" with most Albertans.

By the end of his second term in 1979, Grant had really established himself as the social conscience of the legislature and of Alberta.

Unfortunately his efforts were not to be rewarded electorally in 1979. This was not because of a lack of work in the party. Several key people worked hard during this period. Perhaps the hardest worker was Ray Martin, who was Provincial Secretary. His task was not an enviable one. The NDP had put all of its efforts, financially and organizationally, into the 1975 election. Although Grant was re-elected, and there was still a feeling of victory, the natural letdown began by late 1975. Everyone in the Executive knew that this was a crucial time. If the party could keep buoyant until 1977, the natural momentum associated with new candidates, the disintegration of Social Credit, and the continued excellent performance by Grant, would begin to take over.

The remedy proposed by Grant was predictable. First, he and Ray went on the road raising money, having meetings, and keeping constituencies active. Second, the party planned for a good convention in early 1976, where the Executive could be revamped and enthusiasm renewed. Third, Grant continued to use his base as an MLA to further the interests of the party throughout Alberta. The first part of the strategy was implemented immediately. As Ray recalls, he went "on the road" with Grant in what he describes as the "Grant and Ray Show." Grant would give the political speech, and Ray would give the "pitch" for money. In so doing, Ray was following the honourable tradition of many previous Secretaries. One of the things that Ray remembers most about that period was the personal relationship that grew between the two men. Grant always treated Ray as an equal, and Ray reciprocated by working hard and being completely loyal. Again, in so doing, he was following a tradition.

Another key player in the organizational and fiscal rescue plan was Alex McEachern. Alex and his wife, Ethne, became active in the NDP in 1972. His father had been a staunch CCFer, but Alex had been little interested in politics. His first real experience with the party came at the 1973 convention, which he said "underwhelmed" him. However, he was very impressed with Grant, and went on to become a candidate in Edmonton Kingsway in 1975, the constituency where he would eventually be elected in 1986. At the 1976 provincial convention, he was elected Treasurer, a job which he held for the next seven years. Alex provided stability in the Executive with his thoughtful and patient counsel, something that became much more important after Nancy Eng left the Executive in 1977. Together with Grant and Ray, Alex became one of the inner circle of decision makers.

The 1976 convention itself was very successful. Held in Red Deer, in March, it was a big convention, and Grant took advantage of it to refurbish the Executive. There were several new faces, as Nancy Eng stepped down and long-time supporters like Anne Dryden were defeated. In his speech to the convention Grant emphasized the issues which would become the general theme of the next three years. Some people were not sharing in the new found wealth of Alberta, and Peter Lougheed was creating a quasi-separatist Alberta.

Lougheed's new west scares the hell out of me . . . . How shall we build this province? People must come first, and no Tory government will begin with people.[12]

The convention was a big success, sending people home with new enthusiasm, and Grant back to the Legislature in the same mood.

Throughout the next two years the process continued. The strategy was the same as it had been in the previous several elections: concentrate on six or seven ridings, hope to elect five or six people, and become the Official Opposition. All of the key players in the party were convinced that this was the right strategy. No one questioned the fact that this strategy had been unsuccessful for at least six or seven elections, and that the premise involved ought to be examined. Not only had the party never become the Official Opposition, it had never elected more than one member. This, despite the fact that the Government had fallen in 1971, and Social Credit had disintegrated in 1975. No one wanted to face the prospect that the people of Alberta simply did not want the NDP, either as the government or the opposition. Like rats in a maze, the NDP continued down the same old familiar passage, leading to the same blank wall, returned, regrouped, and planned to go down the same trail again next time.

To be fair, there were few alternatives. At least in one instance the strategy had been successful, in Spirit River-Fairview. The hope was that although the party might not be acceptable, individual MLAs would be. The problem with this strategy was that it also did not work. Other political parties, like the Liberals in Alberta, had attempted to capitalize on a few locally popular MLAs and failed. By contrast, the Conservatives had become successful overnight between 1967 and 1971. The time, as they say, had to be "right."

The only way to keep an electoral party active in the face of such a lack of success, is to constantly replenish activists before they become cynical with defeat. Grant realized this and consciously or unconsciously did this every four years. As well, he knew that his own role, however superb, would also be subject to a time limit. But in 1977, this seemed far away. Indeed, everyone believed with some justification that the breakthrough would come in 1979. It would be the beginning of a third term for the Tories, a time when they should be vulnerable. Social Credit, although still the Official Opposition under Bob Clark, seemed to have suffered a mortal blow in 1975. In the scheme of things, the same old strategy seemed finally to be consistent with the electoral cycle. By 1978, then, everyone in the Alberta NDP had themselves convinced that 1979 was their year.

The second part of the concentration strategy involved the selection of constituencies. Again, there was unanimity in the Executive behind Grant's analysis. If there were pockets of discontent that could be exploited to elect five or six MLAs, they would most likely be found in the rural areas. Therefore the selection of target ridings focused on five or six rural constituencies. These included Spirit River-Fairview, St. Paul, Drayton Valley, Smoky River, Athabasca, and one on two others. In Edmonton, Norwood and Strathcona were thought to be the best bets. Once again, no one challenged a strategy which had essentially failed in the past. More importantly, the recent history of electoral swings indicated that when a desire for change and discontent began to manifest themselves, they did so mainly in the cities, as with the Tories in 1967. If Grant had really believed that the Lougheed government was in some early electoral trouble, it would have been more appropriate to concentrate on some urban ridings. In fact, it is most likely that Grant really did not believe that any substantial erosion had begun. In his report to the Provincial Council in February 1978 in Edmonton he emphasized the fact that the Conservatives had begun to look very "blue," moving away from red Tory policies of the past. He acknowledged that there was a "right wing swing" in Alberta, but dismissed it as a short-lived phenomenon.

But liberal-democratic societies were entering a profoundly right-wing decade led by Margaret Thatcher and Ronald Reagan. Grant had no way of knowing how far-reaching this would be, but it is clear that he sensed that some change had taken place. The conclusion one must come to is that Grant realized that there would be no substantial erosion of the Lougheed government support, and the rural strategy remained as the only viable alternative. This did not keep him from being optimistic however, since the other part of the equation, Social Credit, seemed to have collapsed completely. Anne Dryden remembers that even in private he was still "high" and believed that the breakthrough would finally come the next year.

There were some small danger signals however. As Myron Johnson recalls they had no money for professional polling, so there was no hard evidence about their real position.

In some ways we were fooling ourselves. We had no polling, and we assumed that rural discontent was stronger than it was.

As well, the party continued to have financial problems despite the best efforts of Grant, Ray, Alex McEachern, and the new Director of Organization, Tom Brook. At the beginning of 1978, Alex reported as Treasurer that the party had slid further into debt in 1977, by $30,000, bringing the total to $90,000. Myron Johnson remembers that the financial situation concerned Grant in this period.

In terms of candidates, the party was still dependent on people who had a high internal profile in the NDP, but had few community contacts. Anne Hemmingway, who was now President, was nominated in Smoky River. Tacitly, this was an admission of defeat from the party, since Anne did not live in the riding. No strong local person would come forward. Ray Martin, although Provincial Secretary, was recruited to run Edmonton Norwood, again a tacit admission that the riding probably would not be won. Although Ray had a high profile within the NDP, he was a transplanted Calgarian, who had lived in St. Albert during the previous two years. He recalls that there was a long way to go in Norwood, since he started in 1978 with only 22 members.

Edmonton Strathcona seemed to have some possibility, but it wound up in a close fight for the nomination between Gordon Wright, long-time Executive member, and John McInnis, Executive Assistant to Grant. Grant stayed scrupulously out of the contest, which Gordon won by two votes. Alex McEachern, party Treasurer, was nominated again in Edmonton Kingsway. In all three Edmonton ridings these candidates would do much better, but they would be far off the pace in 1979. Thus, in finances, candidates, and timing, 1979 was not the year that Grant thought it would be.

In his own riding during this period, things went very well. Shortly after the election Grant and Sandy moved to a quarter section overlooking the Peace River Valley at Dunvegan, a site between Rycroft and Fairview. It was a beautiful piece of land, with a side valley, and a gorgeous view of the river and valley. They built a Cape Cod House, complete with shutters and entry way. It was considerably different from the house in Fairview. Anne Hemmingway thought that politically it was a good move. The people in the towns now thought of him as a country squire, and those on the farm thought that he had "come down to their level."

Grant, Sandy, and the three children settled in comfortably in the new house. As he stayed longer in the community, Grant became more at home. Sandy was quite active with the local Anglican church, and by 1978 Grant was also regularly attending. Sandy did not believe that he had changed his mind about organized religion, but he liked to socialize with the congregation after services. His taste in music, which had been quite "vague" earlier, now tended toward classical. But most of all he loved to walk on his property, to be alone with trees, animals, with nature. His own solitary, rural nature drew him back to this kind of communion with rural Alberta.

During this four-year period, Grant took on a new dimension with the membership. Through his constant efforts and obvious ability, he grew in stature in their eyes. Anne Hemmingway thought that he became one of the few top politicians in Canada. He was not only capable, but also sophisticated in everything from his speaking style to his public presence. Graham Thomlinson remembers it as a good time, as one where things went smoothly. They all agreed that his win in 1975 took the "steam" out of the Conservatives. The NDP was ready for the 1979 election, probably as ready as they would ever be.

While things almost always went smoothly for the Lougheed Conservatives, Spirit River was a thorn for them. In the Legislature Grant was someone they would rather not have there. Unlike the period before 1975, Tory members in the House were less tolerant of Grant, attacking him often. Some members, like Mr. Batiuk from Vegreville, made a point of trying to harass Grant whenever possible. "Notley baiting" was certainly approved of after 1975. In the riding there was an equal animosity, and a determination to defeat him. One of the ways of doing this was to withhold certain government services, like road repairs, to reinforce the government argument that the constituency would fare much better if it had a government member to pressure from the government caucus. In the run-up to the 1979 election the local Conservatives decided to emphasize this during the visit of Premier Lougheed. He was in the Peace River country, and came to Fairview by helicopter. The day did not start off well. The Premier's helicopter was forced to make an emergency landing in a field which was soaked with rain. This meant that the Premier's entourage went by car to Fairview, over terrible muddy roads. When the Premier arrived at the Hall, there were only a hundred people in a hall that could hold seven or eight hundred. To make matters even worse, the first presentation was from local Conservatives, who wanted to reinforce the idea that the roads in the area were in a mess. Grant used to chuckle when he recalled the incident.

> They wanted to make the point about the roads with the television cameras there. The very first presentation is from a good local Tory who gets up . . . with the Premier there, . . . and says Mr. Premier I am in the repair business, and on behalf of all of the businesses in the repair business, I want to thank you and your government because of the roads in this area, which are so bad that we do a land office business. And he presented the Premier with a broken muffler. The Premier was convinced that it was an NDP plot, but it was the local Tories that did it trying to be funny.

Notwithstanding these troubles, the Conservatives were willing to try once again to defeat Grant.

Throughout the whole four-year period the NDP had gotten only indifferent media coverage. In the national media the coming election was already conceded to the Conservatives. The only question was, who would form the Official Opposition. Grant exuded optimism in every interview. In the *Globe and Mail* he was quoted as "the most optimistic he's ever been." The paper talked about the "cocky NDP."[13] The *Financial Post* conceded that it looked as if the NDP would form the Opposition.[14] But some of the local media were not as kind as the national media. Indeed, in some cases there was outright bias. In his book on Peter Lougheed, Allan Hustak quoted Doug Shepherd, a former CFRN (Edmonton) news reporter, as saying that coverage of Grant was downgraded.

> Shepherd claims he even received a memo from his boss, Bruce Hogle, stating that Grant Notley, the NDP leader, was not to be given exposure on CFRN's highly rated 6:00 p.m. Eyewitness New Show.[15]

Another former reporter, Geoff Davy confirmed the existence of media bias, saying, "It was an unwritten law that Notley would be downplayed . . . ."[16] It was still a difficult task for Grant to muster favourable reaction from the owners of media outlets.

Nevertheless, when the election was called in February of 1979, the NDP was ready. Once again there was a full slate of candidates. The party also had more money than in 1975, and was prepared to put on a full-scale campaign. People like Ross Harvey (now an Edmonton MP), who had done an excellent job as Editor of the Alberta *Democrat* for four years, were pressed into publicity service.

As usual the campaign started well, amid bouyant enthusiasm. Grant was on the road and in the air immediately. This time he was prepared to spend quite a bit more time outside of Spirit River. Grant asked Anne Hopp (formerly Dryden) to travel with him the whole time as a personal assistant, and as a "warm-up" for the crowd. Increasingly he relied on her for personal and political advice in the campaign. She recalls that Grant was very upbeat in the beginning. Despite the new organization and more money, however, they still did everything "on the cheap." Staying at the Notley house on one return trip to the constituency, Grant and Anne were about ready to go to a meeting, Grant was on the phone, but when he crossed his legs, suddenly he split the crotch in his pants.

> Sandy was gone . . . . The guy is coming any minute. So I tell him, take off your pants. And of course I always carry a sewing kit with me, and shoelaces, etc. So out of his pants he comes, and he's sitting there in his shorts, and I'm sewing up his pants. The guy comes up

outside and toots the horn, so Grant had to jump into his pants and get his coat on and out the door we go on yet another meeting.

Although the NDP had changed, and the approach was more sophisticated, some things about Grant's wardrobe seemed fixed in time. However, it should be reported that during this period one member of the media conceded that Grant "had raised the Woolco look to new heights of perfection."

The campaign was not without its scarey moments. At one time, on the highway near Edson, Grant's car slid off of the road in a snowstorm. Another time during the campaign the pilot of his plane had to abort a landing when a snowplow suddenly appeared on the runway. It was just one of several close calls Grant had before 1984.

The NDP concentrated its campaign on two major issues. The first was the use of the Heritage Trust Fund, which Grant had so successfully criticized after 1976. The NDP proposed a new set of priorities for the fund, including agricultural diversification, research, and public ownership. As well, he proposed a new, open style of management, consistent with his remarks in the Legislature. The second area of concentration surrounded the dispossessed and powerless in Alberta society, the groups that Grant had tried hard to gather support from during the previous four years. For them the NDP made a series of proposals in housing, agriculture, and social services. The campaign platform seemed to be well received and the campaign itself was in high gear.

By mid campaign, however, it became obvious that the early expectations were not going to be fulfilled. As Myron Johnson recalled, crowds in the key ridings were thinner than expected in weeks three and four, especially in ridings like Red Water-Andrew and Drayton Valley. Grant became very pessimistic and downgraded his predictions to just two seats, his and St. Paul. Myron, who by this time thought Grant was being more than his normal pessimistic self, chided him for being negative.

Articles written for the newspapers in the final days of the campaign were quite positive for Grant and the party. Most of them portrayed Social Credit as a fading party, and the Liberals as in even worse shape. The *Financial Post* declared that the NDP "had a good chance of wresting the official Opposition title from the Social Credit Party."[17] Other observers were a bit more circumspect, but thought that the NDP had a good chance.

For their part the Conservatives ran a vigorous, high profile campaign, with promises that totalled over three billion dollars. Peter Lougheed was taking no chances that his party might crumble even a little. The unofficial slogan was "79 in 79" the same as Social Credit's "63 in 63," sixteen years previous.

On election night, it was a triumph for the Conservatives. They took 74 of 79 seats. But most importantly for Grant, Social Credit retained its four seats, and Grant alone was elected for the NDP. Although his own personal margin was 990, ten times as high as in 1975, it was, as Ray Martin put it, "fairly devastating for us." Not only was the NDP not the Official Opposition, it had failed to gain any seats, although coming close in some. After eight brilliant years in the Legislature it seemed to Grant that he was no closer to making a breakthrough than he had been in 1971.

In retrospect, it is obvious that he had expected too much. There was virtually no fundamental discontent with the government, nor with the representation in the Legislature. Albertans were generally satisfied. Where Opposition members had established good reputations, as with Grant and Bob Clark, they were re-elected. But there was no swing to elect any new people outside the government caucus. There simply was no political momentum for anyone.

Personally, Grant was crushed. For the first time in his career he had to face the prospect that his calculations might be wrong, the strategies incorrect. He had to face the possibility that there might never be a breakthrough.

8 THE LEADER OF THE OFFICIAL OPPOSITION

IT IS DIFFICULT NOW to accurately assess the impact of the 1979 election on Grant. From comments by Ray Martin and others we know that it was substantial. He was quoted in *Macleans* as saying:

I feel like the little boy who fell and stubbed his toe. I'm too old to cry . . . but it hurts too much to laugh.[1]

The magazine article also talked about the shattering of a dream for the NDP. Myron Johnson says that Grant was extremely disappointed. He had expected much more, and even in his most pessimistic moments did not think that he would come back alone. In private interviews Grant said little about the 1979 election, which to those familiar with Grant reinforces Myron's conclusion. But if he was disappointed he bounced back quickly. Although the big breakthrough had not come, he had won his own constituency by the largest margin ever, and provincially the party had some strong second place finishers, especially in Edmonton. As Ray Martin said, planning for the next election began almost immediately.

In what was almost a four-year ritual, wholesale changes in staff took place. Ray Martin wanted to go back to teaching, and left as Provincial Secretary right after the federal election. The Director of Organization, Tom Brook, was appointed Provincial Secretary. Other people were also changed in the party office. At the Legislature, Myron Johnson and John McInnis both left, John going to the BC NDP as Director of Research. Ross Harvey, who had been Editor of the *Democrat,* was placed on staff

199

with Grant in research and communications. For those who knew Ross as an "unorthodox" person, it seemed like an unlikely appointment, but Ross did an excellent job for Grant and was one of his most trusted people. Grant's chief assistant was a bright young man named Peter Puxley, a Rhodes Scholar, who had come to Grant via some work with native organizations. He was an excellent addition, and together with Henry Mandelbaum made up the heart of Grant's staff. Peter later went on to work with Peter Gzowski at CBC and Ross Harvey was elected to the House of Commons in 1988.

Among Grant's colleagues, there was also a changing of the guard. Ray Martin continued to be Grant's chief political ally. However, Grant continued to develop other contacts as he had always done, especially among younger New Democrats. One of these was Davis Swan from Calgary, a geophysicist who worked in the oil industry. He and Grant became very close for the next four years. Davis had both the time and the inclination for politics, something that Grant always appreciated. It took Grant only a short time to lure Davis onto the provincial Executive as a Vice-President, and into a major role as a policy person in the area of energy, oil, natural gas and the constitution. Like Steven Galen and the Engs before him, Davis became one of the Calgary crowd with whom Grant stayed when he was there on party business. Another person Grant worked closely with after 1980 was Tom Sigurdson, who came from BC to organize for the Alberta party in 1980. Tom was assigned to the Peace River country, and came to know Grant as well as anyone during this period. Like Tom McLeod before him, Tom Sigurdson was thrown into the job of winning another election. Together with others they all formed another "Notley's Crew" in 1979/80.

While Grant remained the heart of the party, his own heart was increasingly in the Legislature, and not in the details of party work. He spent less and less time on administrative detail, and more on policy issues in the House. He wanted to depend on Ray Martin to pilot the party itself. The problem was that Ray had stepped down as Secretary, and had no official position. Grant sought to rectify this by electing Ray as President of the Alberta NDP. The problem was that a staunch supporter of his, Anne Hemmingway from his own riding, had been President for two years. In typical Notley fashion he decided that a change was needed, and proceeded to engineer it in a way that would most benefit the party.

There are several versions of the great presidential race in October, 1979, which pitted Anne Hemmingway against Ray Martin and Alex

McEachern. Ray Martin recalls that Grant asked him point-blank to run against Anne at the convention. Ray refused at first, because he really was not interested. Later, after much pressure from Grant, he acceded, but only if he would not be in a two way race with Anne. Alex McEachern was also encouraged by Grant to run, but at the time he was not told that he was providing the third candidacy, which would allow Ray to run. Later, when Alex discovered the manoeuvre, he was quite disappointed and hurt. Anne Hemmingway contends that she actually started the chain of events. In her version she told Grant that she had a basic conflict with the new Provincial Secretary Tom Brook, and did not believe that she could work effectively with him. However, she did not want to face the questions that would come from a resignation and urged Grant to convince Ray to run against her, without telling Ray. Grant, therefore, became pivotal to the race, and succeeded in the task of getting all three to run, something that he thought was good for the party in any case. Ray Martin won the presidency rather handily.

By 1980 all of the key personnel for the next three years were in place. However, unlike the previous four-year period, only two issues were to really dominate the political agenda. The first was national unity and the constitution, and the second was round two of the energy dispute between Edmonton and Ottawa. It was the latter dispute more than anything which solidified in the public mind the image of a single man, Grant Notley, standing alone in the Legislature against the Lougheed government, a classic David and Goliath.

The Alberta-Ottawa energy dispute, which had begun with the export tax on oil in 1973, had simmered between 1975 and 1980. Occasionally it had flared on minor fronts, at constitutional conferences, or in some of the other producing provinces, most notably Saskatchewan. At the heart of the dispute was control of the energy industry and the enormous revenues flowing from it. With prices predicted to reach astronomical levels in the 1980s, perhaps as high as $80 per barrel, the revenues involved seemed staggering. At that time most oil in western Canada was being produced for less than $5 per barrel, leaving enormous profits for someone. Ottawa had moved during the mid-1970s to control the price of oil and to take some of the revenue. This policy was motivated by a desire to keep down consumer prices and to give central Canadian manufacturing interests an international competitive advantage through low energy prices. The producing provinces of Saskatchewan, Alberta, and BC had responded by claiming complete jurisdiction over natural resources and consequently the right to the revenues generated from the industry. The British North America Act gave them ownership of resources, but important powers over taxation and interprovincial and international trade were within federal jurisdiction. The result of the initial conflict was a temporary agreement in 1974/75, which in reality was only a truce. The issue of jurisdiction was hotly discussed at the constitutional conferences of 1978 and 1979.

For Grant and the Alberta NDP it was a problematic issue. Complicating matters was the fact that the industry was almost completely privately owned, and foreign dominated, making Lougheed's strong provincial rights position anathema, since it perpetuated these two undesirable conditions. There was close agreement with the federal NDP on a major role for Petro-Canada, lower prices to consumers, and more Canadian control over the industry. However, there was also a persistent streak of alienation, pragmatism, and good sense in the Alberta party, which led it to agree with the obvious argument that no other industry was treated like the oil industry in Canada, that Alberta and the West had always been the poor cousins of Confederation, and that the windfall profits from the industry ought to go to the people of Alberta. It was a conundrum which pitted Grant against the federal NDP, the federal government, and Lougheed government—all in all, an unenviable position to be in.

As a result the Alberta party tended to support the Saskatchewan NDP government which took a middle ground between Lougheed and the federal government, albeit a middle ground heavily slanted toward provincial rights. It was a position which infuriated David Lewis, and later Ed Broadbent, who had little sympathy for, and less understanding of, the role of Western NDP sections. The view of the federal NDP leadership was dominated by a lifetime of politics that dictated strong central government, national public ownership, and the reduction of provincial government influence. The latter they defined as anti-civil rights, anti-Canadian, and parochial. It was a view which relegated the provincial sections in the regions, and especially in Quebec, to the role of minor players, although in the latter stages of his leadership Ed Broadbent worked hard to establish a viable section in Quebec. The exceptions were BC, Saskatchewan, and Manitoba, where provincial parties had flourished for other reasons. It led to some bitter internal fights at key NDP national councils and conventions in the 1970s, fights in which Alberta tended to agree with the larger and more influential Saskatchewan section.

In the Legislature Grant made energy his key area of attack. He usually hit hard on issues relating to profits and control of the industry. Often he clashed with both Peter Lougheed and the Speaker of the House, Gerald Amerongen, as he attacked the Lougheed government.

Mr. Notley: Mr. Speaker, on a point of order first, if your ruling is that when members of the Legislature ask questions they are not to provoke debate, the same must also apply to the answers. For the last half hour we've seen one answer after another designed to provoke debate.

Mr. Speaker: Order please, I must draw the Hon. member's attention to the fact that very many of the questions asked today have provided ample provocation for debate. The Hon. member may recall that his last question started out, "in view of the record profits of the oil companies," and went on from there.

Mr. Notley: Mr. Speaker, I have absolutely no concern about making those questions if we have it on both sides. If it's all open on both sides, that fair enough with me.

Mr. Speaker: It's been on both sides. It's a very simple matter. The rules of the question period are quite clear. If we're going to have no further debate in questions, then of course there shouldn't be any further debate in answers.[2]

But Grant was equally as scathing on some federal government actions, and in defense of provincial interests.

Mr. Notley: I welcome the opportunity to participate in the debate this afternoon, Mr. Speaker. As I look at the resolution, I certainly agree that the force majeure clause was unilaterally and arbitrarily enacted by the federal government. I believe this government has made some very serious errors in its negotiation of future energy prices in Canada. But in my judgement, that does not in any way justify the action of the federal minister a few days ago in unilaterally indicating that the federal government was going to impose this particular provision of the 1975 and 1976 agreements.

Mr. Speaker, this is particularly unfortunate, coming as it does from Mr. Lalonde. I think many people hoped, when he assumed the office of federal Minister of Energy, Mines and Resources, that he would bring to the particular duty a degree of statesmanship which is obviously going to be required if Canada is to reach a new energy pricing package. But unfortunately, there is clearly no question that the minister's announcement the other day was pure and simply provocation. What is even more regrettable is that while that kind of action is not directly associated with the equally unilateral decision of the Minister of Transport to renege on the previous government's position with respect to the infrastructure costs at Prince Rupert, the two taken in total can only lead to increased bitterness among people in western Canada at this time. I find that very difficult to understand, because I know the present leaders of the federal government are concerned about preserving Canadian national unity, and to react in two very significant ways that strike at the heart of western Canadian development one in the grain industry and the other in the question of the force majeure clause in my view is really playing with fire.[3]

As you might expect, Grant found himself in a difficult "middle" position. The second energy crisis which began in 1980 was really the result of two federal elections which took Pierre Trudeau out of power, and then brought him back less than a year later. The election of the Levesque government in Quebec in 1976 tended to concentrate the federal Liberals' attention on that province. All other decisions about Canada and Canadian federalism were viewed through the prism of Quebec nationalism. This was particularly true of western Canadian provincial governments which were viewed by the Trudeau cabinet as motivated by crass commercial interests, rather than high principle. In the Liberal view of the world, Quebec nationalists at least had principle and a cause. By contrast western premiers were viewed as largely unprincipled and avaricious, with little concern for the impact of their actions on the fabric of Canada. This, it was thought, was particularly true of Peter Lougheed although they also believed that Allan Blakeney of Saskatchewan acted in a parochial manner often enough to be the target of federal government legal action.

In 1978, however, the Trudeau Liberals found themselves in trouble with the electorate and even Trudeau's reputation as a bulwark against Quebec nationalism was not able to save the Liberals. When the First Ministers failed to agree on the constitution in February of 1979, Trudeau went to the electorate in the Spring. He was defeated, and the Clark Conservatives took over with a minority government. However, this short lived regime suffered from over confidence and an inability to count during the month of December, and was defeated in the House on a budgetary motion in December 1979.

Previous to this, in November, Trudeau had announced his retirement, but as a result of the quick vote in the House, he was persuaded to come back and lead the party one more time. The result was a Liberal majority in the February election. Unfortunately, like the Bourbons of royal France, the Prime Minister had neither learned anything during his sabbatical, nor forgotten anything. Indeed, his position regarding the dangers of provincial power and separatism had hardened. His government entered into a three pronged strategy, the elements of which were defeat of the PQ in the Spring referendum in Quebec, patriation of the Canadian constitution with or without the approval of the provinces, and a new National Energy Programme to ensure federal control in this vital area. The unabashed objective of the strategy was to tilt the balance of power decisively in favour of the federal government forever.

The first objective was achieved in the Spring of 1980. Levesque was defeated and humiliated. The second objective was implemented through the summer of 1980, and when no agreement on the constitution was forthcoming at the First Ministers' conference in September of 1980, unilateral patriation was announced in early October. The third objective, the National Energy Policy, was announced October 26, 1980.

Prior to the beginning of a year long confrontation, Grant had staked out his political ground clearly. Although he had always taken the "middle ground" between Edmonton and Ottawa, he had never attacked Lougheed directly for "separatist views." The focus of his attack had always been class based, concentrating on the fact that Peter Lougheed was the handmaiden of a foreign dominated oil industry. This strategy changed in the Fall of 1980. Grant became very concerned that the PC government in Edmonton was playing with fire by fuelling the alienation which already existed in Alberta. Worse, Lougheed seemed to be doing it for foreign controlled oil interests that had little loyalty to the province. The result, in Grant's opinion would be irreparable damage to the fabric of Canada and Alberta.

Ironically, Grant's response can be traced to his analysis of the role of Social Credit in the history of Alberta. He firmly believed that Aberhart and Manning had entrenched the politics of alienation and hate in

Alberta. Prior to 1935, in his analysis, there had been a participatory system, one in which both government and opposition had a legitimate position. After 1935, however, politics and elections became plebiscites and the fabric of the political system slowly became plebiscitarian, resulting in a one-party state. This led, he reasoned, to an unthinking electorate which did not debate issues, leaving them to the "experts" who were, of course, in the government. In this kind of polity the opposition became mere "politicians," self-seeking and self-aggrandizing while the government worked selflessly in the public interest. In Grant's opinion, Peter Lougheed had inherited this tradition and perfected it, making him even more dangerous than Social Credit had been. For Grant the fight was not only for Canada but also for Alberta, a more participatory Alberta in which the legislature could become the centre for debate and ideas rather than a rubber stamp for a one-party dictatorship. The fight was for an Alberta that would diversify and grow socially and politically as well as economically. He wanted to remove forever the Social Credit legacy which had prevented Albertans from being mainstream and Canadian.

This meant that when Peter Lougheed announced oil cutbacks to the rest of Canada on October 30, 1980, as a result of the federal budget, Grant was caught squarely between the two sides. He attacked the Alberta government's decision to cut oil supplies, and to postpone heavy oil plants in northern Alberta as "punishing each and every individual Canadian from coast to coast," and as disastrous for Albertans who would suffer in conjunction with their fellow Canadians. He was aided in this position by the Government of Saskatchewan which also opposed the federal energy programme. However, he was hampered by the federal NDP, led by Ed Broadbent, which supported Trudeau on both the energy programme and unilateral patriation of the constitution.

In the Legislature in November, 1980 the government forced a vote on its cutback programme. Grant remembers that time very well:

When it came to the resolution in the Legislature in the fall of 1980 to cut back [oil production] as a consequence of the national energy programme, I voted against it. I took the view that it was just not acceptable to use economic warfare, to make Canadians the hostages in a form of economic warfare with the federal government.

It was one of the most difficult times I've had in the Legislature. Seldom have I gotten so much in the way of hate mail. I don't think I've ever gotten such a sustained barrage of hate mail and phone calls.

We had some people resign [from the party] on both things, the cutbacks and the whole constitution business where we lost a lot of support.

We had to do it. It was the right thing to do. I don't regret it in any respect. [The Government members] were quite vicious: "Are you an Albertan or not?" [they said].

It was quite an experience. It was probably the toughest time I'd had in the Legislature, during that period of time. [But], it goes with the turf sometimes. It would have been nice to have some colleagues to stand with.

About the only small support that Grant received was from party members. Tommy Douglas wrote him immediately after the vote:

This is a note to tell you how proud I was when I heard . . . that you were the only member of the Alberta Legislature to vote in opposition to Lougheed's cutback in oil production. I know that you were under terrific pressure to succumb . . . .

What makes it tough is the fact that we both understand why people are resentful of Central Canada . . . .

Keep up the good work and be of good cheer. No man can ever be defeated ultimately by fighting for the things in which he devoutly believes.[4]

Because he believed that Lougheed was fuelling the fires of separatism, and to take some of the pressure off of himself, Grant introduced a motion declaring separatism "is not an option that will be considered for Alberta by this Assembly." The Lougheed government had some of the backbenchers "talk it out" when it was debated on November 27, 1980. The Edmonton *Journal* criticized the government for this action. They concluded that there was "no excuse for Mr. Lougheed not entering the debate, that by doing so he arrogantly abuses that [public] support by placing himself above the Opposition and beyond legislative debate." At the time Lougheed was unwilling to foreclose any options, and used the western separatists to increase pressure on Ottawa.

In support of his own position Grant went on a gruelling two week tour of Alberta, dubbed the "pro-Canada" tour. In so doing he solidified his position as the only reasonable voice for federalism in Alberta.

The battle continued into the new year, when in the Olds-Disbury riding, Gordon Kessler, an oil scout, was elected for the Western Canada Concept Party, a quasi-separatist party. It was ironic that Grant's birth place became the home of the first and ultimately the only avowed separatist elected to the House.

Coupled with the oil issue was the Trudeau initiative to unilaterally patriate the constitution. Like Blakeney in Saskatchewan, Grant was initially inclined to support Broadbent, but as the details emerged he too became quite concerned about the NDP position. Grant had been a constant critic of Lougheed's confrontationist approach to bargaining on the constitution. After the defeat of the PQ referendum in May of 1980, Grant disagreed with both Lougheed and Blakeney on the question of language rights and a Charter of Rights, calling for more flexibility and compromise on the issue.

When unilateral action was announced in October, Grant was caught between the federal NDP and Lougheed again. For three months the Alberta party worked on a new position, developing a policy. In early December they agreed on an approach which leaned heavily on the concept of economic and social democracy, something which was probably out of tune with Alberta at the time, but allowed the NDP to develop a distinct position. By early 1981, the split between the federal NDP and Saskatchewan had widened considerably. In a secret meeting in Calgary attended by Ed Broadbent, Grant Notley, Howard Pawley and Allan Blakeney, the leaders tried to patch together a compromise.

At a meeting prior to Broadbent's arrival, Howard Pawley, Allan Blakeney and Grant sorted out a position to put to Ed Broadbent. They wanted the federal NDP to agree to something which would reunite the party. They agreed to urge Ed Broadbent to pressure Trudeau to call one more federal-provincial conference to discuss the resolution before the House of Commons.

The next day the proposal was put to Broadbent by Grant. Broadbent called it "laughable," saying several times that the federal NDP would be "laughed at" if they proposed it. He was very hard line, saying that the federal NDP was committed publicly and would support passage of the resolution even if the Supreme Court had not ruled on the issue. Most unsettling for Grant and Allan Blakeney, the federal Leader seemed convinced that Trudeau had gone "the extra mile" with Blakeney and the West, something which neither of them accepted.

Despite Broadbent's sense of fairplay and passion for social justice, he could be infuriatingly inflexible at times. At this meeting he was at his pugnacious worst. Grant left the meeting depressed and worried.

As a result of the failure, the Alberta NDP adopted a policy which declined to support the resolution before the House of Commons. It was in direct opposition to the federal NDP position, a tough decision for Grant and the Alberta party given their generally fearless position on most other issues. As might be expected, the resolution also condemned the Conservative government of Alberta for the "obstructive, negative, and ultimately self-defeating nature of the Lougheed government's participation in the constitutional process."

When these two issues were finally resolved in the Fall of 1981, it removed from the political agenda of Alberta two matters which were extremely divisive and problematic for Grant. It is probably true, however, that November 1980 was the pinnacle of his legislative career. If one measures leadership and personal commitment to principle by the difficulty involved for the person taking the stand, Grant surely passed the test with more than flying colours. All of the questions about his commitment, lack of policy sense, and self-admitted pragmatism, were answered in the Legislature by the single act of standing alone to oppose the oil cuts to the rest of Canada. It was indeed his finest hour.

With the two problems of energy and the constitution temporarily out of the way, but only temporarily because with the Alberta government there would always be the issue of alienation, Grant and the party began to concentrate on the next election. They all expected it early since the federal-provincial fight was over.

The loss of the Blakeney government in Saskatchewan in April of 1982 was a great shock to Grant. It was totally unexpected and raised fundamental questions about the role of the NDP in Western Canada. Grant had concentrated most of his attention on the Legislature and on policy issues, but as both Davis Swan and Tom Sigurdson recall, after the Blakeney loss he became quite concerned about the state of readiness for a coming Alberta election. Financially the party was carrying a large debt and organizers like Tom Sigurdson had to be laid off in the summer of 1982, only months before the election. As Sigurdson said, "NDP cheques were bouncing all over." In particular Tom was concerned both with provincial organization and with the state of readiness in Spirit River-Fairview. He felt there was far too much complacency, illustrated most importantly the previous Fall when it had been difficult to get people out for a picnic to celebrate Grant's tenth anniversary in the Legislature. Publically the party exuded confidence. With Social Credit almost irrelevant, and the Liberals destroyed by confrontations on constitution and energy, it seemed that the electorate had little other choice than to opt for the NDP if it wanted to vote against Lougheed.

The 1982 election campaign began well enough, although Tom Sigurdson thought that the party was not well organized on the ground. Anne Hopp (previously Anne Dryden), recalled that there was much more money for the campaign. There was a chartered plane with paid seats for the media and a recreational vehicle for closer activities. There were rules for those who went along, good accessbility for the media, and even an attempt at a clandestine taping by one of the radio reporters. The result was excellent coverage and considerably more media exposure. It was a far cry from 1971 or 1975.

Davis Swan recalled that Grant had tempered his own optimism as a result of 1979. At the beginning he hoped for six to eight seats, but Grant respected the power of Peter Lougheed in an election campaign, telling Davis that he worried that nothing could really be done while Lougheed remained as leader. Times were still good, although the recession was beginning, and the people were willing to forgive the Premier for much. In a way, elections had become ritualized and predictable, with Lougheed playing the benign Goliath, and Grant the lonely, strong David. Indeed, for either of them to have changed positon at this time would have shocked most Albertans, and maybe even Grant.

One other part of the electoral equation looked very promising for the NDP. The Social Credit party, which had for eleven years died a long, slow agonizing death, ceased to be a party in 1982. Its demise, and the retirement of Bob Clark its leader, left the last two MLAs to run as independents. The Liberal Party, still led by Nick Taylor, had been unable to shed its attachment to Ottawa leaving it in a hopeless position as well. Only the Western Canada Concept party, with its sole MLA Gordon Kessler, elected in a by-election in 1981, seemed to be attracting support. However, most of this support appeared to be coming from Tory voters, not the opposition. In Grant's estimation, the WCC was a bonus for the NDP, likely to provide some good splits that might elect people much as Grant had been elected in 1971.

Judged by this, it ought to have been the best campaign of all for Grant. Unfortunately, his own length of tenure began to work against him. Just before the campaign the Edmonton *Journal* ran a story which indicated some New Democrats questioned Grant's ability to lead the NDP. The article mentioned Winston Gereluk, a former political science student at the University of Alberta, party activist, and employee of the Alberta Union of Public Employees. There was an indication that some other high profile New Democrats, including the candidate in St. Paul agreed. It caused a minor sensation in the press and within the NDP.

Two things were curious about the story. First, the timing could not have been worse. It was calculated to do maximum damage, which it probably did. Second, there had been no hint at conventions or within the party that such a sentiment existed. All indications were that Grant was firmly in control of the party. Nevertheless, it shocked and angered Grant, although it died as an issue rather quickly. According to Davis Swan and others, there was not even minimal support for the position. He attributed it to the "mischievousness" of Winston Gereluk. Ray Martin agrees, declining to comment publicly on who might have been involved with the group.

It was an ominous sign however, made even more important because the issue of Grant's length of tenure found some resonance in his own constituency of Spirit River-Fairview. For the first time, organizers were finding it hard to recruit people to work. In the west of the constituency the WCC seemed to be attracting voters. The NDP organization had a dangerous air of complacency about it, partly as a result of the large 1979 win.

On the day the writ was dropped, very little was ready in Spirit River-Fairview. The office was not open, there were no telephones, and no pamphlet was ready. Tom Sigurdson, charged initially with running the campaign, was depressed.

> We couldn't get workers. It was tough getting workers. A lot of people just felt that nothing was going to change. How could anybody not vote for Grant Notley? You know, he's done a wonderful job. But, I've got to get the crop off . . . . There were a lot of farmers out there trying to get the crop off . . . before the last snow. But, the first part of the campaign was very, very difficult to get workers.

As well, there were organizational difficulties. Although some of the "old standby's" like Ted Chudyk were there, it was not clear who was in charge. At first Sigurdson thought he, not Chudyk, was in charge, but he was soon supplanted by a BC organizer. On the south side of the constituency the original organizers had to leave, and two relatively in-experienced people were put in charge. At E-20 (twenty days before election day) Tom Sigurdson confided to his fiancee that he felt the election was lost.

Grant was very concerned by the end of the first week. Anne Hopp watched him become increasingly worried. He had trouble sleeping, and finally took some medication. He thought that everything was falling apart in his own riding, that too many local people were not working. Their hearts were not in it. As a result, he did two things. First, he had a long and "loud" conversation with Tom Sigurdson. He told Tom that campaign was not going as it should. He was feeling exhausted, and even a little betrayed, not only in Fairview, but also in the rest of the province. He felt the weight of the party on him. He "told" Tom that much more needed to be done, and that meant that Tom had to do it. For the first time he confided to Tom that he was worried about losing.

The second thing that he did was to call me in Saskatchewan, and ask me to come to his riding for two days to give him an realistic assessment of what the situation really was. As a result I went up to Spirit River, where he asked me to review the canvass results for the south half of the riding. Two young, inexperienced organizers were in charge of that portion. After only a few hours it became apparent to me that there was little hard evidence about the real state of affairs, and that a lot of work needed to be done. Two days later when I communicated this to Grant he asked me to stay on and take charge in the south, which I did, staying until two days before election day. It was typical of Grant, that he would reach into the past and resurrect a member of a previous generation of "Notley's Crew" to come to his rescue, and even more typical that we would respond.

In contrast the rest of the campaign went well after the Gereluk story. The Leader's tour was smooth, the various constituencies seemed to be well organized, and there was optimism in the key or target ridings. Despite this Grant remained pessimistic about any breakthrough. Perhaps because of so many past defeats he was unwilling to allow himself to get too optimistic. Alex McEachern, who was running again in Kingsway, met Grant just five days before the election as he swung through Edmonton. By this time Peter Lougheed had begun to put his election campaign in high gear. He was on television throughout the province every night, pleading for a large renewed mandate to secure Alberta's future against any incursion from Ottawa. It was by now the tried and true Tory approach, which Alex thought had a profound effect.

You could just feel it at the door. I did a lot of door knocking, you could just feel people backing away. I remember Grant came into my riding with about five days to go. I said how's it going, because I was pretty upbeat even at that stage even though I was getting a little backing away.

Grant just said "disaster" He knew already that it was a disaster. I said "Really, I could win this seat." And he kind of [chuckled], "Nice try, Alex, but no cigar." I came within 415 votes.

So Grant knew in the last week of the campaign that we weren't going to get our beachhead.

In fact, Lougheed's intervention was decisive. The electoral script in Alberta was about to follow the "normal" routine. At this point what was still unclear was whether or not some familiar faces would be back, particularly from Spirit River-Fairview.

By election day Grant was convinced that he had lost his own riding. He expected it to be close, but he expected defeat. In preparation he refused to go down to the school where the party was to take place. He stayed in the office. He wanted time to compose himself for the loss.

On election night Tom Sigurdson was designated to handle the press at the "victory" headquarters. It was felt that Tom had the best chance to "bring Grant down" if the loss occurred. The first polls were not good. The WCC was taking votes in the west, but mainly from the Conservatives. With three polls to report, Grant was still behind by 50 votes, but the polls that were left were traditionally strong for Grant. However, several formerly strong polls had already proven weak. CBC was projecting a Notley loss. Tom Sigurdson was forced to give a live interview with them at this point.

I was standing there, and the tears started to well up in my eyes. I could feel them. I didn't know why they would have said that. Then I heard the crowd behind me roar, and Harry [the CBC reporter] said, "Well it looks like Grant is going down to defeat." I said, "well, I don't know where you got your results from, but it's wrong, and by the end of tonight your going to know its wrong, because we're going to win."

When Grant showed up he was in good spirits. He had won by 193 votes. In Norwood, Ray Martin had won by just 75 votes. More importantly, only two other opposition members in the province, both former

Socreds running as independents, had won. It was an incredible victory for Lougheed, all the more impressive because it was unexpected. For Grant the extra seat in Norwood was good news, but it was tempered by the large Tory win and by his own narrow escape in Spirit River-Fairview.

From the vantage point of several years (and two elections) later, it is now apparent that this election presaged several important changes. The first was that it was the last election for Peter Lougheed, and the last in which the PCs would completely dominate the electoral scene in the province. The history of Alberta politics, the tradition of one party government which Peter Lougheed had inherited from Social Credit, would not outlive his leadership. It was a tradition rooted in the plebisciterian politics of Social Credit after 1935 and the alienation of Albertans from the rest of Canada. The latter attitude, a profound alienation from ''the east,'' continued and grew under the Lougheed regime, fed in a robust self-confidence by petro-dollars and fuelled by the cockiness that often results when people are newly empowered or enriched. Albertans were the *nouveau riche* of Canada and were determined to let the rest of Canada know it. The economic recession of 1982 shattered that juvenile self-confidence, and caused Albertans to look inward, to begin to ask questions about how their new wealth was being distributed, who benefitted, and by how much. The politics of class began to assert itself, as bankruptcies became commonplace, and debts ballooned.

Understandably, these division surfaced first in Edmonton. Edmonton had less of the macho oil complex to shed than Calgary, as well as more ethnic diversity. It also had a history of electing left wing mayors and councillors. It had less fear of the politics of scarcity. In ridings like Edmonton Strathcona, Kingsway, Beverly, and Calder, all inner city ridings, Tory wins were very narrow, signalling that future electoral behaviour would be rooted less in historical attitudes and more in attitudes familiar to other developed countries. Politically, Alberta emerged into the twentieth century in 1982. The have-nots of Alberta were no longer content to sell their vote for a bowl of future dreams, and this meant the end of one-party dominance in the province.

The second lesson was more personal and disturbing for Grant. His whole political strategy had been predicated on trying to win in a few ridings where the NDP had shown some strength, to try and form the Official Opposition and then expand to become the Government. In large part these ridings were rural, where discontent was high and people were not sharing in the huge oil wealth; where the CCF/NDP had shown an ability to get votes in the past. It was this strategy, the trademark of the Notley years, which had again failed. More importantly, it was apparent that the NDP was losing strength in the rural ridings, including Grant's, while gaining in urban ridings in Edmonton. The Reimers and Baskens of the world seemed now to be vindicated in their predictions (albeit fifteen years later), while Grant's strategy was now openly in question.

In fact, it is likely that the rise of the NDP in Edmonton would not have started any earlier than it did, regardless of how the NDP might have concentrated its resources. The social changes which underpinned such a change had not yet occurred in the 1970s. But by 1982 it was also clear that Grant's strategy, indeed Grant's dream of a progressive coalition which spanned urban and rural Alberta, was unlikely to come about. This was the bitter lesson of the 1982 election for Grant. Not that he had almost lost. Not that he was rejected by over half of the electorate in Spirit River-Fairview, despite providing the most conscientious and complete service of any MLA in the province. Not even that some in the NDP like Neil Reimer might gain some advantage over him in the party. Rather, it was the realization that his own vision of the party, and of the people of Alberta, a vision of unity between urban and rural people, fuelled by a realization of their own powerlessness and sacrifice, was not going to be attained. At the very time that Alberta politics was set to turn again, it would not turn in the direction that Grant had anticipated.

In many ways the 1982 election shattered Grant's drive and self-confidence. The election of Ray Martin meant that the NDP would likely do better in the future, but it was a narrow win, and could easily be erased in the next election. Ray's win was also more than balanced by the fact that Lougheed's grip on the electorate seemed unbreakable, and by the fact that Grant's seat was very much in question. At just 44% of the popular vote, the lowest since 1971, only 1093 votes for the WCC candidate had saved him.

Although Grant did not speak openly about the results, much can be inferred from his own changed behaviour after 1982. Close friends like Mike Cooper, Anne Hopp, Davis Swan, and others, all commented on his more relaxed attitude. He was less intense, less driven, betraying the fact that he also had come to some of these same conclusions. Alex McEachern recalled that Grant was very disappointed with the results, putting up a bold front, but knowing that it was an important electoral lesson. For the first time he began to discuss options for his own personal future with a select few. There was no talk of immediate resignation, but there was considerable talk about whether or not to lead the party in one more election. With political associates like Ray Martin and Alex McEachern he was careful to say that he wanted one more election as leader. To say anything else would have been to precipitate a premature leadership contest. But he openly discussed the possibility of running federally with Tom Sigurdson, perhaps after one more provincial election, perhaps before. The options discussed were always political. That is, Grant could not conceive of himself in any other capacity at this point. He had no other career to return to, nothing that really interested him. His chances of working for government elsewhere were quite limited, and other opportunities even more remote. The possibility of his provincial political career ending when he was still a relatively young man was quite disturbing for Grant during this period. But it was a possibility that he had to face, and one which he was well aware of. Many of Grant's friends noticed the change in him. He had always had a love of nature, but now he began to spend more time in the country at farms like Mike Cooper's in the Pincher Creek area. At home there was more time to walk, and to play with the horses. He was much more relaxed at parties and could be enticed into conversations about something other than politics.

But immediate problems faced him in early 1983, however. Superficially, with two MLAs from the only organized party in the legislature, it looked as if Grant and the NDP would become the Official (albeit tiny) Opposition in the province. However, the two independents in the House, both former Socreds, also laid claim to the role and more importantly, the money that went with it. Grant was outraged by this manoeuvre and even angrier when the Speaker of the House, Gerald Amerongen, refused to make a decision about the matter. For the NDP it was obvious. Two independents could not claim to be a party in the House. They had not run in the election as an organized party, and the NDP had secured by far the second largest number of votes in the election. Although the Conservatives had dominated the election, it seemed perfectly clear that the main opposition party was the NDP. However, Ray Speaker and Walter Buck claimed the office on the basis that they were equal in numbers to the NDP and had occupied the position previous to the election. It was March, 1983, at the opening of the Legislature, before Amerongen announced that he would recognize Grant as the Leader of the Official Opposition.

It is difficult to understand why Amerongen waited so long. The two men did not like each other, or at least that was Grant's perception. He was convinced that Peter Lougheed had ordered Amerongen to make the NDP wait, something denied by both the Speaker and the Premier. Whatever the real circumstances, Grant thought it was extremely vicious, and never forgave the Premier for what he considered to be petty harassment.

Grant's relations with Ed Broadbent and the federal party, already strained by the meeting in Calgary in 1981, and the federal convention of that year, were stretched even further by Grant's open participation in the "June 22" movement at the federal convention in Regina in 1983. Ed Broadbent's support of Pierre Trudeau and the federal party's split with Saskatchewan, had left an unhealed breach. The June 22 movement was a group of disgruntled western New Democrats, led by Allan Blakeney and Grant Notley, who wanted to make some changes in the federal party. One of the possibilities discussed was running Grant for the Presidency of the Federal party against the incumbent President. In the end the movement came to nothing, and Grant did not run for a position. However, it did tear open the wounds of 1981 again, and left a gap between Notley and Broadbent.

The rest of 1983 and 1984 were spent in taking the measure of the NDP's new position in the Alberta House, in trying to get the party into shape for the next election. As might be expected, the relationship between Ray Martin and Grant had new hurdles to overcome. The two men were good friends and had worked well together in the past. But things were now changed. Ray had always been aware of the fact that Grant was the Leader and an elected member. Now that they were both elected Ray viewed their relationship as more equal than in the past, as a partnership. Grant, long used to being the only MLA in the House, was unsure of how to treat Ray in their new situation, perceiving himself to be the Leader and not an equal partner with Ray. These natural tensions led to some chafing by both men, but all reports indicated that, like a married couple, they were "working it out."

Of more importance to Grant was his own feeling that he had lost some control and contact over the party. The Gereluk affair during the 1982 campaign indicated to Grant that he needed to reassert himself in party affairs. In order to do so he again reached into the past to pull up one of "Notley's Crew," Bill Dryden, who had been Provincial Secretary from 1971 to 1973. He hired Bill in a position at the Legislature with the intention of having him "clean up" party office, and reassert Grant's presence there. Sandy Notley recalled that Grant was much more relaxed and at ease about party affairs after Bill's return.

The political agenda in Alberta was hectic in 1984, dominated by the federal election. Pierre Trudeau's unseemly departure, and John Turner's pathetic performance led to an enormous Tory victory, one in which all of the federal seats in Alberta went to the national PCs. Intuitively Grant understood that this meant the end of a particular style of politics in Alberta. It meant the end of the ability of the provincial PCs to run effectively against the federal government instead of the local opposition. The glimmer of hope in Edmonton in 1982 might become a ray of light in the next provincial election after the Tories had been in office federally for two years. As a result Grant's own immediate future seemed set. He seemed ready to lead the party in one more election.

The Fall Session of the Legislature opened on October, 1984. On October 18, 1984 Grant spoke to the Assembly on a motion to approve the government's operations since the Spring. He concentrated on a number of subjects, but as usual he also attempted to put everyday concerns into some kind of larger social democratic framework.

> As we reflect upon these observations Mr. Speaker, it seems to me that one has to ask: has the time come on this continent to look at whether we shouldn't restructure the economy so that there is a primacy of people over things.[5]

On Friday October 19, 1984 his first set of questions revolved around compensation for the wrongly convicted. His closing questions were on the status of unemployment action centres in Alberta. During the afternoon Grant attended to some party business, sending Sandy on to Fairview with the car. He had decided to fly to Fairview on the Wapiti Airline evening flight.

Later that evening I arrived at the Airport. I had hoped to meet Grant, since I was flying into Edmonton to visit my family, but my plane was late and I thought that he would be gone. As I walked down the aisle of the lower airport I saw Grant and Bill Dryden coming toward me. It had been some time since we had seen each other and his greeting was quite warm. His flight had been delayed, otherwise we would have missed one another. He had only a few minutes before departure. We talked about all of the usual political matters. He was most interested about the trial of Colin Thatcher, a Saskatchewan Cabinet Minister, for the murder of his wife. It was the kind of political gossip that he thrived on. He wanted to know my plans, and when I indicated that I would be in Edmonton, and had to rent a car, he insisted that I use his government vehicle. He chatted a bit more, until it became obvious that he would miss the flight if he did not board.

Bill and I waved to him as he went through the door.

Less than an hour later, he was killed as the plane crashed near Lesser Slave Lake.

EPILOGUE

THE NEWS OF Grant Notley's death brought a spontaneous outpouring of grief and praise that was unexpected and unprecedented. It was clear from the reaction that he had touched many people in a way that none of us suspected. The reaction was too genuine for it to be ignored.

Why? Why, as we asked at the beginning, did this man forge such a relationship with the people of Alberta? Part of it had to do with the loneliness of his position, the solitary fighter in the legislature, the NDP David against the Tory Goliath. Albertans voted for Peter Lougheed because they liked his strength and his toughness. But they admired Grant Notley for his courage and his dedication to the powerless, the dispossessed. He was their conscience, their social barometer. They could count on him to nag them about what was right or wrong. In a fickle sort of way he was their electoral ombudsman, the institutionalized embodiment of their own social conscience. His loss was a genuine loss for all of them.

Perhaps that is too idealized a conclusion. But how else does one explain the depth of feeling that was so evident upon his death? Even amongst his political enemies he incurred no jealousy as a result of the praise heaped upon him. In a truly generous gesture of humanity Peter Lougheed put the resources of the Alberta government at the disposal of those organizing the funeral, and ensured that colleagues of Grant like Alan Blakeney, Roy Romanow, myself, and others were brought in by special plane to be at the funeral. Absent from the speeches of those

221

outside of the NDP was the artificiality that accompanies such speeches at the funerals of public figures. He was, in death, respected by all.

What was his legacy? Did he leave something for his party, for Albertans? What was the conclusion of all of those years of hard work? He was never Premier. He did not head a government. He was never appointed to high office. Although he was Leader of the Official Opposition, it was such a tiny accomplishment, one extra member, as to require only a footnote in the political history of any jurisdiction. He built no buildings, no dams, no constitutions. He did not sit astride the history of Alberta as did E.C. Manning or Peter Lougheed. And yet, intuitively one has a sense that he was important.

This book began by saying that he was a living link between the progressive forces of yesterday and the new left of today. He was not the only link. He shared that position with a large number of people; with his parents, with Neil Reimer, with Ivor Dent, Henry Thomaschuk, Irene Dyck; and the list could go on into the hundreds, and thousands. They all forged a new political movement. But unlike them, he came to be the embodiment of that link. He became the single shining star of those searching for a new voice for their political concerns. His own hard work, however selflessly or selfishly motivated, was a living symbol in the years when this effort could have been extinguished. Would the NDP have been active and successful in Alberta without him? Perhaps. Would there have been a stronger and more eloquent spokesman for the movement during this period? Probably not. Standing as his single most important legacy is his contribution to the body politic of Alberta. Had he not been there, his example of humane, issue-oriented politics would have been absent, and we would have been the less for it.

In an ironic way, he succeeded because he was never too successful. In his solitary position he could afford to speak out for the powerless, for the mistreated, for the disadvantaged. Not with impunity, because he was always an electoral politician, but with an ideological understanding, an understanding which reflected his own social origins, his own background in Alberta.

In the final analysis it was his connection to Alberta, to Albertans, which seemed to strike a resonance with them. As he said:

I'm comfortable with being an Albertan. I think that I'm at home in Alberta.

NOTES

INTRODUCTION

1. *Debates and Proceedings*, 1st Session of the 17th Legislature of Alberta, March 6, 1972, pp. 3-29 and 3-30.
2. Doug Owram, *The Promise of Eden: The Canadian Expansionist Movement and the Idea of the West, 1856-1900* (Toronto: University of Toronto Press, 1980), p. 219.
3. Quoted in Anthony Mardiros, *The Life of a Prairie Radical: William Irvine* (Toronto: James Lorimer and Company, 1979), p. 244.
4. This is a quotation from a personal interview done with Grant Notley in 1981. Quotations from taped interviews are not individually footnoted, but rather, indicated in the text as to individual time or place where appropriate. A general note in the Bibliography explains this more fully.

2 UNIVERSITY YEARS

1. See a variety of publications, including John Irvine, *The Social Credit Movement in Alberta* (Toronto: University of Toronto Press, 1959), C.B. McPherson, *Democracy in Alberta, The Theory and Practice of the Quasi-Party System* (Toronto: University of Toronto Press, 1953) or articles like "The Social Credit in Alberta, 1935-1971," in Carlo Caldarola, ed., *Society and Politics in Alberta* (Agincourt, Ontario: Methuen, 1979).
2. Myron Johnson, "The Failure of the CCF in Alberta," in Carlo Caldarola, ed., *Society and Politics in Alberta* (Agincourt, Ontario: Methuen, 1979), p. 104.
3. Anthony Mardiros, *The Life of a Prairie Radical: William Irvine* (Toronto: James Lorimer and Company, 1979), p. 237.
4. Betty's husband Anthony wrote the biography of Bill Irvine; cited above.
5. The following quotations are from copies of material held by the University of Alberta Archives. In most cases the pages of this material were not

223

numbered and the issues irregular. Where possible indications of dates and position are given in the text.

6. *Edmonton Journal*, January 9, 1960, p. 5.
7. Walter D. Young, *Anatomy of a Party; The National CCF, 1932 - 1961* (Toronto: University of Toronto Press, 1969), p. 137.

3   THE EARLY NDP

1. Actually Notley and Dan de Vlieger "created" Irwin Weeks, who was from Jamaica, hoping to capitalize on reverse discrimination at the campus.
2. Stanley Knowles, *The New Party* (Toronto: McClelland and Stewart, 1961), p. 46.
3. Ibid.
4. Mardiros, pp. 248-49.
5. Ibid.
6. Letter, Notley to Iwaasa, August 11, 1961, No. 84.178, Provincial Archives of Alberta.
7. Desmond Morton, *NDP: The Dream of Power* (Toronto: Hakkert, 1974), p. 24.
8. Minutes, Alberta NDP Provincial Council, November 5, 1961, No. 84.178, Provincial Archives of Alberta.
9. Mardiros, p. 250.
10. *Edmonton Journal*, January 20, 1961, p. 5.
11. Ibid.
12. Ibid., p. 28.
13. Ibid., January 22, 1961, pp. 1-3.
14. *Edmonton Journal*, January 18, 1961, p. 1.
15. Ibid., January 20, 1961.
16. Ibid., January 12, 1962, p. 29.
17. Ibid.
18. Ibid., June 22, 1962, p. 24.
19. Minutes, Alberta NDP Provincial Council, February 1, 1962, No. 84.178, Provincial Archives of Alberta.
20. Report, Gilroy to Notley, May 1, 1962, No. 84.178, Provincial Archives of Alberta.
21. Letter, Notley to Iwaasa, April 10, 1962, No. 84.178, Provincial Archives of Alberta.
22. Letter, Gilroy to Power, April 6, 1962, No. 84.178, Provincial Archives of Alberta.
23. Report, de Vlieger to Notley, June 28, 1962, No. 84.178, Provincial Archives of Alberta.
24. Minutes, Alberta NDP Executive, June 4, 1962, No. 84.178, Provincial Archives of Alberta.
25. Organizational Report, Alberta NDP, July 27, 1962, No. 84.178, Provincial Archives of Alberta.
26. Ibid.

27. Letter Notley to de Vlieger, December 10, 1962, No. 84.178, Provincial Archives of Alberta.
28. Letter, Gilroy to de Vlieger, October 9, 1962, No. 84.178, Provincial Archives of Alberta.
29. Letter, Gilroy to Dyck, No. 84.178, Provincial Archives of Alberta.
30. Letter, Notley to de Vlieger, December 10, 1962, No. 894.178, Provincial Archives of Alberta.
31. Minutes, Alberta NDP Executive, Nov. 18, 1962, No. 84.178, Provincial Archives of Alberta.
32. Letter, Yanchula to Reimer, September 24, 1962, No. 84.178, Provincial Archives of Alberta.
33. Minutes, Alberta NDP Executive, November 18, 1962, No. 84.178, Provincial Archives of Alberta.
34. Minutes, Alberta NDP Executive, January 4, 1963, No. 84.178, Provincial Archives of Alberta.
35. CCF/NDP papers, Vol. 379, National Archives of Canada.

4 PROVINCIAL SECRETARY

1. Minutes, Alberta NDP Executive, February 9, 1963, No. 84.178, Provincial Archives of Alberta.
2. Letter, Notley to Dent, February 19, 1963, No. 84.178, Provincial Archives of Alberta.
3. Ibid.
4. Letter, Notley to *Calgary Herald,* February 28, 1963, No. 84.178, Provincial Archives of Alberta.
5. Organizational Report, Alberta NDP, April 21, 1963, No. 84.178, Provincial Archives of Alberta.
6. Ibid.
7. It really is unfortunate that Grant Notley did not live to see Ross Harvey elected in Edmonton East in 1988.
8. Letter, MacDonald to Notley, April 6, 1963, No. 84.178, Provincial Archives of Alberta.
9. Minutes, Alberta NDP Executive, April 21, 1963, No. 84.178, Provincial Archives of Alberta.
10. *Edmonton Journal,* June 17, 1963, p. 3.
11. Ibid., June 10, 1963, p. 1.
12. Ibid., p. 10.
13. Ibid.
14. Ibid.
15. "Four Year Plan," Alberta NDP, January, 1964, p. 1, No. 84.178, Provincial Archives of Alberta.
16. Ibid., p. 2.
17. Larry Pratt, "Grant Notley: Politics as a Calling," in *Essays in Honour of Grant Notley: Socialism and Democracy in Alberta*, Larry Pratt, ed. (Edmonton: NeWest Publishers, 1988), p. 15.

18. Minutes, Alberta NDP Executive, January 25, 1964, No. 84.178, Provincial Archives of Alberta.
19. Ibid., p. 2.
20. Minutes, Alberta NDP Executive, October 25, 1964, No. 84.178, Provincial Archives of Alberta.
21. Alf Hooke, *Thirty Plus Five: I Was There* (Edmonton: Coop Press Ltd., 1971), p. 224.
22. Provincial Planning Memorandum, Alberta NDP, 1967, No. 84.178, Provincial Archives of Alberta.
23. Carlo Caldarola and G.S. Paul, "Voting in Edmonton," in *Society and Politics in Alberta*, Carlo Calderola, ed. (Agincourt, Ontario: Methuen, 1979), pp. 322-56.
24. *Edmonton Journal*, May 12, 1967, p. 4.
25. Ibid.
26. *Edmonton Journal*, May 19, 1967, p. 4.
27. *Edmonton Journal*, May 24, 1967, p. 4.

5 THE LEADER

1. David K. Elton, Arthur M. Goddard, "The Conservative Takeover 1971," in Carlo Caldarola, ed., *Society and Politics in Alberta* (Agincourt, Ontario: Methuen, 1979), p. 52.
2. Allan Hustak, *Peter Lougheed* (Toronto: McClelland and Stewart, 1979), p. 116.

6 THE MEMBER FOR SPIRIT RIVER-FAIRVIEW

1. *Debates and Proceedings*, 1st Session of the 17th Legislature of Alberta, March 6, 1972, pp. 3-29 & 3-30.
2. *Debates and Proceedings*, 1st Session of the 17th Legislature of Alberta, March 6, 1972, p. 3-35.
3. *Edmonton Journal*, March 7, 1972, p. 5.
4. *Edmonton Journal*, April 5, 1972, p. 4.
5. *Debates and Proceedings*, 1st Session of the 17th Legislature of Alberta, May 15, 1972, p. 34-50.
6. *Edmonton Journal*, April 15, 1972, p. 4.
7. *Debates and Proceedings*, 2nd Session of the Legislature of Alberta, March 8, 1973, p. 16-663.
8. Press Release, Alberta NDP, Notley to all media, October 9, 1973.
9. *Debates and Proceedings*, 3rd Session of the 17th Legislature of Alberta, April 3, 1974, p. 951.
10. Personal Diary, Tom McLeod, May 26, 1974.
11. Ibid., May 31, June 1, June 2, June 5, 1974.
12. Ibid., p. 23.
13. Ibid., p. 23.

7   THE SOCIAL CONSCIENCE OF ALBERTA

1. *Debates and Proceedings*, 2nd Session of the 17th Legislature of Alberta, March 21, 1973, p. 25-1140.
2. *Debates and Proceedings*, 3rd Session of the 18th Legislature of Alberta, May 6, 1977, p. 1211.
3. *Debates and Proceedings*, 4th Session of the 18th Legislature of Alberta, May 15, 1978, p. 1231.
4. Ibid., April 27, 1978, p. 872.
5. *Debates and Proceedings*, 2nd Session of the 17th Legislature of Alberta, April 3, 1973, p. 34-1671.
6. *Debates and Proceedings*, 2nd Session of the 18th Legislature of Alberta, April 23, 1976, p. 825.
7. Ibid., p. 839.
8. *Alberta Democrat*, November 1976, p. 17.
9. *Debates and Proceedings*, 2nd Session of the 17th Legislature of Alberta, March 8, 1973, p. 17-677.
10. *Debates and Proceedings*, 3rd Session of the 17th Legislature of Alberta, March 14, 1974, p. 209.
11. *Debates and Proceedings*, 4th Session of the 18th Legislature of Alberta, May 10, 1978, p. 1183.
12. *Alberta Democrat*, April/May, 1976, p. 11.
13. *Globe and Mail*, October 30, 1978, p. 11.
14. *Financial Post*, November 25, 1978, p. 20.
15. Hustak, p. 191.
16. Ibid.
17. *Financial Post*, March 10, 1979, p. 6.

8   THE LEADER OF THE OFFICIAL OPPOSITION

1. *Macleans*, Vol. 92, No. 13, March 26, 1979, pp. 21-22.
2. *Debates and Proceedings*, 1st Session of the 19th Legislature of Alberta, October 30, 1979, pp. 10-19 and 1020.
3. *Debates and Proceedings*, 2nd Session of the 19th Session of the Legislature of Alberta, April 10, 1980, p. 272.
4. Letter, T.C. Douglas to Grant Notley, November 5, 1980.
5. *Debates and Proceedings*, 2nd Session of the 20th Legislature of Alberta, October 18, 1984, p. 1204.

BIBLIOGRAPHY

BOOKS

Caldarola, Carlo, ed. *Society and Politics in Alberta*. Agincourt, Ontario: Methuen, 1979.

Hooke, Alf. *Thirty Plus Five: I Was There*. Edmonton: Coop Press Ltd., 1971.

Hustak, Allan. *Peter Lougheed*. Toronto: McClelland and Stewart, 1979.

Knowles, Stanley. *The New Party*. Toronto: McClelland and Stewart, 1961.

Mardiros, Anthony. *The Life of a Prairie Radical: William Irvine*. Toronto: James Lorimer and Company, 1979.

Morton, Desmond. *NDP: The Dream of Power*. Toronto: Hakkert, 1974.

Owram, Doug. *The Promise of Eden: The Canadian Expansionist Movement and the Idea of the West, 1856-1900*. Toronto: University of Toronto Press, 1980.

Pratt, Larry, ed. *Essays in Honour of Grant Notley: Socialism and Democracy in Alberta*. Edmonton: NeWest Publishers, 1988.

Young, Walter D. *Anatomy of a Party: The National CCF, 1952-1961*. Toronto: University of Toronto Press, 1969.

ARTICLES

Caldarola, Carlo and Paul, G.S. "Voting in Edmonton" in Caldarola, Carlo, ed., *Society and Politics in Alberta*. Agincourt, Ontario: Methuen, 1979.

Elton, David K. and Goddard, Arthur M. "The Conservative Takeover: 1971" in Caldarola, Carlo, ed., *Society and Politics in Alberta*. Agincourt, Ontario: Methuen, 1979.

Johnson, Myron. "The Failure of the CCF in Alberta" in Caldarola, Carlo, ed., *Society and Politics in Alberta*. Agincourt, Ontario: Methuen, 1979.

Pratt, Larry. "Grant Notley: Politics as a Calling" in Pratt, Larry, ed., *Essays In Honour of Grant Notley: Socialism and Democracy in Alberta*. Edmonton: NeWest Publishers, 1988.

229

NEWSPAPERS
Alberta Democrat, April/May, 1976, November, 1976.
Edmonton Journal, January 9, 1960, January 18 & 20, 1961, January 12, 1962, June 22, 1962, June 10 & 17, 1963, May 12 & 19, 1967, March, 7, 1972, April 5 & 15, 1972.
Financial Post, November 25, 1978, March 10, 1979.
Globe and Mail, October 30, 1978.

MAGAZINES
Macleans, Vol. 92, No. 13, March 20, 1979.

PUBLIC DOCUMENTS
Debates and Proceedings, 1st Session of the 17th Legislature of Alberta.
Debates and Proceedings, 2nd Session of the 17th Legislature of Alberta.
Debates and Proceedings, 3rd Session of the 17th Legislature of Alberta.
Debates and Proceedings, 1st Session of the 18th Legislature of Alberta.
Debates and Proceedings, 2st Session of the 18th Legislature of Alberta.
Debates and Proceedings, 3rd Session of the 18th Legislature of Alberta.
Debates and Proceedings, 4th Session of the 18th Legislature of Alberta.
Debates and Proceedings, 1st Session of the 19th Legislature of Alberta.
Debates and Proceedings, 2nd Session of the 19th Legislature of Alberta.
Debates and Proceedings, 2nd Session of the 20th Legislature of Alberta.

ARCHIVES
National Archives of Canada, Volume 379, CCF/NDP Papers.
Provincial Archives of Alberta, No. 84.178. Minutes, Alberta NDP Provincial Council, November 5, 1961.
Provincial Archives of Alberta, No. 84.178. Minutes, Alberta NDP Provincial Council, February 1, 1962.
Provincial Archives of Alberta, No. 84.178. Minutes, Alberta NDP Executive, June 4, 1962.
Provincial Archives of Alberta, No. 84.178. Minutes, Alberta NDP Executive, November 18, 1962.
Provincial Archives of Alberta, No. 84.178. Minutes, Alberta NDP Executive, January 4, 1963.
Provincial Archives of Alberta, No. 84.178. Minutes, Alberta NDP Executive, February 9, 1963.
Provincial Archives of Alberta, No. 84.178. Minutes, Alberta NDP Executive, April 21, 1963.
Provincial Archives of Alberta, No. 84.178. Minutes, Alberta NDP Executive, January 25, 1964.
Provincial Archives of Alberta, No. 84.178. Minutes, Alberta NDP Executive, October 25, 1965.
Provincial Archives of Alberta, No. 84.178. Letter, Notley to Iwaasa, August 11, 1961.

Provincial Archives of Alberta, No. 84.178. Letter, Gilroy to Power, April 6, 1962.
Provincial Archives of Alberta, No. 84.178. Letter, Notley to Iwaasa, April 10, 1962.
Provincial Archives of Alberta, No. 84.178. Letter, Yanchula to Reimer, September 24, 1962.
Provincial Archives of Alberta, No. 84.178. Letter Gilroy to de Vlieger, October 9, 1962.
Provincial Archives of Alberta, No. 84.178. Letter, Gilroy to Dyck, October 14, 1962.
Provincial Archives of Alberta, No. 84.178. Letter, Notley to de Vlieger, December 10, 1962.
Provincial Archives of Alberta, No. 84.178. Letter, Notley to Dent, February 19, 1963.
Provincial Archives of Alberta, No. 84.178. Letter, Notley to *Calgary Herald*, February 28, 1963.
Provincial Archives of Alberta, No. 84.178. Letter, MacDonald to Notley, April 6, 1963.
Provincial Archives of Alberta, No. 84.178. Report, Gilroy to Notley, May 1, 1962.
Provincial Archives of Alberta, No. 84.178. Report, de Vlieger to Notley, June 28, 1962.
Provincial Archives of Alberta, No. 84.178. Organizational Report, July 27, 1962.
Provincial Archives of Alberta, No. 84.178. Organizational Report, Alberta NDP, April 21, 1963.
Provincial Archives of Alberta, No. 84.178. Provincial Planning Memorandum, 1967.
Provincial Archives of Alberta, No. 84.178. Four Year Plan, Alberta NDP, January, 1964.

DIARY
Thomas McLeod, Edmonton, Alberta.

LETTERS
Letter, T.C. Douglas to Grant Notley, 5 November, 1980.

INTERVIEWS
Personal interviews were conducted with a large number of people in Alberta, and in other parts of Canada. These tapes are in my possession. At the appropriate time they will be donated to the Provincial Archives of Alberta. Some material is drawn from interviews conducted by Mr. D. Elliot as part of a history project involving the CCF in Alberta. As well, some interviews with Grant Notley were conducted by Mr. Mark Zwelling, and remain in my possession. The latter sets of tapes will also be given to the Provincial Archives of Alberta at an appropriate time.

INDEX